S.C.U.B.A. director manual

Group's
S.C.U.B.A.
SUPER COOL UNDERSEA BIBLE ADVENTURE

Group
Loveland, Colorado

a SPeciaL THanKS...

Our deepest thanks to the outstanding "school" of VBS Directors who shared their time and talents at our 2003 **SCUBA** field test. Thanks to Wes Boyd, Don Carlson, Judy Hermanski, Scott Klemanchuck, Richard Fitzgerald, Barb Frederiksen, Susie LaFollette, and Barbara Swingle. Your oceans of ideas will help other VBS Directors reach children with God's love.

Group's R.E.A.L. Guarantee to you:

This Group resource incorporates our R.E.A.L. approach to ministry—one that encourages long-term retention and life transformation. It's ministry that's:

Relational
Because learner-to-learner interaction enhances learning and builds Christian friendships.

Experiential
Because what learners experience through discussion and action sticks with them up to 9 times longer than what they simply hear or read.

Applicable
Because the aim of Christian education is to equip learners to be both hearers and doers of God's Word.

Learner-based
Because learners understand and retain more when the learning process takes into consideration how they learn best.

SCUBA DiRecTOR manuaL

Copyright © 2003 Group Publishing, Inc.

Unless otherwise noted, Scripture taken from the HOLY BIBLE, NEW INTERNATIONAL READER'S VERSION. Copyright © 1994, 1996 by International Bible Society. Used by permission of Zondervan Publishing House. All rights reserved.

Visit our Web sites:
www.grouppublishing.com
www.groupvbs.com
www.groupoutlet.com

Credits
SCUBA Dive Master: Jody Brolsma
Chief Creative Officer: Joani Schultz
Copy Editor: Pamela Shoup
Art Director: Kari K. Monson
Print Production Artist: Tracy K. Donaldson
Cover Art Director/Designer: Lisa Chandler
Cover and Interior Photographer: Daniel Treat
Illustrator: Dana Regan
Production Manager: Peggy Naylor

ISBN 0-7644-2500-5
Printed in the United States of America.
10 9 8 7 6 5 4 3 2 1   05 04 03

Contents

PLANNING YOUR SUPER COOL UNDERSEA BIBLE ADVENTURE

Dive In!

Come on in, the Water's fine!

Listen to the crashing waves. Smell the salt air. Feel the warm, soft sand under your toes. Then grab your gear, slip on your flippers, and get ready to immerse yourself in the amazing underwater world of a Super **C**ool **U**ndersea **B**ible **A**dventure! Kids, teenagers, and adults will have oceans of fun on *this* VBS, going deeper into God's Word. As kids dive into awesome Bible adventures, they'll discover how to believe in God, obey God, trust God, love God, and share God's love.

If you haven't used Group's VBS materials before, you're in for a real treat. **SCUBA** is an exciting, fun-filled, Bible-based program your kids will love. (We know, because we tested everything in a field test last summer. Look for the "Field Test Findings" to learn what we discovered and how that will make *your* program the best!) Your leaders will love being divers at **SCUBA**, too, because their roles are so easy! And *you'll* love it because kids will take part in unforgettable Bible adventures that will take them deeper into a relationship with God.

Leader Lifeline

As **SCUBA** Director, you'll want to know what's happening each day. Refer to the **SCUBA** Overview chart on pages 10-11 to get an overview of the Bible stories and biblical truths elementary kids cover. You'll discover how these truths are reinforced creatively throughout each day.

Each day at **SCUBA** is swimming with activities designed to help kids discover more about God's love.

Kids start each day by forming small groups called Scuba Crews. All the Scuba Crews gather at Sing & Play Splash to do fun motions to upbeat Bible songs that introduce kids to the concepts they'll be learning that day. Then Scuba Crews travel to different Scuba Stations: They explore Deep Bible Adventures, meet Chadder Chipmunk™ on video (and use their **SCUBA** Bible Books, too!), have fun playing Splish Splash Games, sample tasty Dive-In Diner snacks, and visit Undersea Crafts and Missions to make oceans of Bible Point Crafts! Then crews gather to participate in each day's Sea Star Finale. And throughout the week, children work on a special project they'll share during Operation Kid-to-Kid™. This missions project allows the kids at your church to impact needy children around the globe!

This **SCUBA** Director Manual contains everything you need to plan a successful program, recruit and train volunteers, publicize your program, and follow up with kids and their families after your **SCUBA** comes to an end.

The Super Cool Undersea Bible Adventure is just beginning! Get ready to dive into an ocean of Bible fun!

FieLD TeSt FinDinGs

Afraid you'll feel lost once you distribute those station leader manuals? Don't worry! The chart on the following pages contains all the information you'll need to have an idea as to what's happening in each station. Veteran VBS directors tell us that it's nice to simply delegate and give some of the responsibility to the Scuba Station Leaders. Don't feel like you need to know every minute detail of every station!

Scuba Overview

This is what everyone else is doing! On your **S**uper **C**ool **U**ndersea **B**ible **A**dventure, the daily Bible Point is carefully integrated into each Scuba Station activity to reinforce Bible learning. Each Station is an important part of kids' overall learning experience.

	BIBLE POINT	BIBLE STORY	TREASURE VERSE	SING & PLAY SPLASH	DEEP BIBLE ADVENTURES	SPLISH SPLASH GAMES
Day 1	Believe in God.	Elijah confronts the prophets of Baal (1 Kings 18:16-39).	"But you are the only true God" (Jeremiah 10:10a).	• Introduce the Bible story about Elijah and the prophets of Baal. • Introduce the flying fish Bible Memory Buddy, Ace. • Lead "Deeper With God." • Lead "Jump, Shout & Sing." • Lead "We Believe in God."	**Elijah confronts the prophets of Baal.** • Help build Elijah's altar. • Get a surprise visit from a firefighter. • Talk about what it means to believe in God.	**Games** • You Are True • Choose Now! • Scuba Talk People may believe in many things today, but we believe in the one, true God.
Day 2	Obey God.	Jonah disobeys God (Jonah 1–3).	"Here is what it means to love God. It means that we obey his commands" (1 John 5:3).	• Introduce the Bible story of Jonah. • Introduce the whale Bible Memory Buddy, Squirt. • Lead "I Will Obey You." • Lead "I Wanna Go Deep." • Lead "Your Everlasting Love."	**Jonah disobeys God.** • Get swallowed up by a giant "fish." • Discover what it might have been like for Jonah inside the fish. • Make bracelets as reminders to go God's way— the right way.	**Games** • The Nineveh Assignment • Runaway Jonah • Jonah Overboard Jonah didn't want to obey God, so he tried to run away. God's plans are always best, so we need to obey God today!
Day 3	Trust God.	Jesus calms a storm (Matthew 8:23-27).	"Trust in the Lord with all your heart. Do not depend on your own understanding" (Proverbs 3:5).	• Introduce the Bible story of Jesus calming a storm. • Introduce the sea turtle Bible Memory Buddy, Tank. • Lead "Trust in the Lord With All Your Heart." • Lead "Rain or Pour." • Lead "Great Is the Lord."	**Jesus calms a storm.** • Pretend to be Jesus' disciples on a wet and stormy sea. • Listen to words of peace from the Bible. • Receive Life Savers candies as reminders that God is our life saver.	**Games** • Stop the Storm • Shark and Turtles • Treasure Hunt Mix-Up Jesus' disciples were afraid when they were caught in a big storm. We can trust God during all the "storms" in our lives.
Day 4	Love God.	Jesus dies on the cross and rises again (Luke 23–24).	"Love the Lord your God with all your heart and with all your soul. Love him with all your strength" (Deuteronomy 6:5).	• Introduce the Bible story of Jesus' death and resurrection. • Introduce the oyster Bible Memory Buddy, Pearl. • Lead "Father, I Adore You." • Lead "Come to the Water."	**Jesus dies on the cross and rises again.** • Sneak through the church to hide from Roman soldiers. • Confront an angry Roman guard. • Talk about what it means to know that God loves us.	**Games** • Dive Danger • Give It All You've Got! • Find the Pearl God loved us and sent Jesus to die for our sins. We love God with everything we've got!
Day 5	Share God's love.	Jesus appears to his followers as they fish (Matthew 28:18-20 and John 21:1-17).	"Go into all the world. Preach the good news to everyone" (Mark 16:15).	• Introduce the Bible story of Jesus appearing to the disciples. • Introduce the sea star Bible Memory Buddy, Starla. • Lead "Yes, I Will Go."	**Jesus appears to his followers as they fish.** • Become "fish," swimming in the Sea of Galilee. • Use a clothesline to discover how we're connected by God's love. • Enjoy a fish "breakfast" like the disciples did.	**Games** • Stuck on You! • Candy Capers • Fish Net Friends Jesus told his disciples to tell everyone the good news about God's love. We can share God's love in so many wonderful ways.

This overview chart shows you the entire program at a glance. Refer to the chart to see how each Scuba Station's activities supplement other activities to help kids go deeper into a relationship with God.

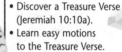

Introduction

DIVE-IN DINER	CHADDER'S UNDERSEA BIBLE ADVENTURE	UNDERSEA CRAFTS AND MISSIONS	SEA STAR FINALE
Elijah's Altar 	**Video Segment** Chadder accidentally finds himself on a research boat, the Collapso. Chadder will have to go under the water to help solve the mystery of who is stealing coral. He'll have to believe that God will show him a way to breathe under water. Jamie assures Chadder that God will take care of him, but Chadder is afraid when he learns that his diving instructor will be the menacing Klaus. 	• Flying Fish • Fish-a-Loon	• Discover a Treasure Verse (Jeremiah 10:10a). • Learn easy motions to the Treasure Verse. • Take part in an experiment in which they sample foods that look alike and determine which is the "real thing." • Sing praise songs to show that they believe in the one, true God.
Fancy Fish 	**Video Segment** When Klaus begins the diving lessons, Chadder has trouble following the instructions. Jamie helps Chadder understand how to communicate with hand signals, and he begins to understand. But when it's time to go under the water, Chadder refuses to obey the rules and is left behind while the others go exploring undersea. While he's alone on the boat, Chadder finds a pile of coral. The thief is someone from the Collapso! Before Chadder can tell Jamie of his discovery, he realizes a huge storm is headed their way.	• Dive Bags	• Experience a fun game show, *The Choice Is Right, Jonah!* • Discover a Treasure Verse (1 John 5:3a). • Act out the Treasure Verse in a memorable way. • Celebrate their love for God by singing praise songs.
Stormy Seas 	**Video Segment** When a storm threatens the Collapso, Chadder discovers that being under the water is the safest and calmest place to be. He trusts God to calm his heart just as Jesus calmed the storm. While undersea Chadder learns about different kinds of coral and sees something shiny that might be a clue to the coral thief. Before he can pick up the clue, someone cuts Chadder's air hose! 	• Trusty Timers • Buzzalong Boats 	• Discover a Treasure Verse (Proverbs 3:5). • Sing the Treasure Verse. • Help make a rainstorm that builds and then calms down. • Pray and affirm that they can trust God all the time.
Treasure Treats	**Video Segment** Chadder shows Jamie the coral he found on the Collapso and tells her about the shiny clue he saw while they were diving. Chadder and Jamie go back to find the shiny object. While they're diving, Jamie runs out of air. Chadder must decide if he will show sacrificial love and buddy breathe, which means he'll share his own air with Jamie. As the two make their way to the surface, they realize they're in danger—a shark is following them!	• Pearl Diver's Paradise • Treasure Books	• Experience a powerful drama and watch as Jesus "takes away" their sins. • Discover a Treasure Verse (Deuteronomy 6:5). • Learn easy motions to the Treasure Verse.
Bunch-o'-Believers	**Video Segment** After examining the shiny object they found on the ocean floor, Chadder and Jamie know who has been stealing the coral. Before they can alert the authorities, the thief chases them around the boat and threatens them—but is captured in the end. Chadder is a hero and must decide if he'll risk being laughed at and tell everyone that it was God who gave him courage. 	• Share Mail Postcards  • SCUBA Snapshot Frames 	• Review what they've learned at **SCUBA**. • Discover a Treasure Verse (Mark 16:15). • Share God's love with each other, and make a human "net." • Present their Operation Kid-to-Kid items as an offering to God.

Inspecting Your Scuba Starter Kit

Before you begin your **SCUBA** program, inspect your **SCUBA** Starter Kit to make sure it contains all the following items:

○ **SCUBA Director Manual (you're reading it now!)**—This is your guide to directing your **SCUBA** production. It includes everything you need to plan, staff, and promote your church's best program ever! In it you'll find photocopiable handouts, letters, certificates, and more. (And don't miss the all-new Crew Leader's Pocket Guide we've tucked inside your manual. It's overflowing with simple, practical helps for your Scuba Crew Leaders!)

○ *Dive Deep! Recruitment, Overview, and Pass-Along Training Video*—You'll reach for this video again and again and again. This three-part video contains a wealth of information—for you *and* your staff! First, you'll find three recruiting commercials that will get church members "hooked" on helping at this VBS! The next two-minute segment is a promotional tool that you can use to publicize **SCUBA** in your church. Finally, you'll *love* the twenty-five-minute "pass-along" training section, filled with invaluable tips and hints from the staff at our **SCUBA** field test. You can feel confident that your staff is well-prepared for its role in **SCUBA**. Plus, you'll see for yourself how much fun Bible learning can be!

○ **Preschool Tide Pool Director Manual**—This manual outlines five days of complete programs for children between the ages of three and five. The manual also contains supply lists, room setup and decoration ideas, exciting Bible-teaching ideas, and more to make your Tide Pool swimming with Bible fun!

○ **seven Scuba Station leader manuals:**
  • **Sing & Play Splash Leader Manual** (includes *Sing & Play Splash Music* CD)
  • **Dive-In Diner Leader Manual**
  • **Undersea Crafts and Missions Leader Manual** *(you can find this inside the craft packet!)*
  • **Deep Bible Adventures Leader Manual**

- **Chadder's Undersea Bible Adventure Leader Manual***
- **Splish Splash Games Leader Manual**
- **Sea Star Finale Leader Manual**

Each leader manual introduction contains detailed instructions for before, during, and after **SCUBA**, plus an overview of the entire program. Leader manuals include clear, step-by-step directions for each activity, guided discussion questions, and valuable "Leader Lifeline" and "Field Test Findings" to make sure everything goes smoothly.

*Requires *Chadder's Undersea Bible Adventure* video (available from Group Publishing, Inc. and your local Christian bookstore).

○ *Sing & Play Splash Music* **CD**—This CD provides Bible songs your kids will love, including the **SCUBA** theme song, "Deeper With God." The CD is recorded in split-track format so you can use just the accompaniment or add kids' voices. After you've listened to the CD, give it to your Sing & Play Splash Leader. He or she will use the CD to teach kids the **SCUBA** songs. You may want to order additional cassettes or CDs so that other leaders (especially those for Undersea Crafts, Dive-In Diner, and Splish Splash Games) can play the songs in the background as kids visit their Scuba Stations.

○ **Operation Kid-to-Kid™ brochure**—On Day 2 kids will learn about an exciting, meaningful missions project called Operation Kid-to-Kid. In Operation Kid-to-Kid, the children at your VBS will send new shoes and/or socks to needy children around the world! This brochure explains what Operation Kid-to-Kid is, how it was developed, whom it will impact, and how the kids at your VBS will carry it out.

○ **SCUBA Bible Book**—Diving into God's Word has never been so exciting...or easy! During Chadder's Undersea Bible Adventure, elementary kids will read, highlight, and journal in these kid-friendly, colorful Bible Books. The kids at your VBS will discover that the Bible is filled with incredible (and true) stories that show us what an amazing God we serve. Plus, each book contains a page of Surprise Stickers—the coolest thing you've *never* seen! Kids will use Surprise Stickers in their Dive Logs as well as for their crafts! And we've even included four take-home pages to reinforce Bible truths at home!

○ **Tide Pool Bible Book**—Preschoolers get to discover God's amazing love in their own age-appropriate children's Bible books. Children will love "reading" the picture Bible stories that reinforce the Bible stories they've learned at **SCUBA**. Tide Pool Bible Books also include exciting activity pages for children to work on during Preschool Tide Pool, plus ideas for family activities

Leader Lifeline

Before you hand the leader manuals to your station leaders, be sure to skim the books to get an idea of what's happening in each area. You'll feel better prepared to answer questions that may arise. We've heard from some directors who simply purchase a set of leader manuals for themselves, so they can be super informed!

that will reinforce the Point at home. And the Tide Pool Bible Book includes a page of eye-popping Surprise Stickers that preschoolers will love!

○ **craft packet**—Use the items in this packet to create samples of all the delightful Bible Point Crafts. Kids will love these irresistible, engaging crafts, like Flying Fish, Trusty Timers, Dive Bags, and Treasure Books. Plus, each Bible Point Craft helps reinforce important Bible truths! (Just flip through the Undersea Crafts and Missions Leader Manual to find simple instructions for creating these cool crafts!)

○ **Bible Memory Buddies**™—You'll make a big splash with these adorable sea creatures. Each squishy squirter reminds kids of the daily Bible Point, *and* has the Treasure Verse inscribed right on it! Bible Memory has never been so fun, easy, or wet!

○ **SCUBA samples**—In this bag you'll find publicity aids to help you build excitement about your program, awards to recognize everyone's contribution, and souvenirs to leave a lasting impression.

○ **Ministry Calendar**—This handy calendar will make it easy to keep your ministry events on track all year long! You'll love the helpful reminders and special offers that we've packed into this essential calendar!

If any **SCUBA** Starter Kit items are missing or damaged, contact your local Christian bookstore or Group Publishing for prompt replacement.

If you checked off everything on this list, you're ready to dive in to a **S**uper **C**ool **U**ndersea **B**ible **A**dventure!

May God Bless you as you plan your Scuba Program!

Scuba BASICS

DON'T HiDE in YOUR SHELL! THiS WiLL answeR aLL of YOUR QUESTiOnS!

WHat's SO DiffeReNt aBout Scuba?

It may seem like all VBS programs are alike. But take a closer look, and you'll see why Group's VBS is the most effective VBS around!

• **At SCUBA, kids learn one important Bible Point each day.** Instead of trying to teach kids more than they can remember or apply, **SCUBA** focuses on one key biblical concept. The Bible Point is reinforced daily through Bible stories, Bible verses, songs, and hands-on activities that help kids know more about God's amazing love. Kids who attend your church regularly will enjoy discovering this important truth in fresh, new ways. And neighborhood kids who come to your VBS will hear the "meat" of the gospel right away. Each day kids will learn something new about how we can have a relationship with God.

Day 1: Believe in God.
Day 2: Obey God.
Day 3: Trust God.
Day 4: Love God.
Day 5: Share God's love.

Bringing Bible truths to everyday life!

We know that you want kids to apply Bible truths to daily life. That's why each lesson is swimming with life-application activities and questions. To help you spot these important activities, just look for the Life Application logo throughout your leader manual.

• **At SCUBA, kids learn the way they learn best.** Not all kids learn the same way, so **SCUBA** offers seven daily Scuba Stations to meet the needs of all kinds of learners. Children will come away from each day remembering the Bible Point because each child will pick it up in a way that matches his or her learning style.

Sing & Play Splash's songs and motions will teach the Bible Point to your **musical learners**. Plus, it's where kids worship their loving God with gusto!

Splish Splash Games, Deep Bible Adventures, and Undersea Crafts and Missions allow **bodily-kinesthetic learners** to wiggle and move as they explore the Bible Point in active ways. Plus, Undersea Crafts and Missions helps kids develop hearts for helping needy children around the world.

Chadder's Undersea Bible Adventure lets **visual learners** discover the Bible Point through watching the high adventure, cliffhanger *Chadder's Undersea Bible Adventure* video. Kids also have a chance to read, think, and journal in colorful, eye-catching **SCUBA** Bible Books! Plus, they'll interact with cool Surprise Stickers—something most kids have never seen before!

Dive-In Diner allows **interpersonal learners** the opportunity to explore Jesus' love as they make and serve snacks for all the explorers at **SCUBA**.

Sea Star Finale's dramatic and interactive programs help **linguistic learners** remember each day's Bible Point and Treasure Verse.

Leaders at every Scuba Station ask meaningful, thought-provoking questions that encourage **logical and introspective learners** to think about and apply the Bible Point. We've even added photocopiable questions that Scuba Station Leaders will give to Scuba Crews to help trigger great discussion!

• **At SCUBA, teachers teach the way they teach best.** Just like kids, not all teachers think alike. Instead of forcing every teacher to teach the same material, **SCUBA** provides opportunities for you to place a variety of teachers in the roles that best suit them. Have a great storyteller in your congregation? Recruit that person to lead Deep Bible Adventures. Have a great athlete? Recruit that person to lead Splish Splash Games. Because each Scuba Station is different, teachers can volunteer in their areas of expertise. And volunteers who are intimidated by the idea of teaching can join your staff as Scuba Crew Leaders.

FieLD TeST FinDinGS

Churches around the country have reported great success with having families travel together as crews. Family crews build unity, encourage communication, and create wonderful memories that families will cherish for years to come. It really works!

FieLD Test FinDinGS

• **At SCUBA, no activity stands alone.** Instead of leading independent, isolated classes, Scuba Station Leaders see all the kids each day. Sing & Play Splash songs play in the background during other activities. Bible characters from Deep Bible Adventures appear at Sea Star Finale. Kids collect shoes and socks at Undersea Crafts and Missions, then donate them as an offering during Sea Star Finale. Bible Memory Buddies™ appear in Sing & Play Splash and Chadder's Undersea Bible Adventure…kids even play with them in Splish Splash Games! The Splish Splash Games Leader serves as an assistant Dive-In Diner chef. All Scuba Station Leaders assist in Sea Star Finale. Each member of your **SCUBA** team provides a unique and important part of kids' total VBS experience. With everyone working together, your staff will float through the week.

• **At SCUBA, kids take responsibility for what they're learning.** Throughout the week, kids travel to Scuba Stations with their Scuba Crews—small groups of three to five kids. On the first day, each child chooses a job that he or she will do throughout the week. Kids may be Readers, Scuba Guides, Materials Managers, Coaches, or Prayer People. From time to time, Scuba Station Leaders will call on kids to complete tasks that are part of their job descriptions.

Each Scuba Crew also has an adult or teenage Scuba Crew Leader. Scuba Crew Leaders aren't teachers. They're simply part of Scuba Crew families—like older brothers or sisters. Scuba Crew Leaders participate in all the activities and encourage kids to talk about and apply what they're learning. Scuba Crew Leaders who participated in **SCUBA** field tests saw kids encouraging other kids during the activities, helping younger crew members with difficult tasks, and reminding each other to use kind words. At **SCUBA**, kids put God's love into action!

• **At SCUBA, everyone is treated with respect.** Because elementary kids travel in combined-age Scuba Crews, big kids and little kids learn to work together. Instead of trying to compete with children their own age, older children help younger children during Undersea Crafts and Missions and Splish Splash Games. Younger children spark older children's imaginations during Deep Bible Adventures and Sea Star Finale.

Think of Scuba Crews as families in which kids naturally learn with and from one another. Social skills improve, self-esteem rises, cooperation increases, and discipline problems diminish.

Combined-age Scuba Crews also allow people of any age (even entire families) to join you for your **SCUBA**. You can even use combined-age crews to teach kids about being part of the body of Christ!

Knowing and understanding these distinctions will help you present **SCUBA** to your church or committee.

Preschoolers have an all-star, special **SCUBA** program of their own.

HOW DO PRESCHOOLeRS Fit in at SCUBa?

Little adventurers join the older kids for opening and closing activities each day, and in between they enjoy fun, age-appropriate, Bible-learning activities in Preschool Tide Pool.

Each day preschoolers hear a fun Bible story and then explore the story with all five senses through Scuba Discovery Stations. At Scuba Discovery Stations, preschoolers make crafts like Fish-a-Loons, Dive Bags, Buzzalong Boats, Treasure Books, and Share Mail Postcards.

Later, children continue their discoveries and work off some energy during Splash and Dash Playtime. They also get to meet Chadder Chipmunk™, collect Bible Memory Buddies, and enjoy Dive-In Diner treats made by the older kids. One day, they even make the snacks for the entire **SCUBA** crew! And preschoolers will dive into bright, colorful, age-appropriate Tide Pool Bible Books, complete with take-home activity pages, "read-along" picture stories, and brilliant Bible art!

The Preschool Tide Pool Director Manual contains complete instructions for setting up, organizing, and running Preschool Tide Pool.

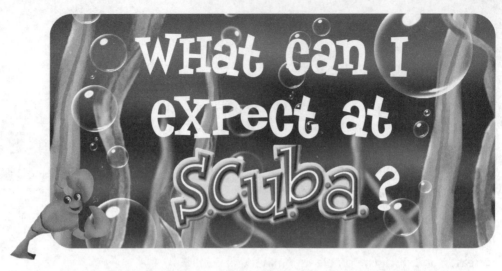

WHat can I eXPect at Scuba?

If this is your first time using Group's VBS, you're in for a real treat. You're also in for some surprises! If you look "beneath the surface," you'll discover that this VBS program is unlike any you've ever seen or experienced.

You might expect to see...	But at SCUBA, you'll see...	That's because...
kids quietly working in workbooks.	kids talking excitedly in their Scuba Crews.	crew leaders and station leaders will encourage kids to talk about important Bible truths, to cement them to their lives.
a traditional school setting, with desks or tables.	kids sitting in small, knee-to-knee circles (maybe even on the floor!).	we want kids to get face to face as they talk about how to apply God's Word to their lives. (And it's just plain easier for kids to sit on the floor instead of in chairs!)
children in age-graded classrooms.	children in mixed-age groups called Scuba Crews.	kids will learn so much more by interacting with children of different ages. Think of each crew as a mini-family!
classes that look neat and orderly.	lots of kid-friendly movement, activity, and energy—and a little clutter, too!	we know that kids have a lot of energy—so each activity is designed to let kids actively participate in fun and exciting ways (the way God designed them!).
kids spending most of their time in one classroom.	Scuba Crews traveling from station to station, about every twenty minutes.	station leaders prepare only about twenty minutes of activities. Not only is that easier on leaders like you, but it keeps kids busy—so there's no time to get into trouble!
kids memorizing Bible verses to receive prizes.	kids learning—and understanding—God's Word like you've never seen before!	Bible learning should be meaningful, delightful, and unforgettable.

HOW WILL KIDS LEARN THE BIBLE?

Each day kids will be exposed to a Bible Point as well as to a corresponding Bible story and Treasure Verse. The chart below shows the Bible content kids will cover each day.

Day	✝ BIBLE POINT	BIBLE STORY	🔺 TREASURE VERSE
1	Believe in God.	Elijah confronts the prophets of Baal (1 Kings 18:16-39).	"But you are the only true God" (Jeremiah 10:10a).
2	Obey God.	Jonah disobeys God (Jonah 1–3).	"Here is what it means to love God. It means that we obey his commands" (1 John 5:3).
3	Trust God.	Jesus calms a storm (Matthew 8:23-27).	"Trust in the Lord with all your heart. Do not depend on your own understanding" (Proverbs 3:5).
4	Love God.	Jesus dies on the cross and rises again (Luke 23–24).	"Love the Lord your God with all your heart and with all your soul. Love him with all your strength" (Deuteronomy 6:5).
5	Share God's love.	Jesus appears to his followers as they fish (Matthew 28:18-20; John 21:1-17).	"Go into all the world. Preach the good news to everyone" (Mark 16:15).

FIELD TEST FINDINGS

At each Scuba Station, kids will be carefully listening to hear the Bible Point so that they can respond by shouting "OK!" (OK is a sign given by scuba divers, indicating that everything is…well, OK!) Watch their excitement and enthusiasm—and listening skills—build throughout the week. It'll be awesome!

If you usually incorporate memory verses into your program, you can have kids memorize the daily Bible verses provided in this chart. Since children actually look up and read the Treasure Verses during Chadder's Undersea Bible Adventure, it's a natural connection. At Splish Splash Games, kids also collect the daily Bible Memory Buddies that have the daily Treasure verse inscribed right on them! That makes learning the verse even more fun.

At each Scuba Station, kids will encounter a different presentation of the Bible Point, Bible story, or Bible verse.

Leader Lifeline

You'll need to be available during Sing & Play Splash. The Sing & Play Splash Leader will send all the Scuba Crew Leaders out of the room for a brief time of prayer with you. Then you'll come forward at the end of Sing & Play Splash to give announcements, pray, and send Scuba Crews to their first stations.

Field Test Findings

Chadder's Undersea Bible Adventure is more than just time to watch a video; this is where kids *really* dig into Bible reading and life-application. In our field tests, we've discovered that the mix of video and Deep Bible Adventures is an excellent tool for reaching a variety of learners. Kids have the opportunity to work with entire portions of Scripture, as well as make the life-application connections that cement Bible learning.

Sing & Play Splash

• The Sing & Play Splash Leader repeats the Bible Point each day.

• In addition to fun praise songs, kids sing at least one song each day that specifically ties to that day's Bible Point.

• Each day kids sing the **SCUBA** theme song, "Deeper With God," which connects with the daily Bible Points.

• Each day the Sing & Play Splash Leader summarizes the daily Bible story.

Undersea Crafts and Missions

• The Undersea Crafts and Missions Leader repeats the Bible Point each day.

• Kids make Bible Point Crafts that remind them of each day's Bible story and Point. For example, on Day 3 kids make Trusty Timers. These see-through sand timers remind children that we can trust God all the time, any time.

• Kids listen to the Sing & Play Splash songs as they're working.

• The Undersea Crafts Leader asks questions to help kids review and apply the Bible Point and the Bible story.

• Through Operation Kid-to-Kid, kids experience what it means to share God's love.

Chadder's Undersea Bible Adventure

• In each day's exciting, cliffhanger video segment, Chadder Chipmunk™ explains the daily Bible Point.

• The Chadder's Undersea Bible Adventure Leader repeats the Bible Point each day.

• Kids read and explore key Bible verses to discover more about God and what it means to love and follow him. Then kids do meaningful, memorable journaling activities to help them apply what they've learned about God to their daily lives.

Dive-In Diner

• The Dive-In Diner Leader repeats the Bible Point each day.

• Kids make and eat snacks to reinforce the daily Bible Point. For example, on Day 5 when kids are learning to share God's love, they make a Bunch-o'-Believers from grapes, cheese, and toothpicks.

• Kids show Jesus' love by serving others. Each day one set of Scuba Crews makes the snacks for the entire VBS—even the preschoolers get a chance to serve others!

• Kids listen to Sing & Play Splash songs as they make and eat their snacks.

Splish Splash Games

• The Splish Splash Games Leader repeats the Bible Point each day.

• Kids play games that encourage them to apply what they've learned. For example, on Day 1 kids play a game in which they tell two things about themselves that are true…and one thing they *wish* were true. Then kids talk about how we can believe everything that God does.

• Kids listen to Sing & Play Splash songs as they play games.

• The Splish Splash Games Leader gives each child a Bible Memory Buddy to help reinforce the day's Treasure Verse.

• The Splish Splash Games Leader connects each game to the daily Bible Point.

Deep Bible Adventures

• The Deep Bible Adventures Leader repeats the Bible Point each day.

• Kids experience the daily Bible story in a hands-on way. For example, on Day 2 they are swallowed by a giant fish and discover what happened when Jonah didn't obey. On Day 3 they experience what it might have been like to be in the boat when Jesus calmed a raging storm.

• Scuba Crew Leaders guide small-group discussions in which kids connect their unforgettable Bible experiences with real life.

Sea Star Finale

• The Sea Star Finale Leader repeats the Bible Point each day.

• Kids repeat the Sing & Play Splash songs they've learned that day.

• Kids use drama to apply what they've learned throughout the day and to remember the day's Treasure Verse. For example, on Day 4, kids hold red streamers that represent their sins. Then crew leaders drape the sins over "Jesus' " outstretched arms.

Preschool Tide Pool

• Preschoolers sing the Sing & Play Splash songs with the older kids.

• The Tide Pool Director tells each day's Bible story in a fun, involving way.

• The Tide Pool Director repeats the Bible Point during each Scuba Discovery Station and Splash and Dash Playtime activity.

• Preschoolers hear the Bible story and the Bible Point as they watch *Chadder's Undersea Bible Adventure* video.

• Preschoolers work on interactive pages in their Tide Pool Bible Books. These books are also filled with picture stories that give little ones the ability to "read," and eye-popping Surprise Stickers that preschoolers will play with again and again.

• Preschoolers make and eat snacks that reinforce the daily Bible story.

• Preschoolers sing additional songs that reinforce the daily Bible Point or Bible story.

• Preschoolers participate in Sea Star Finale with the older kids.

LeaDeR LifeLine

On Day 1 only, preschoolers skip Sing & Play Splash and go straight to Preschool Tide Pool. This allows little ones to meet their preschool director, Scuba Crew Leaders, and Scuba Crew members. Plus preschoolers get to make Dive-In Diner snacks on Day 1, and the extra time helps them accomplish this big task.

As you can see, **SCUBA** is swimming with Bible-based activities your kids will love!

What's a Scuba Station?

At **SCUBA**, kids dive into Bible learning as they visit various Scuba Stations each day. Each Scuba Station is staffed by an adult leader and features a different Bible-learning activity. Some Scuba Stations—such as Sing & Play Splash, Dive-In Diner, and Sea Star Finale—accommodate all the **SCUBA** "divers" simultaneously. Kids will visit other Scuba Stations in smaller groups.

Elementary-age kids visit the following Scuba Stations each day:

- Sing & Play Splash
- Undersea Crafts and Missions
- Splish Splash Games
- Dive-In Diner
- Chadder's Undersea Bible Adventure
- Deep Bible Adventures
- Sea Star Finale

Preschoolers spend most of their time in Preschool Tide Pool, but they visit the following Scuba Stations each day:

- Sing & Play Splash
- Sea Star Finale

Preschoolers also enjoy the same Dive-In Diner treats, *and* watch the same *Chadder's Undersea Bible Adventure* video as the older children.

SCUBA Fits Churches of all Sizes!

Small...

If you have fewer than forty children, they can all swim through the Scuba Stations together.

This means that your Scuba Station Leaders will teach their area only one time! (Station leaders may find this so easy that they'll volunteer to teach more than one station, so you'll have fewer leaders to recruit!) Since you can set up multiple stations at one location, your church might be set up like this:

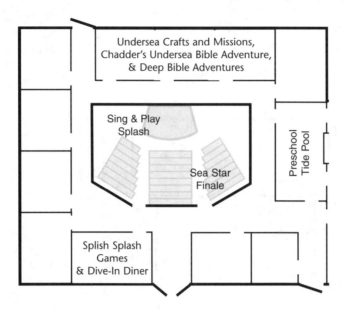

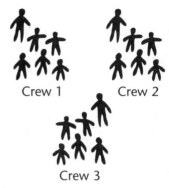

Your daily schedule might look as simple as this:

All Crews

Sing & Play Splash (9:00-9:25)

Allow five minutes to travel to your next station.

Deep Bible Adventures (9:30-9:50)

Allow five minutes to travel to your next station.

Undersea Crafts and Missions (9:55-10:15)

Allow five minutes to travel to your next station.

Dive-In Diner (10:20-10:40)

Allow five minutes to travel to your next station.

Splish Splash Games (10:45-11:05)

Allow five minutes to travel to your next station.

Chadder's Undersea Bible Adventure (11:10-11:30)

Allow five minutes to travel to your next station.

Sea Star Finale (11:35-12:00)

FieLD TeSt FinDinGs

We've heard from VBS directors who use this program and are delighted at how simple it is for smaller churches. Their leaders love teaching only one or two rotations, and it's easy to find leaders who will teach more than one. Your job has never been easier!

Medium...

If you have 50 to 150 kids at your **SCUBA**, you'll set up six Scuba Stations, so your church might be set up like this:

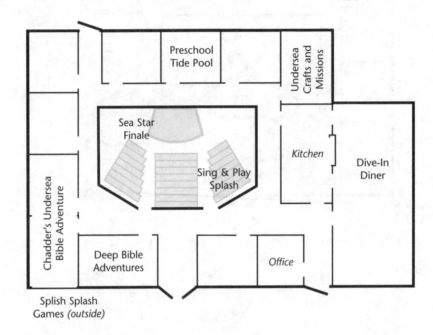

Preschool Tide Pool

Undersea Crafts and Missions

Sea Star Finale

Kitchen

Dive-In Diner

Chadder's Undersea Bible Adventure

Sing & Play Splash

Deep Bible Adventures

Office

Splish Splash Games *(outside)*

Divide your total number of elementary Scuba Crews by four to form four large groups.

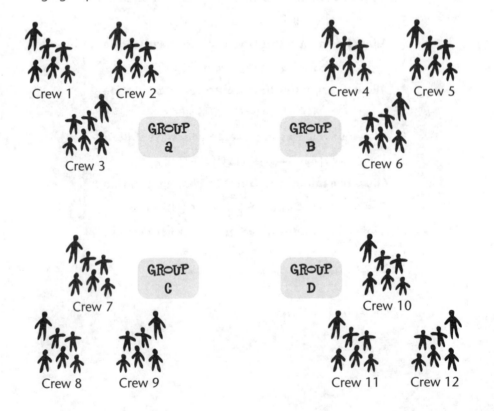

Crew 1   Crew 2   Crew 4   Crew 5

Crew 3   GROUP a   GROUP B   Crew 6

Crew 7   GROUP C   GROUP D   Crew 10

Crew 8   Crew 9   Crew 11   Crew 12

These groups will travel to each Scuba Station, following a schedule that looks like this:

Time	Group A Crews 1-3	Group B Crews 4-6	Group C Crews 7-9	Group D Crews 10-12	Preschool
9:00-9:25	Sing & Play Splash	Sing & Play Splash	Sing & Play Splash	Sing & Play Splash	Sing & Play Splash
	Allow five minutes to dive to your next Scuba Station.				
9:30-9:50	Deep Bible Adventures	Undersea Crafts and Missions	Dine-In Diner	Chadder's Undersea Bible Adventure	Preschool Tide Pool
	Allow five minutes to dive to your next Scuba Station.				
9:55-10:15	Undersea Crafts and Missions	Splish Splash Games	Chadder's Undersea Bible Adventure	Deep Bible Adventures	Preschool Tide Pool
	Allow five minutes to dive to your next Scuba Station.				
10:20-10:40	Dive-In Diner	Dive-In Diner	Dive-In Diner	Dive-In Diner	Chadder's Undersea Bible Adventure
	Allow five minutes to dive to your next Scuba Station.				
10:45-11:05	Splish Splash Games	Chadder's Undersea Bible Adventure	Deep Bible Adventures	Undersea Crafts and Missions	Preschool Tide Pool
	Allow five minutes to dive to your next Scuba Station.				
11:10-11:30	Chadder's Undersea Bible Adventure	Deep Bible Adventures	Undersea Crafts and Missions	Splish Splash Games	Preschool Tide Pool
	Allow five minutes to dive to your next Scuba Station.				
11:35-12:00	Sea Star Finale	Sea Star Finale	Sea Star Finale	Sea Star Finale	Sea Star Finale

Large!

If you have more than 150 kids, your church might be set up like this:

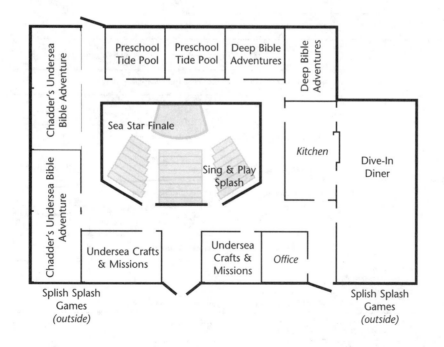

LeaDeR LifeLine

Don't worry if you need to set up duplicate stations—it's easy and really works best. If at all possible, place the duplicate stations next to each other. Then, when Scuba Crews arrive at the stations, station leaders can simply direct half of them into each station.

LeaDeR LifeLine

For another large-group option, run a morning and evening program. Simply have participants sign up for the daytime or evening program; then decorate once and run two "shifts."

Divide your total number of elementary Scuba Crews by eight to form eight large groups. These groups will travel to each Scuba Station, following a schedule that looks like this:

Time	Group A Crews 1-3	Group B Crews 4-6	Group C Crews 7-9	Group D Crews 10-12	Preschool
9:00-9:25	Sing & Play Splash	Sing & Play Splash	Sing & Play Splash	Sing & Play Splash	Sing & Play Splash
	Allow five minutes to dive to your next Scuba Station.				
9:30-9:50	Deep Bible Adventures #1	Undersea Crafts and Missions #1	Dive-In Diner #1	Chadder's Undersea Bible Adventure #1	Preschool Tide Pool #1
	Allow five minutes to dive to your next Scuba Station.				
9:55-10:15	Undersea Crafts and Missions #1	Splish Splash Games #1	Chadder's Undersea Bible Adventure #1	Deep Bible Adventures #1	Preschool Tide Pool #1
	Allow five minutes to dive to your next Scuba Station.				
10:20-10:40	Dive-In Diner	Dive-In Diner	Dive-In Diner	Dive-In Diner	Chadder's Undersea Bible Adventure #1
	Allow five minutes to dive to your next Scuba Station.				
10:45-11:05	Splish Splash Games #1	Chadder's Undersea Bible Adventure #1	Deep Bible Adventures #1	Undersea Crafts and Missions #1	Preschool Tide Pool #1
	Allow five minutes to dive to your next Scuba Station.				
11:10-11:30	Chadder's Undersea Bible Adventure #1	Deep Bible Adventures #1	Undersea Crafts and Missions #1	Splish Splash Games #1	Preschool Tide Pool #1
	Allow five minutes to dive to your next Scuba Station.				
11:35-12:00	Sea Star Finale	Sea Star Finale	Sea Star Finale	Sea Star Finale	Sea Star Finale

Time	Group E Crews 21-25	Group F Crews 26-30	Group G Crews 31-35	Group H Crews 36-40	Preschool
9:00-9:25	Sing & Play Splash	Sing & Play Splash	Sing & Play Splash	Sing & Play Splash	Sing & Play Splash
	Allow five minutes to dive to your next Scuba Station.				
9:30-9:50	Deep Bible Adventures #2	Undersea Crafts and Missions #2	Dive-In Diner #2	Chadder's Undersea Bible Adventure #2	Preschool Tide Pool #2
	Allow five minutes to dive to your next Scuba Station.				
9:55-10:15	Undersea Crafts and Missions #2	Splish Splash Games #2	Chadder's Undersea Bible Adventure #2	Deep Bible Adventures #2	Preschool Tide Pool #2
	Allow five minutes to dive to your next Scuba Station.				
10:20-10:40	Dive-In Diner	Dive-In Diner	Dive-In Diner	Dive-In Diner	Chadder's Undersea Bible Adventure #2
	Allow five minutes to dive to your next Scuba Station.				
10:45-11:05	Splish Splash Games #2	Chadder's Undersea Bible Adventure #2	Deep Bible Adventures #2	Undersea Crafts and Missions #2	Preschool Tide Pool #2
	Allow five minutes to dive to your next Scuba Station.				
11:10-11:30	Chadder's Undersea Bible Adventure #2	Deep Bible Adventures #2	Undersea Crafts and Missions #2	Splish Splash Games #2	Preschool Tide Pool #2
	Allow five minutes to dive to your next Scuba Station.				
11:35-12:00	Sea Star Finale	Sea Star Finale	Sea Star Finale	Sea Star Finale	Sea Star Finale

What's a Scuba Crew?

As you set up your **S**uper **C**ool **U**ndersea **B**ible **A**dventure, you assign kids to Scuba Crews. On Day 1 kids report to their Scuba Crews right away to start getting acquainted. Since Scuba Crew members work closely during the week, Scuba Crews encourage kids to make new friends at VBS. They also provide an organizational structure that helps kids progress from station to station in an orderly manner.

Scuba Crews consist of three to five children and an adult or teenage Scuba Crew Leader. If you're expecting visitors or want to encourage outreach, assign three children to each Scuba Crew. Then encourage children to invite their friends to "fill up" their crews. If your attendance is pretty steady, assign up to five children to each crew. If possible, assign one child from each age level to each crew. "Your Elementary Scuba Crew 'Family' " (p. 30), a developmental chart and illustrations, highlights the unique contribution children from each age level can make to a Scuba Crew. The "Who's Who on the Crew?" chart on page 32 lists the five jobs elementary Scuba Crew members may fill during **SCUBA**.

Preschoolers' Scuba Crews consist of up to five preschoolers and an adult or teenage crew leader.

Detailed instructions for setting up Scuba Crews begin on page 155. Qualifications for crew leaders are listed on page 135.

Field Test Findings

Try to structure your crews so that they contain no more than six members. Through field testing and customer feedback, we've discovered that larger crews can get unmanageable and become a frustration for the crew leaders. Plus, smaller crews maximize important relationship-building time in the crew.

Leader Lifeline

Be sure to distribute the "Crew Leader's Pocket Guide" to all crew leaders during your leader training time. Have extras available at **SCUBA** for crew leaders who are unable to attend leader training. These guidebooks are a valuable source of helpful information to those who work closely with children!

YOUR ELEMENTARY S.C.U.B.A. CREW "FAMILY"

I just finished second grade. I'm a unique and important part of my Scuba Crew because I want everything to be fair. I can help make sure we all take turns and treat one another fairly.

I just finished fifth grade. I'm a unique and important part of my Scuba Crew because I like to make choices. I can help my Scuba Crew make choices about a crew name, jobs, and activities.

I just finished first grade. I'm a unique and important part of my Scuba Crew because I like to be the best. I can help encourage my Scuba Crew to be the best it can be.

I just finished kindergarten. I'm a unique and important part of my Scuba Crew because I have a great imagination. I can help my Scuba Crew pretend we're really exploring undersea!

I just finished third grade. I'm a unique and important part of my Scuba Crew because I like to be challenged. I can help younger members of my Scuba Crew with challenging projects.

I just finished fourth grade. I'm a unique and important part of my Scuba Crew because I like to ask questions. I can help my Scuba Crew ask questions to make sure we understand what we're learning.

WHY aRe Scuba CReWS ComBineD-age?

FielD Test FinDings

"The older kids at my church like being with their friends. They'll complain if they have to be with the 'little' kids." Many people are hesitant to try teaching combined-age groups because they're afraid kids will balk at something new. You *can* let kids partner with same-age friends if they're really reluctant. But at our field tests, we discovered that kids enjoyed being in combined-age Scuba Crews. Sure, it was a little different at first, but as kids warmed up to their crew mates, we saw them working together, helping one another, and forming friendships. There were few complaints, and discipline problems were almost nonexistent.

You may be skeptical about placing kids in mixed-age groups. After all, that's probably not how your other children's ministry functions are structured. And the school system is set up to be age-graded too. So why should you shake things up and try combining ages? Here's why!

Combined-age Scuba Crews encourage teamwork, rather than competition. When kids are grouped in age-graded classes, there's more emphasis on comparison ("I can do it better!") and competition ("I can do it faster!"). However, by placing children in mixed-age crews, you nearly eliminate the unspoken desire for kids to compare or compete. Instead, older kids help younger ones with challenging tasks. Younger kids seek to emulate the older, "cool" kids in their crews.

Combined-age Scuba Crews reduce discipline problems. Now we *love* kids of all ages, but there's something intimidating about that group of fifth-grade boys. But when you split up that daunting bunch of preteen kids, they suddenly lose their "audience" (that is, one another), and your discipline problems nearly vanish. You'll get the same delightful effect when you split up middle-elementary cliques, some siblings, and other "troublesome twosomes."

Combined-age Scuba Crews encourage relationship-building. By mixing ages to form small groups, you provide a rare opportunity for kids of all ages to get to know one another. Most kids are with one another during school, sports, and other activities. Multi-age Scuba Crews give kids the chance to build meaningful relationships with new friends.

Combined-age Scuba Crews are easier to work with. Your Scuba Crew Leaders will *love* how easy it is to work with kids of mixed ages. Rather than trying to assist a group of six-year-olds with reading or crafts, a crew leader can give one-on-one attention to one six-year-old. And (believe it or not) older kids will relish their helping role as they lead with their strengths.

But don't take our word for it! Log onto www.groupvbs.com and ask other directors who have tried this method.

DiD you KnoW?

Studies show that children learn as much—or more— when they're linked with kids of different ages. In fact, one study observed that children naturally chose to play with other children their age only 6 percent of the time. They played with children at least one year older or younger than them 55 percent of the time.

FiELD TesT FinDinGS

It's true that kids may protest when they discover that they won't be with their group of very best friends. But we've discovered that it's really the *parents* who complain the loudest! That's why we've created a photocopiable parent information letter on page 170. Keep several copies on hand to help parents understand why you're setting up your **SCUBA** this way.

FiELD TesT FinDinGS

As VBS director, you'll find that open, clear communication is your best friend! Be sure to touch base with the Sing & Play Splash Leader to remind him or her to allow time for children to choose their roles on Day 1. Although this process is written into the Sing & Play Splash Leader Manual, it's good to double-check and be sure the leader understands the importance of this process.

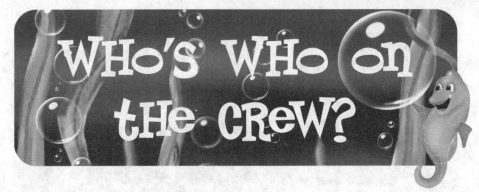

WHO'S WHO on the CREW?

During Sing & Play Splash on Day 1, kids choose Scuba Crew jobs. You can expect each of the following jobs to be represented in each Scuba Crew. If crews have fewer than five kids, some kids may have more than one job.

In addition to the five jobs listed below, each crew should have an adult or teenage Scuba Crew Leader. You can count on the crew leader to help kids complete the activities at each Scuba Station.

Kids are excited about having special jobs! Each leader manual suggests ways Scuba Station Leaders can call on kids to fulfill the job responsibilities they've chosen.

JOBS	DUTIES
Reader	• likes to read • reads Bible passages aloud
Scuba Guide	• chooses action ideas for traveling between Scuba Stations (such as "swimming," rowing, hopping, galloping, or marching) • helps monitor the daily schedule to let the Scuba Crew know what's coming next
Materials Manager	• likes to distribute and collect supplies • distributes and collects **SCUBA** Bible Books • carries the crew's bag until the day is over
Coach	• likes to smile and make people happy • makes sure people use kind words and actions • leads group in cheering during Splish Splash Games
Prayer Person	• likes to pray and isn't afraid to pray aloud • makes sure the group takes time to pray each day • leads or opens prayer times

WHERE DO MIDDLE SCHOOLERS Fit In?

Many churches are unsure how to handle upper-elementary kids; they seem too old for some children's ministry programs and too young for youth group. With **SCUBA**, upper-elementary kids can fill a number of roles. (In fact, middle schoolers at our field test reported that they loved helping because it gave them the chance to be adults...*and* kids.) Check out the following options to find the perfect fit for your middle schoolers. They can

• **join Scuba Crews as Assistant Scuba Crew Leaders.** Many upper-elementary kids are ready for simple leadership roles, but they still enjoy participating in activities such as games, snack times, crafts, and biblical dramas. As Assistant Scuba Crew Leaders, they can help their crew leaders by keeping kids together, working with younger children during Undersea Crafts and Missions or doing the more difficult jobs during Dive-In Diner Service.

• **become assistant station leaders.** Your middle schoolers are developing their gifts and talents and are discovering the things they excel at and enjoy. Being an assistant station leader is a great way to encourage kids toward this discovery. Do you know an older child who's developing a love for drama and storytelling? Use him or her as an Assistant Sea Star Finale Leader or an Assistant Deep Bible Adventures Leader. What about a child who enjoys sports and other athletic activities? Ask him or her to be an Assistant Splish Splash Games Leader. Your station leaders will love the extra help, and older kids will enjoy the added responsibility.

• **help with Preschool Tide Pool registration.** Some middle schoolers are nurturing and caring—great qualities for helping preschoolers find their way at **SCUBA**. For the first day or two, have a few middle schoolers available to act as guides, helping preschoolers find their Scuba Crew Leaders, showing preschoolers the restrooms, or playing with shy children to get them accustomed to Preschool Tide Pool.

• **create an upper-elementary Sing-Along Crew.** Older children (who might normally hesitate to sing and move to music) will enjoy teaching song motions and leading younger children in Sing & Play Splash. Ask a group of upper-elementary kids to work with the Sing & Play Splash Leader to learn the words and motions to all twelve **SCUBA** songs. The Sing-Along Crew will add visual excitement and energy to your singing time.

FieLD TesT FinDinGS

It's important that middle school kids understand the specifics of their jobs. We discovered that assigning kids this age as "floaters" who could fill in wherever there were needs gave them too much freedom and not enough direction. When we gave them specific roles, such as Assistant Chef or Assistant Undersea Crafts Leader, they did super jobs to help us out!

LeaDeR LifeLine

Make sure you choose more mature fifth- and sixth-graders for leadership roles. Many kids this age still enjoy being crew members and participating in all activities. Some upper-elementary kids will feel left out if they can't make their own crafts or participate fully in other activities. Be sure to ask kids what they'd like to do instead of assuming they'd rather "opt out."

Middle schoolers have so much to offer (and gain from) your program! We've heard countless stories of middle schoolers and teenagers whose lives were changed because of their experiences in leading or assisting in VBS. The more these kids are involved in your program, the more opportunities you have to touch their lives.

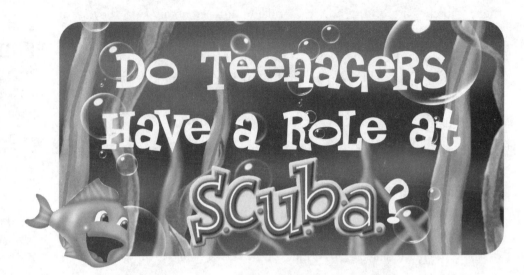

Teenagers have an important role in making **SCUBA** a success! Use the following suggestions to involve teenagers (or college students) in your program.

• **Have them act as Scuba Crew Leaders.** Many young adults have younger siblings or baby-sit frequently and are comfortable working with children. Young adults will have a great time leading their crews—and will love how easy it is. (Teenagers will actually get as much out of the Bible stories and discussions as the young children will!)

• **Let teenagers and young adults help with registration.** Believe it or not, some young people have excellent organizational skills. These young people enjoy forming crews, greeting children, and helping kids find their Scuba Crew Leaders. (These helpers make a great first impression for adults as well as kids.) After the first day, your registration helpers can register newcomers, count the daily attendance and report the number to the Dive-In Diner Leader, and fill in for crew leaders who are absent.

• **Have qualified teenagers run your sound system or act as photographers.** Some high school drama programs train young people to run sound, lighting, and video equipment. These teenagers make excellent **SCUBA** technical staff members. You may even ask them to put together a slide show or video production of your program.

FieLD TeST FinDinGS

Who says VBS is just for little kids? We've heard so many stories of how teenagers' lives were touched by past VBS programs. Young adults who volunteered had such a great time and were so moved by the Bible experiences that they made life-changing decisions!

• **Ask teenagers to act as Deep Bible Adventures volunteers.** The Deep Bible Adventures Leader needs several volunteers to act as Bible characters in simple dramas. Teenagers with dramatic flair enjoy playing Scuba-Do (in Sing & Play Splash) or the Roman guard (during Deep Bible Adventures).

• **If your church's youth group has a choir or worship band, let it help with Sing & Play Splash and Sea Star Finale.** Kids at **SCUBA** love singing with the "big kids," and young adults will never have such a receptive and friendly audience again. Your station leaders enjoy the extra backup and enthusiasm. Plus, teenagers learn and grow right along with the children!

There are countless ways to involve youth in **SCUBA**. Just let teenagers find roles in which their gifts, talents, or interests lead them. You'll be surprised at how committed and enthusiastic these young volunteers are.

WHAT'S A SCUBA BIBLE BOOK?

Each child at **SCUBA** will need a **SCUBA** Bible Book. The Bible Book includes five Bible stories (taken directly from the kid-friendly New International Reader's Version), spectacular sea stuff, journal activities, and take-home newsletters to extend learning into the home. While traditional student pages are filled with pointless puzzles and word searches, the **SCUBA** Bible Book allows kids to dig in to practical Bible study skills—learning how to read the Bible, apply it to their lives, and find answers to their questions in God's Word.

Preschoolers have their own age-appropriate Tide Pool Bible Books, each complete with five illustrated Bible stories and five activity pages to make Bible learning fun and memorable at VBS. Preschoolers' parents will appreciate the take-home newsletters—full of easy follow-up ideas, fun Bible-learning songs, and simple crafts that reinforce each day's Bible story and Point.

And don't forget Surprise Stickers! Kids will really go "below the surface" with these awesome two-in-one stickers! That's why we've placed one sheet of Surprise Stickers inside each Bible Book (elementary and preschool). Ordinary stickers have a cool picture on top...but *these* have another picture or message underneath! (And the top sticker will re-stick again and again!) For example, on Day 1, elementary kids will place the Ace sticker inside their Bible Books...but when they peel back the picture of Ace, they'll find an *ichthus*. The Chadder's Undersea Bible Adventure Leader will explain that early Christians used the *ichthus* to tell that they believed in God. Kids use Surprise Stickers during Chadder's Undersea Bible Adventure and Undersea Crafts and Missions.

WHAT ARE BIBLE POINT CRAFTS?

OK, you're right...every VBS program includes crafts. (And you've probably got a few crafty folks at your church who could pull together some nifty projects on their own.) So what makes these crafts so special?

○ **Each Bible Point Craft connects with the Bible story and Bible Point.** Now *that's* different! In fact, everything at **SCUBA** ties together to reinforce one simple, memorable Bible Point—and crafts are no exception. Not only do these crafts tie into the scuba theme, but they will be lasting mementos of important *Bible* truths. We've heard from VBS directors who substituted a more generic or theme-oriented craft...and were disappointed at how disconnected it felt from the Bible Point.

○ **Bible Point Crafts are irresistible to kids.** We know because we've tested these crafts in a real VBS setting! We asked kids what they liked about the crafts, listened to kids' conversations as they worked on the crafts, and watched what kids did with the crafts during (and after) **SCUBA**. These are *all* kid-pleasers—even for those hard-to-please fifth-grade boys!

○ **Bible Point Crafts are downright fun!** You may run across crafts that look adorable when they're finished...but all they do is hang on a refrigerator or sit on a shelf. Forget those boring mosaics, pencil toppers, or paperweights. We figure that kids are active so their crafts should be too! Kids will definitely dive for *these* craft "toys" that soar, store, sail, sift, swim, and stretch!

○ **Bible Point Crafts are "doable."** Flip through some craft magazines, and you'll be amazed at the crafts they tout as "kid-friendly." (At least they're not friendly to many kids *we* know!) Since groups of "real" kids have tested these crafts, we know that these projects won't frustrate or bore the kids at your **SCUBA**. And the crafts are relatively no-mess, so you don't have to wait for the glue or paint to dry overnight. Kids can use and play with these amazing crafts right away!

○ **Bible Point Crafts are exclusive.** These keepsakes are available only with our special VBS. That means you'll delight and surprise kids with these unique projects they can get nowhere else! Kids will be excited to get their hands on these never-been-done crafts.

○ **Bible Point Crafts give you more options.** VBS directors and craft leaders asked us to provide more options so they could choose the best crafts for their particular church setting. So now you have two choices for each day. Can't decide which to do? Then do them all! Just purchase extra craft options to use at summer Sunday school, children's church, day camp, family camp, or midweek programs. Or save them for the fall and use them for other special children's ministry events.

○ **Bible Point Crafts are cost-effective.** Whatever your budget, there's something for you in this manual. On a tight budget? Check out our fund-raising ideas in this **SCUBA** Director Manual. You'll find fun, easy, creative ways to stretch your VBS dollars. And since kids make keepsake reminders of the Bible truths they've learned, you know that these crafts won't end up in the trash. Your dollars are being used wisely!

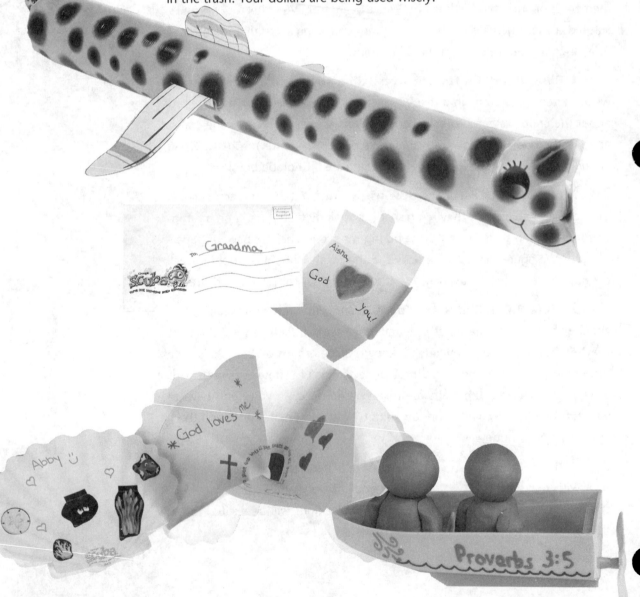

WHO IS CHADDER CHIPMUNK?

Chadder Chipmunk™ is a lovable, mischievous character the kids love. Each day when kids visit Chadder's Undersea Bible Adventure, they view a segment of *Chadder's Undersea Bible Adventure* video.

Chadder mistakenly hops aboard the Collapso, a research ship headed for the coral reefs. It seems that someone is stealing the coral and endangering the reef! Chadder and his new friend, Jamie, face an amazing adventure as they find out. Is it kooky Captain Jock Crusteau? Or that menacing Klaus? It couldn't be crazy Cookie! Tag along with Chadder on his mystery of the coral reef thief to find out! Kids won't want to miss the daily cliffhangers in *this* adventure!

As Chadder explores God's amazing creation undersea, he discovers what it means to believe in God and to obey God's commands. Chadder also finds that he can trust and love God and share the wonderful news of God's love.

Chadder's Undersea Bible Adventure Leader Manual contains discussion questions that go along with each day's segment of *Chadder's Undersea Bible Adventure* video. The video is available from Group Publishing and your local Christian bookstore.

FIELD TEST FINDINGS

Our field test kids couldn't wait to see each day's adventure! The continuing drama, comical characters, and cliffhanger endings built great anticipation and kept kids coming back for more each day.

FIELD TEST FINDINGS

Your kids will love Chadder and will look forward to seeing him. Not only will they enjoy the humorous characters Chadder meets, but they'll also appreciate the wonderful downtime during a busy day at **SCUBA**. Kids are so active during VBS that it's nice for them to have a few moments to sit down, rest, and watch. (Your Scuba Crew Leaders will appreciate it too.)

LOOK WHO'S MAKING A SPLASH AT YOUR S.C.U.B.A.

Nobody should ever dive without a dive buddy. So each day at **SCUBA**, kids meet a fishy friend who reminds them of the day's Bible Point. They're Bible Memory Buddies™! We'll let this wet set speak for themselves!

I'm Ace! Believe it or not, I'm a flying fish! There's only one, true God who can *really* make a fish that can fly. I'll remind kids to believe in God. Wahoo!

It's me...Squirt! We whales make cool sounds when we talk to each other. And it's super important that we listen and obey what other whales say. Otherwise we'll end up lost, hungry, or hurt! I want kids to learn to obey God.

Tank here! Sea turtles have a built-in protection system that keeps us safe from danger. Kids don't have a shell...but they *do* have God. I'll help kids discover that they can trust God.

I'm Pearl. God gave me a way to make a precious treasure from a tiny grain of sand. I want kids to know Jesus is God's Son— *God's* precious treasure! I'll remind kids to love God!

My name's Starla, and I love reaching out to share God's love with others! When kids see my arms stretched out, they'll want to share God's love too!

To help kids remember these important Bible truths, the Splish Splash Games Leader will give each child a Bible Memory Buddy every day to keep in his or her Dive Bag (an awesome craft that kids make on Day 2). And each Buddy has the Key Verse inscribed on it. Kids will *love* collecting these squirty sea critters! And you'll be amazed at how the Bible Memory Buddies help kids dive deeper into a relationship with God.

Can Kids Really Make Their Own Snacks?

Each day at **SCUBA**, a different group of kids skips its Splish Splash Games time so it can prepare snacks for the entire VBS. Snack preparation provides kids with a unique opportunity to live out the daily Bible Point by serving others. And it makes your job easier because you don't have to recruit additional volunteers to make snacks. (Some churches have said snack preparation was the biggest hurdle to overcome. But after letting kids try it, snack preparation became one of the best parts of their VBS experience.)

Believe it or not, one-fourth of your kids *can* prepare snacks for everyone else—if you follow the field-tested, step-by-step instructions provided in the Dive-In Diner Leader Manual. Each day snack preparation will follow the simple procedures outlined below.

1. Before kids arrive, the Dive-In Diner Leader sets out supplies according to the diagrams provided in the Dive-In Diner Leader Manual.

2. After kids arrive and wash their hands, the leader explains each step of the snack preparation and invites kids to choose which steps they'd like to work on.

3. Kids work in assembly lines to prepare the snacks. Scuba Crew Leaders are assigned the more difficult tasks such as handling sharp knives or pouring drinks.

4. Kids set out the completed snacks on tables, where they'll be picked up and gobbled down during Dive-In Diner.

Leader Lifeline

Of course it sounds simpler to just distribute cookies and juice at snack time. But isn't it worth a little extra effort to give kids the opportunity to actually serve others? You'll be amazed to see children working together, and the kids will be delighted to see what a big job they can accomplish. Don't rob them of a valuable (and fun) learning and serving experience.

41

Field Test Findings

Kids who serve on the Dive-In Diner Service Crew report for snack preparation right after Sing & Play Splash. They'll take twenty to twenty-five minutes to prepare snacks before moving on to their next Scuba Station. And just in case kids don't finish in time, the Dive-In Diner Leader has an additional twenty to twenty-five minutes to make final preparations before all the children arrive to eat. In **SCUBA** field tests, even preschoolers were able to complete their snack preparation within the allotted time.

As director, you'll want to drop in on the Dive-In Diner Service Crew each day. Ask the leader how kids' work is progressing, and affirm the children for a job well done. But don't linger too long; you may distract kids from completing their work. Be sure to return at snack time to see children explain the meaning of the snack as *they* teach the Bible Point. Then watch the Dive-In Diner Service Crew kids' faces light up as they're recognized for their accomplishment.

THIS HANDS-ON
MISSION PROJECT
ALLOWS KIDS TO REACH
OUT TO CHILDREN
AROUND THE WORLD!

What Is Operation Kid-to-Kid™?

Operation Kid-to-Kid

Leader LifeLine

You may be used to having children bring money for missions offering or toward a mission project. However, most children don't understand the value of money—it's not a tangible "need" for them. Therefore, it's difficult to make a concrete connection to how they're really making a difference in the life of another child. Shoes and socks are simple, everyday objects that children are familiar with. Kids can easily identify with this need! This mission project is designed to have a big impact—on the kids who give and on the kids who receive!

More Than an Offering

Several years ago, the VBS team at Group Publishing wanted to include a meaningful service project to help kids realize that with God's help, even children can impact the world. We knew that today's kids are service-minded and want to make a difference, both globally and within their communities. From customer feedback, we also learned that VBS directors (like you) wanted kids to give more than money. They wanted kids to give something that was meaningful and tangible—something that would meet the needs of children across the world. So in 1998, we launched the first Operation Kid-to-Kid™ program as an integral part of our Space Mission Bible Camp VBS.

Since then, Operation Kid-to-Kid has been an exciting part of each Group VBS program. We've partnered with a different mission organization each year, finding new ways for kids in North America to reach out in meaningful ways. Through Operation Kid-to-Kid, millions of kids in North America have sent God's love around the world!

> Operation Kid-to-Kid™ is an international mission project that allows hundreds of thousands of kids in North America to serve children around the world. What a great way to splash God's light and love around the globe!

Put Your Best Foot Forward

Buckner Orphan Care International (BOCI) is part of one of the largest Christian social-care ministries of its kind in the nation, serving approximately 80,000 children and families each year. One dynamic ministry Buckner has developed is Shoes for Orphan Souls. With this project, children in North America collect brand-new

shoes and socks to send to orphans all over the world. In 2001, Shoes for Orphan Souls collected over 500,000 pairs of shoes! Those shoes were sent to orphans in twenty-five countries, such as China, Kenya, Ukraine, India, Guatemala and Russia. And along with a new pair of shoes, these children also receive the life-changing message of God's love.

When the shoes and socks are distributed in the orphanages, a team of volunteers will also hold a VBS program for the children there. Loving volunteers explain that these gifts are sent from friends in North America as a way to show how much God loves us! The orphans will learn Bible songs, hear life-changing Bible stories, and experience a touch of God's love.

We want to give the kids at **SCUBA** the opportunity to share God's love with children across the globe. Operation Kid-to-Kid is a practical, meaningful way for kids to demonstrate God's love through giving and service.

LeadeR LifeLine

For more information about Operation Kid-to-Kid, check out www.ok2k.org or www.shoesfororphansouls.org.

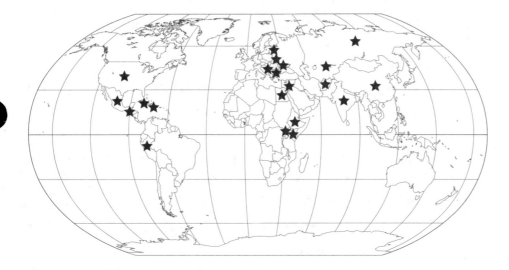

HoW youR KidS can HeLP

Before you begin your **S**uper **C**ool **U**ndersea **B**ible **A**dventure, decide how to focus your Operation Kid-to-Kid program. With this flexible program, you have a few options:

Just collect brand-new shoes. Kids can bring in boots, sandals, or sturdy athletic shoes in any size!

Just collect brand-new socks. Kids can bring colorful socks; silly socks; plain, white socks; or athletic socks in any size!

Collect both brand-new shoes *and* socks! Kids can decide which they'd like to bring in.

Wow! Look what kids have done through Operation Kid-to-Kid!

- **1998** Kids in North America sent more than 91,000 school supply kits to children around the world.

- **1999** Children involved in Operation Kid-to-Kid sent approximately 400,000 Spanish translations of the Gospel of John to Spanish-speaking children around the world.

- **2000** Film Crews at Group's HolyWord Studios created more than 100,000 Care Kits that were distributed in countries such as Thailand, Vietnam, and Albania.

- **2001** Cool Crews who took part in Polar Expedition sent more than 380,000 Gift Boxes to needy children across the globe!

- **2002** The numbers aren't in, but as this manual is being written, churches are still taking part in Operation Kid-to-Kid 2002. It's estimated that children in North America will send almost 1 million Bible coloring books to orphans in Russia and Romania! Wow!

- **2003** Who knows what we can accomplish together!

Leader Lifeline

We discovered that kids need a small-group setting to discuss, understand, and focus on Operation Kid-to-Kid. Undersea Crafts and Missions is a natural "Operation Kid-to-Kid Headquarters." There, children learn about the project and its impact, then "meet" three children (through Operation Kid-to-Kid posters) who are representatives of the children who will receive the shoes and socks.

You might even want to have elementary kids bring shoes and the preschoolers bring socks. Be creative and choose the item that will work best for *your* church and community!

On the second day of **SCUBA**, the Undersea Crafts and Missions Leader will explain Operation Kid-to-Kid to the elementary kids when they come to do crafts. He or she will string a hammock "fishing net" in a corner of the room to collect the items children bring in. (This is a *great* way to watch the "catch" grow!)

The Preschool Tide Pool Leader will explain the project to preschoolers on Day 2. Preschoolers will use their own hammock "fishing net" to collect shoes or socks!

At the end of Day 2, preschoolers and elementary children will take home a special letter that explains the program to parents. (Although their leader manuals direct these leaders to make and distribute the letters, we've included the letter in this manual if you prefer to take that responsibility.)

Just circle the appropriate box on the "Have You Ever Thought About..." letter (p. 49). Make enough photocopies of the letter for each child to take one home.

Then the Undersea Crafts and Missions Leader (as well as the Preschool Tide Pool Leader) will ask each day which children have brought in their Kid-to-Kid items. Those children will write a short note or draw a simple picture for the child who will receive the shoes or socks. Kids will tuck their notes inside the shoes or socks, then bring them forward and place their items in the hammock "net."

At the last Sea Star Finale (on Day 5), your Undersea Crafts and Missions Leader and the Preschool Tide Pool Leader will drag in the overflowing nets to present the shoes and socks as an offering. This is a powerful, moving ceremony. Kids and leaders will be amazed as they see how their fishing net is bursting with gifts for other children! It's a very concrete way for kids to see that it's easy to share God's love.

LeaDeR LifeLine

Operation Kid-to-Kid is a super way to involve your entire church in SCUBA. A few weeks before VBS, let church members know that you'll be collecting shoes and socks to send to needy orphans across the globe. Hold a shoe (or sock) drive before SCUBA even starts! Use these additional shoes for kids who weren't able to bring any to donate. What an easy way to get everyone hooked on VBS!

Field Test Findings

When the shoes and socks were brought forward, the huge pile was amazing...but we couldn't tell what it was because kids had left the shoes in shoe boxes! Then, in talking with our friends at Buckner Orphan Care International, it turns out that they need the shoes out of the packaging anyway! So we changed the instructions in the Undersea Craft and Missions Manual, as well as in the Preschool Tide Pool Director Manual, to direct children to remove shoes from the shoe boxes. (Seeing the variety of shoes and socks makes a wonderful visual of all God's children!)

Leader Lifeline

These shoes and socks *do* go a long way in reaching hurting children with a touch of God's love. You're welcome to include a larger monetary gift with your shoes, allowing Shoes for Orphan Souls to do even more as they minister to these children.

and Your Job Is Easy Too!

After your **SCUBA** ends, it's time to send your shoes and/or socks to Shoes for Orphan Souls for distribution. Follow these simple steps to ensure that your shoes and socks will be a special part of this world-changing project.

1. Take the shoes out of any boxes and remove all tags and paper. Fasten shoes together with a plastic tie (can be purchased at a hardware store). Leave the socks in their original packaging. Place the shoes and/or socks in a sturdy shipping box. Detailed shipping information can be found at www.shoesfororphansouls.org or call 1-877-7ORPHAN with questions.

2. Mark an envelope with "Operation Kid-to-Kid."

3. Place a check for $15 in the envelope. (Make checks payable to: Shoes for Orphan Souls.) This money helps cover the cost of distribution and ministry in these hard-to-reach areas of the world.

4. Include in the envelope your contact name, church name, and your mailing address and phone number. (Buckner will send out a follow-up newsletter, letting you know the outcome of this exciting project!)

5. Place the sealed envelope in the box, seal the box, and mail it to:

Operation Kid-to-Kid
c/o Shoes for Orphan Souls
4828 S. Buckner Blvd
Dallas, Texas 75227

Or in Canada:
Shoes for Orphan Souls c/o Arms of Jesus
364 Kingston Road
Pickering, Ontario
L1V 1A2

Shoes for Orphan Souls will take care of the rest!

If You Want a Deeper Ministry...

Every year Shoes for Orphan Souls takes teams of volunteers on mission trips to help deliver the shoes. You may want to encourage someone from your church to raise support to travel with BOCI and hand deliver your church's message of God's love to the orphans. If you're interested, check out www.shoesfororphansouls.org or call 1-877-7ORPHAN.

Thanks for Joining Us in this Exciting World-Changing Project!

HaVe you eVeR THOUGHt aBOUt...

...how it would feel to walk on a hot desert landscape...without shoes?

...what it would be like to face a Ukrainian winter...without shoes?

...allowing your child to walk to school...without shoes?

In North America, many of us take shoes and socks for granted. For the most part, our feet stay clean and protected. But that's not the case for hundreds of thousands of orphans around the world.

During our **S**uper **C**ool **U**ndersea **B**ible **A**dventure, not only will your kids go deeper into God's love, they'll take the news of God's love and share it with these children! This hands-on mission project, called Operation Kid-to-Kid™, will allow kids in North America to send brand-new shoes and socks to needy children around the globe. (In 2001, this project allowed 500,000 orphans in twenty-five countries to have a pair of shoes! Just think what we can do in 2003!)

○ We're collecting brand-new shoes!

○ We're collecting brand-new socks!

○ We're collecting brand-new shoes *and* socks...
   so bring whichever you'd like!

During the week, each child will bring in a brand-new pair of shoes or socks that would fit a child ages 2 to 18 years. We don't expect you to purchase the most expensive, trendy brand out there! The following types of shoes are acceptable, as long as they're **brand new:**

Sandals   Athletic shoes   Canvas shoes   Boots   Flip-Flops

To make this project more meaningful, we ask that you allow your child to help select the shoes that he or she will donate. Then have your child bring the shoes to **SCUBA** before the last day.

If you would like to donate extra shoes, please feel free to do so. We'll need extras for children who are unable to bring their own.

Contact_____at _____for

　　　　　　　　SCUBA Director　　　　　　　　　　　　　Phone

more information. You can read about this project at www.shoesfororphansouls.org or call

1-877-7ORPHAN for more information.

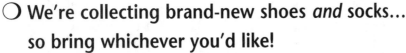

Planning for Operation Kid-to-Kid™

Field Test Findings

A picture really is worth a thousand words! The Operation Kid-to-Kid posters and video help kids connect the face of a child to this project. By posting these pictures for kids to see, you help Operation Kid-to-Kid take on a more personal feeling for kids. It's a great way to build enthusiasm and make outreach meaningful. The Operation Kid-to-Kid™ Missions Kit is available from Group Publishing or your local Christian bookstore.

Before SCUBA

• **Inform your congregation.** Let your congregation know that the kids in your church will be sharing God's love with orphans around the world. Photocopy the "500,000 Feet Undersea!" bulletin insert (p. 52), and distribute it at a worship service. This handout explains Operation Kid-to-Kid and lets church members know about this awesome project for VBS kids. (Church members can start collecting new shoes right away!)

• **Inform your community.** Photocopy the "Operation Kid-to-Kid™ News Release" (p. 53), and fill in the information regarding your church's program. Send the news release to local newspapers, television stations, and radio stations (especially your Christian radio station) so they can let others in your community know about your participation in Operation Kid-to-Kid.

During SCUBA

• **Remind kids of the importance of their mission.** It's likely that kids in North America take their shoes and socks for granted. Most children have more than one pair...and have many hardly-used shoes sitting on closet shelves. Help kids understand that shoes and socks help children's feet feel warm and protected. Explain that the children in orphanages around the world need to know that God loves and protects them in the same way.

• **Check in with the Scuba Crew Leaders.** During your opening huddle and prayer with the Scuba Crew Leaders, ask them how kids are responding to Operation Kid-to-Kid. Encourage them to talk with their kids about how important it is for everyone to know about God's love.

• **Connect with your Undersea Crafts and Missions Leader.** Remind your leader to have kids remove the shoes from any packaging, connect the shoes with a plastic tie, and tuck a special note inside the shoes.

• **Encourage kids to pray for their "foot friends."** During Sing & Play Splash, Undersea Crafts and Missions, or Sea Star Finale, allow a short time for kids to pray for the children who will receive the shoes and socks. Children can pray that these children will discover how much God loves each of us.

After SCUBA

• **Send your shoes and socks to the Kid-to-Kid Send-Off Center.** All shoes should be removed from shoe boxes and be free of tags and paper. Fasten shoes together with a plastic tie, and leave the socks in their original packaging. (These steps should have happened in Undersea Crafts and Missions already.) Place the shoes and/or socks in a sturdy shipping box. Place a check for $15 in an envelope (this money helps cover distribution and ministry costs) along with your contact name, church name, and your mailing address and phone number. Place the sealed envelope in the box, seal the box, and mail it to:

Operation Kid-to-Kid
c/o Shoes for Orphan Souls
4828 S. Buckner Blvd.
Dallas, Texas 75227

Or in Canada:
Shoes for Orphan Souls c/o Arms of Jesus
364 Kingston Road
Pickering, Ontario
L1V 1A2

• **Look for your Operation Kid-to-Kid update**. Shoes for Orphan Souls will send your church a newsletter about Operation Kid-to-Kid several months after your program. You'll learn how this outreach program affected thousands of children around the world. Share this powerful information with your children; they'll love hearing that their gifts went around the world to share the message of God's love! (We'll try to keep you posted on any distribution news at www.ok2k.org.)

500,000 Feet UNDeRSea!

On our **S**uper **C**ool **U**ndersea **B**ible **A**dventure, not only will your kids dive into God's love, but they'll also send the good news across the globe! This hands-on mission project, called Operation Kid-to-Kid™, will allow kids in North America to send new shoes and/or socks to orphans around the world. These shoes and socks are desperately needed by children who have virtually nothing. What a tangible way of showing God's love and care for us!

During **SCUBA**, kids will be asked to bring in either a new pair of shoes or socks (for a child, ages two through eighteen). Due to customs regulations, only brand-new shoes are acceptable. Although boots or sturdy winter shoes are preferred, other shoes are also acceptable. Kids at our **SCUBA** VBS will collect the shoes and present them as an offering at the end of the week. Then we'll send them to Shoes for Orphan Souls for worldwide distribution. We're hoping that Operation Kid-to-Kid can collect 500,000 pairs of shoes!

We're collecting brand-new shoes. Kids can bring in boots, sandals, or sturdy athletic shoes in any size!

We're collecting brand-new socks. Kids can bring colorful socks; silly socks; plain, white socks; or athletic socks in any size!

We're collecting *both* brand-new shoes *and* socks! Kids can decide which they'd like to bring in.

We'Re eXCiTeD aBOuT tHiS Life-CHaNGiNG MiSSioN PROJeCT!

If you have any questions or would like to donate additional funds, shoes, or socks for Operation Kid-to-Kid, please contact:

_____
SCUBA Director

_____
Phone

or log on to www.shoesfororphansouls.org.

Operation Kid-to-Kid

Operation Kid-to Kid™
News Release

*Adapt the information in this news release to fit your church's **SCUBA**. Then submit typed, double-spaced copies to your local newspapers, radio stations (especially your Christian radio station), and TV stations. You may want to check with them for any other specific requirements regarding news releases.*

[Name of church] will be involved in a worldwide mission project called Operation Kid-to-Kid™. For this project, children attending [name of church]'s **SCUBA**: Super Cool Undersea Bible Adventure vacation Bible school will provide new shoes and socks for orphans around the world.

Operation Kid-to-Kid will show kids that even though we're separated by language and distance, everyone can share God's love! The shoes and socks will be shipped to Shoes for Orphan Souls, who will then distribute them to children in orphanages across the globe. Past Operation Kid-to-Kid programs have allowed over a million children in North America to send hundreds of thousands of hygiene items, school supplies, and Spanish-translations of the Gospel of John to children around the world. (For more information about Operation Kid-to-Kid, visit www.ok2k.org or www.shoesfororphansouls.org.)

Operation Kid-to-Kid is just one part of **SCUBA**, a Super Cool Undersea Bible Adventure! **SCUBA** begins [starting date] and continues through [ending date]. It's located at [name of church and church address]. Registration opens each day at [starting time] and closes at [ending time]. For more information, call [church phone number].

PLANNING YOUR

S·C·U·B·a

SUPER COOL UNDERSEA BIBLE ADVENTURE

FOLLOW THESE STEPS TO MAKE SCUBA A SWIMMING SUCCESS!

PLANNING CALENDAR

THREE to SIX MONTHS BEFORE YOUR SUPER COOL UNDERSEA BIBLE ADVENTURE

○ **Begin praying for your church's SCUBA.** Ask God to prepare the hearts of church members, workers, and children who will attend.

○ **Choose a format for your SCUBA.**
- ✔ Will you meet in the morning, afternoon, or evening?
- ✔ Will you meet every day for a week or once a week for several weeks?
- ✔ Will your program be for children only, or will entire families be invited to attend?
- ✔ Will you meet at your church or another location?

○ **Set SCUBA dates.** As you're considering dates, you may want to find out about other summer programs offered by your church or your community so you can avoid conflicts.

○ **Choose a director.** If you're reading this manual, that's you! The director is responsible for planning, recruiting staff, and overseeing all details to ensure that **SCUBA** goes smoothly. For an even easier dive, consider recruiting a Crew Leader Director who will train, encourage, and check in on crew leaders throughout **SCUBA**. (Remember, your new favorite word is "delegate"!)

○ **Set a budget.** Look through the entire **SCUBA** catalog to get an idea of what you'll need for your program. Write down the cost of each item you'll need, then tally the total cost to set your budget. Your church may already include VBS in its budget. If so, find out what funds are available. If your church doesn't have a VBS budget in place, don't worry! Money for a quality VBS program needn't be a stumbling block. There are countless ways that you can easily (and painlessly) raise the funds you need. Consider the following ideas:
- ✔ Collect an offering to cover expenses.
- ✔ Charge a per-child registration fee for **SCUBA**. Give discounts to families that register more than one child.
- ✔ Invite congregation members to "sponsor" children by contributing

Leader Lifeline

We frequently hear back from customers who hold a very nontraditional VBS—using different settings, times, or dates. Be creative and choose the best VBS setting for your church situation.

Planning

a per-child amount. (See the "Registration" section on pp. 151-172 for more specifics on this idea.)

✔ Hold a creative fund-raiser! Open the Coral Café—just a basic bake sale, complete with adorable fish-shaped goodies. Be sure your hosts are decked out in scuba masks, flippers, or sea-creature costumes. Not only will this raise funds for your program, but it will also get everyone bubbling about your **SCUBA**.

○ **Start collecting decorations.** Hit those early summer sales to round up things like inflatable fish, swimming flippers, fish stickers, and large, fish-shaped balloons. You might even let members of your congregation know what you're looking for so that they can keep their eyes and ears open for potential decorations. (Check out our **SCUBA** store at www.groupoutlet.com. You'll find oceans of decorating delights at bargain prices.)

TWO to THRee MontHS BefoRe youR SuPeR cooL undeRsea BiBLe adventuRe

○ **Plan SCUBA publicity.** Decide how you'll promote **SCUBA** in your church and community. Refer to the "Publicity" section (pp. 141-150) in this manual for publicity ideas and resources.

○ **Begin recruiting Scuba Station Leaders.** Use the recruiting helps detailed in the Recruiting section (p. 99) to catch your **SCUBA** volunteers. The Recruiting section also includes bonus ideas that will captivate people's hearts and minds, while allowing you to flex those creative muscles (in an easy way—with great results). And the photocopiable job descriptions, handouts, and bulletin inserts make your job a breeze.

○ **Estimate your SCUBA enrollment.** Use figures from your church's Sunday school or figures from last year's VBS program. Once you've estimated how many children will attend, figure out how many Scuba Crew Leaders you'll need. You'll need one adult or teenage Scuba Crew Leader for every five children, including preschoolers. Be sure to have extra Scuba Crew Leaders ready in case you need to form Scuba Crews for last-minute registrants.

○ **Order SCUBA materials.** If you purchased the **SCUBA** Starter Kit, you already have a leader manual for every Scuba Station. You may want to order additional leader manuals for team teaching—and a copy of each leader manual for yourself, if you'd like. Your Chadder's Undersea Bible Adventure Leader will need a copy of the *Chadder's Undersea Bible Adventure* video.

PLANNING

LeaDeR LifeLine

Networking will stretch your time and dollars. Find other churches in your community who are doing **SCUBA**. Get together and brainstorm decorating, fund-raisers, and publicity ideas that will get your whole community excited about VBS. This year Group Publishing is sponsoring over 400 **SCUBA** Splash Parties around the country…just for you! A **SCUBA** Splash Party will be a time for networking, idea-sharing, and support. Check out the VBS catalog for a location near you! Or visit www.groupvbs.com, where you can gather ideas from **SCUBA** Directors from across North America.

FieLD TesT FinDinGS

Important! As we've said, people who have used Group's VBS in the past tell us that their VBS programs are growing. To avoid stress and disappointment, order early and order extra!

For every elementary-age child, you'll *need* to order

✔ a **SCUBA** Bible Book (includes a sheet of way-cool Surprise Stickers!);

✔ a **SCUBA** name badge;

✔ a set of Bible Memory Buddies; and

✔ Bible Point Craft items:
  • a Flying Fish or a Fish-a-Loon,
  • a Dive Bag,
  • a Trusty Timer or a Buzzalong Boat,
  • a Treasure Book or a Pearl Diver's Paradise, and
  • a Share Mail Postcard or a **SCUBA** Snapshot Frame.

For every preschooler, you'll *need* to order

✔ a Tide Pool Bible Book (includes a set of eye-catching Surprise Stickers);

✔ a **SCUBA** name badge;

✔ a set of Bible Memory Buddies; and
  • Bible Point Craft items:
  • a Fish-a-Loon,
  • a Dive Bag,
  • a Buzzalong Boat,
  • a Treasure Book, and
  • a Share Mail Postcard.

Even if you're planning a late-summer program, it's not too early to order materials. As you update your registration count, you can order additional student supplies as needed.

○ **Explore your church facilities.** You'll want to be deliberate in selecting your station areas. You'll need to set up a separate room or area for each station. Use the following guidelines:

○ **Sing & Play Splash**

✔ large room to accommodate entire VBS (possibly a sanctuary or fellowship hall)

✔ sound system/microphone (helpful)

✔ outlet to plug in audiocassette player or CD player (or a sound system to play *Sing & Play Splash Music* audiocassette or CD)

✔ outlet to plug in overhead projector (if using Sing & Play Splash song lyrics transparencies)

○ **Chadder's Undersea Bible Adventure**

✔ classroom to accommodate all the preschoolers at once and to accommodate one-fourth of the elementary-age kids (helpful if room can be darkened)

✔ outlet to plug in TV/VCR

○ **Undersea Crafts and Missions**
- ✔ classroom to accommodate one-fourth of the elementary-age kids
- ✔ 1 or 2 low tables (helpful for supplies)
- ✔ wall space for Operation Kid-to-Kid posters
- ✔ outlet to plug in audiocassette player or CD player when using *Sing & Play Splash Music* audiocassette or CD
- ✔ TV/VCR for showing the *Operation Kid-to-Kid* video

○ **Dive-In Diner**
- ✔ large room to accommodate entire VBS (possibly a fellowship hall or gymnasium)
- ✔ church kitchen or other noncarpeted area for Dive-In Diner Service

○ **Splish Splash Games**
- ✔ room or outdoor area to accommodate one-fourth of the elementary-age kids (a fellowship hall, gymnasium, or lawn)
- ✔ room enough for children to run around
- ✔ outlet to plug in audiocassette player or CD player if using *Sing & Play Splash Music* audiocassette or CD

○ **Deep Bible Adventures**
- ✔ classroom that can comfortably accommodate one-fourth of the elementary-age kids and that can be darkened
- ✔ classroom that's in a quiet area of your facility (helpful for storytelling)
- ✔ outlet to plug in CD player

○ **Sea Star Finale**
- ✔ large room to accommodate entire VBS (possibly a sanctuary or fellowship hall; could use the same room as Sing & Play Splash)
- ✔ sound system/microphone (helpful)
- ✔ outlet to plug in audiocassette or CD player
- ✔ stage (helpful)

○ **Preschool Tide Pool**
- ✔ classroom(s) to accommodate all preschoolers
- ✔ outlet to plug in audiocassette player
- ✔ restroom facilities in room or nearby
- ✔ child-sized furniture
- ✔ preschool toys such as blocks, modeling dough, dress-up clothes, and stuffed animals

○ **Plan and schedule a leader training meeting using the guidelines in the "Leader Training Meeting" section (p. 125).** This outline incorporates the *Dive Deep! Video*, which contains clips from **SCUBA** field tests.

LeaDeR LifeLine

You'll notice that there are two craft options for elementary kids. Check out your **SCUBA** catalog as well as the Undersea Crafts and Missions Leader Manual to learn more about Bible Point Crafts!

LeaDeR LifeLine

If your plans involve more than 150 children, consider running two or more simultaneous stations. For more information on how to do this, see "What's a Station?" (p. 24).

LeaDeR LifeLine

Remember, kids will need ample space between their crews. In close quarters, kids will be bumping into other crews, making it nearly impossible for them to focus on the life-application discussions. A good guideline is to estimate that you'll need at least one yard between each crew. If your classrooms are small, divide into two smaller rooms so children can stretch out and have some privacy for discussion within their crews. It will make a world of difference!

Your Scuba Station Leaders will enjoy seeing **SCUBA** in action. Be sure to include Scuba Crew Leaders in your training so that they can better understand their role. The video is filled with helpful, practical tips to make station leaders and crew leaders the best staff around. Plan to meet for at least two hours.

eiGHt WeeKS BeFoRe YoUR SUPeR CooL UNDeRSea BiBLe aDVeNtURe

○ **Begin recruiting Scuba Crew Leaders.** Scuba Crew Leaders are like older brothers and sisters in the Scuba Crew family. They aren't responsible for teaching, and they don't have to prepare anything. Scuba Crew Leaders can be teenagers, college students, parents, or grandparents. They need only to love the Lord and love children. For more information on recruiting, see the Recruitment section beginning on page 99.

Scuba Crew Leaders should plan to participate in **SCUBA** for the entire adventure. If they need to be absent one or more days, encourage them to find their own substitutes.

○ **Begin publicity.** Fill in your program's dates and times on the **SCUBA** outdoor banner (available from Group Publishing and your local Christian bookstore). Display the banner in a prominent outdoor location.

Hang **SCUBA** theme posters (available from Group Publishing and your local Christian bookstore) in your church and community.

Show the promotional segment of the *Dive Deep! Recruitment, Overview, and Pass-Along Training Video* during a worship service or other church gathering. This two-minute segment, found at the beginning of your video, gives people a glimpse at how **SCUBA** works and what kids will learn at this awesome VBS. You'll find that the video helps build enthusiasm, recruit volunteers, and promote attendance for your program.

○ **Begin gathering supplies.** Refer to the master supply list in the Daily Supplies section (p. 78). Consult with station leaders to inform them of how you'll handle supply collection. Will you gather all supplies, or will each leader gather his or her own supplies? You may want to ask church members to donate food supplies (such as whipped topping and cupcakes) or easy-to-find items (such as box fans).

○ **Determine (and publicize) your Operation Kid-to-Kid focus.** This Kid-to-Kid project has the potential to involve your entire congregation! Will you collect shoes, socks, or both? Do you need to have congregation members bring in extra shoes or socks ahead of time? It's a good idea to let families know about Kid-to-Kid ahead of time, so they can be scouting sales early on.

○ **Plan your SCUBA schedule.** The average VBS program runs for up to three hours each day. Group's **SCUBA** materials have been developed with these parameters in mind. For a three-hour program, Sing & Play Splash and Sea Star Finale should last twenty-five minutes each, and every other Scuba Station should last twenty minutes. See the daily schedules on pages 84-97 to see how this works. If your program will meet for more or less time than three hours each day, you'll need to adapt these times accordingly.

FouR WeeKS BefoRe youR SuPeR CooL unDeRSea BiBLe aDventuRe

○ **Recruit additional volunteers.** In addition to Scuba Station Leaders and Scuba Crew Leaders, you may want to recruit volunteers to help with registration, transportation, photography, and child care for the staff. Refer to the Recruiting section for more ideas.

○ **Determine whether you'll do the Closing Production.** This year you have the option of putting on a Closing Production at the end of your **SCUBA** program. The Closing Production *Scuba-Do's Dive* is a fun, audience-involving musical that allows kids to share the oceans of exciting Bible adventures they've experienced at **SCUBA!** Every child who attends your **SCUBA** can take part in presenting this musical drama (and it's so easy, you'll need only one or two brief rehearsals).

○ **Continue publicity.** Mail **SCUBA** invitation postcards to children in your church and community. Distribute **SCUBA** doorknob danglers in your community. Write your church's name and when your **SCUBA** will begin. (Invitation postcards and doorknob danglers are available from Group Publishing or your local Christian bookstore.)

○ **Begin preregistration.** Photocopy the "**SCUBA** Registration Form" (p. 169). Insert copies in your church bulletins, distribute copies in Sunday school classes, and keep a supply in your church office. Encourage parents from your church to preregister their children and their children's friends. This will make your first day more manageable.

LeaDeR LifeLine

Trimming time from your **SCUBA** doesn't have to be a challenge. You can shave a few minutes from Sing & Play Splash and Sea Star Finale by simply reducing the number of songs kids sing. Cut back on travel time between stations, as well as the time needed for kids to eat snacks. Please don't cut out important things like Chadder's Undersea Bible Adventure (where kids make important life-application Bible connections) or Operation Kid-to-Kid (which allows kids to share God's love in a tangible way). Each element of this program is there for a reason. Cutting out these elements is like throwing away pieces of a puzzle.

LeaDeR LifeLine

Preregistration really does make things run more smoothly. To get more kids preregistered, you might offer incentives. For example, provide a **SCUBA** T-shirt or a *Sing & Play Splash* Music audiocassette for each child who registers early. Or fill a large jar with gummy fish. Children who preregister can submit a "guess" as to how many fish are in the jar. (The winner gets to keep the entire jar of candy! Yum!) These incentives will build enthusiasm for your VBS too.

Planning

LeaDeR LifeLine

Although station leaders may want to add their flair or creativity to an activity, drama, or craft, encourage them to stick as closely as possible to the written material. Remind your staff members that each element of the **SCUBA** program has been designed to fit with the others—sort of like a jigsaw puzzle. Remember, we want to make VBS easy for your staff. There's no need to re-create or reinvent the wheel!

LeaDeR LifeLine

It's a good idea to line up a few extra Scuba Crew Leaders who will be available in case you have lots of walk-in registrants. Be sure these Scuba Crew Leaders arrive early on Day 1 so that they can step in if necessary. (Because no preparation is needed for Scuba Crew Leaders, it's easy for people to step in at any point.)

○ **Hold the scheduled leader training meeting.** Plan to meet in a large room where you'll be able to try out some **SCUBA** snacks and activities. Before the meeting, set up a TV and VCR, and decorate the room using the suggestions provided in the leader training outline (p. 125). Bring the station leader manuals, Crew Leader's Pocket Guides, and photocopies of the "For Scuba Crew Leaders Only" handouts (pp. 135-140).

○ **Meet with each Scuba Station Leader.** It's a good idea to touch base with each station leader on a one-on-one basis. Take each person to lunch or out for ice cream, or simply go for a walk together as you discuss what supplies the leader needs, what concerns he or she may have, or any aspects of the program he or she is not clear on. Not only will this prevent miscommunication, but it will also help your volunteers know how much you appreciate them.

○ **Provide SCUBA information to your church office.** Fill in your church's information on the community flier on page 149, and photocopy a stack of completed fliers on brightly colored paper to put in your church office. Someone in the office can refer to the fliers if people call with questions about your program and can distribute fliers to people who stop by the office.

If your church has a phone answering machine, you may also want to include **SCUBA** information in your recorded message. If your church has its own Web site, be sure to add **SCUBA** information there, too.

TWO WeeKS BefoRe youR SUPeR CooL UNDeRSea BiBLe aDVeNtuRe

○ **Check your registration count.** Make sure you have enough Bible Books for each child to have one. Order extras just in case; many churches experience last-minute additions, first-day surprises, and unexpected increases as kids bring their friends throughout the week. Also double-check that you have enough Scuba Crew Leaders, assigning one crew leader to five children.

○ **Check your supply collection.** Make a final announcement, or put a final supply list in your church bulletin. Gather or purchase additional supplies as necessary.

○ **Set up Closing Production rehearsal times.** The Closing Production *Scuba-Do's Dive* is so simple that kids will really only need to run through it once or twice. Actors with "speaking" parts should be a bit more familiar with the program. (Although, by using the scripted CD, they won't need to memorize their lines.) You can set up a run-through an hour or two before your actual production, or have the five main actors practice briefly during Dive-In Diner.

○ **Continue publicity.** Photocopy and fill out the news release (p. 148), and send copies to your local newspapers, radio stations, and TV stations. Use the snazzy clip art found on the *SCUBA Clip Art, Song Lyrics, and Decorating* CD to create fliers, bulletins, posters, and more. This CD works with Macintosh and PC-compatible computers.

Announce **SCUBA** in worship services and other church gatherings. Put bulletin inserts (p. 146) in your church's worship bulletins.

As church members enter your facility, distribute theme-oriented snacks, such as gummy fish, fish-shaped crackers, or bottles of water.

Before your worship service, have a few volunteers perform the publicity skit on page 150. Show the promotional segment of the *Dive Deep! Video* again.

Mail additional **SCUBA** invitation postcards as necessary.

○ **Make backup and emergency plans.** What if it rains during your program? Plan in advance how you'll handle bad weather. You may also want to line up backup Scuba Crew Leaders in case some drop out.

Inform Scuba Station Leaders and Scuba Crew Leaders of procedures you'll follow if there's a fire or other emergency.

One Week Before your Super Cool Undersea Bible Adventure

○ **Dedicate SCUBA staff.** Introduce Scuba Station Leaders, Scuba Crew Leaders, and other volunteers during your church service. Then have your pastor or other church members pray that God will use these workers to touch kids' lives with his love during **SCUBA**.

○ **Assign kids to Scuba Crews.** Photocopy the "Scuba Crew Roster" (p. 167). You'll need one roster for each crew. Using the preregistration forms you've received, assign children to elementary and preschool Scuba Crews. Each Scuba Crew should have no more than five children and one adult or teenage Scuba Crew Leader. Be sure that each preschool Scuba Crew has a mix of three-, four-, and five-year-olds.

Field Test Findings

Our Scuba Station Leaders needed a way to quickly identify the Scuba Crew Leaders in each group. We provided crew leader hats and T-shirts for the crew leaders to wear during the week. Crew leaders used metallic paint pens to write their names on their hats, and they even wrote the names of their Scuba Crew members on the hats. And they were fun thank-you souvenirs for crew leaders to take home at the end of the week. Crew leader hats are available from Group Publishing and your local Christian bookstore.

Here are some additional guidelines for assigning crews:

✔ Fill in the "Scuba Crew Roster" (p. 167) in pencil—you'll probably make changes as you work.

✔ Whenever possible, place a child from each age level in each Scuba Crew. If the age distribution at your program is uneven, include as wide an age range as you can. Avoid forming single-age Scuba Crews.

✔ Include a good mix of boys and girls in each Scuba Crew.

✔ If a child is bringing a friend, assign the two children to the same Scuba Crew if possible. If a child is bringing several friends, assign pairs of kids to different Scuba Crews.

✔ In general, it works best to assign siblings to different Scuba Crews. However, you know the children in your church. Use your judgment as to whether siblings should be together.

✔ If you anticipate behavior problems with certain children or have children with special needs, assign them to Scuba Crews that have more experienced adult Scuba Crew Leaders.

✔ If you have children who are particularly helpful or cooperative, assign them to Scuba Crews that have teenage Scuba Crew Leaders.

✔ If you want your program to have a strong outreach emphasis, limit each Scuba Crew to three or four children. Then encourage kids to fill their crews by bringing their friends.

✔ Remember to leave open spaces in a few crews for kids who haven't preregistered.

✔ After you've assigned elementary children to Scuba Crews, assign each crew to one of four larger groups. (Remember, one-fourth of the kids at VBS travel together at a time.) Label these four groups A, B, C, and D—or use your creativity to name them something that fits the undersea theme, such as Clownfish, Sea Stars, or Blue Whales. (This may seem obvious, but it's a good idea to avoid "scary" names such as sharks or stingrays.) Scuba Crews travel with their larger groups as they visit the stations each day. For more information about assigning Scuba Crews to groups, see page 155.

✔ Once you've finished assigning crews, double-check that you haven't forgotten anyone or double-booked anyone.

○ **Meet with Scuba Station Leaders again.** Check with each leader to make sure he or she has all the required supplies, and answer any questions he or she may have. Work together to smooth out any last-minute details.

○ **Decide when and where Scuba Station Leaders and Scuba Crew Leaders will meet each day.** It's a good idea to have your staff arrive early on

Day 1 to greet children and assist with registration. Be sure each Scuba Crew Leader has a large sign with his or her crew number or crew name written on it.

○ **Help Scuba Station Leaders decorate their rooms.** Use the decorating ideas found in the colorful VBS catalog, leader manuals, or the general decorating suggestions in the "Facilities" section of this manual (pp. 73-76) to plunge your church undersea! (Or check out www.groupoutlet.com for a sea of decorating items!)

DURING YOUR SUPER COOL UNDERSEA BIBLE ADVENTURE

○ **Meet with Scuba Crew Leaders during Sing & Play Splash.** Each day the Sing & Play Splash Leader will excuse Scuba Crew Leaders for a quick huddle and prayer with you outside the Sing & Play Splash area. This is a great time to ask crew leaders if they have any needs or concerns, to make last-minute announcements or schedule changes, and to encourage your crew leaders. Lead a prayer, asking God to bless your day, protect everyone, and give all leaders wisdom as they work with each child.

○ **Register new children.** Make sure you have plenty of workers on hand to register kids the first day. (This is an excellent way to use volunteers who aren't available to help the entire week.) Set up separate registration sites for preregistration check-in and walk-in registration. Follow the Day 1 registration procedures outlined on pages 159-162.

After Day 1, maintain a registration table to register kids who join your program midweek.

○ **Meet with Scuba Station Leaders and Scuba Crew Leaders after each day's program.** Check in with all **SCUBA** staff to see what went smoothly and what could be improved for future days. Be prepared to change schedules, rooms, or procedures. You may even need to reassign some Scuba Crews. Work together to make any necessary changes to ensure that everything runs smoothly.

○ **Give announcements during Sing & Play Splash or Sea Star Finale.** During the course of the program, you may need to change schedules, stations, or Scuba Crew assignments. You also may have personal messages or lost-and-found items to deliver to participants. Each day check with the Sing & Play Splash Leader and Sea Star Finale Leader to schedule any announcements you'd like everyone to hear.

PLANNING

FieLD TeST FinDinGS

During our field test, we met each afternoon for prayer and lunch and to talk about the highlights of the day. This was a fun time for volunteers to relax and share stories about what had happened at their stations or about what the kids in their Scuba Crews had done. Not only did we glean important information (to include in the finished program), but it also gave everyone a peek at the other fun things going on at SCUBA.

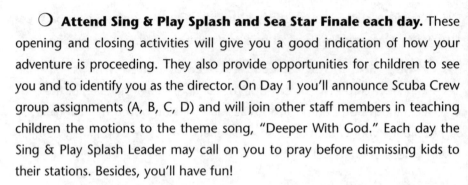

FieLD TeST FinDinGS

Our SCUBA Director got everyone hooked on her corny fish jokes! The kids loved them and even approached her throughout the week with their own "invented" jokes! It was a fun, silly way to get everyone grinning. For a whale of a good time, check out the page of fish jokes on page 88!

○ **Attend Sing & Play Splash and Sea Star Finale each day.** These opening and closing activities will give you a good indication of how your adventure is proceeding. They also provide opportunities for children to see you and to identify you as the director. On Day 1 you'll announce Scuba Crew group assignments (A, B, C, D) and will join other staff members in teaching children the motions to the theme song, "Deeper With God." Each day the Sing & Play Splash Leader may call on you to pray before dismissing kids to their stations. Besides, you'll have fun!

○ **Make sure all Scuba Station Leaders and Scuba Crew Leaders are present each day.** Arrange for substitutes if necessary. If you're in a pinch for Scuba Crew Leaders, ask the Sing & Play Splash Leader and Sea Star Finale Leader to fill in—or appoint yourself crew leader for a day.

○ **Make sure Scuba Station Leaders and Scuba Crew Leaders have the supplies they need each day.** Have a runner available to collect or purchase additional supplies if necessary.

○ **Help with discipline problems as necessary.** In **SCUBA** field tests (and from real programs across the country), workers encountered virtually no discipline problems. Each day was so full of fun Bible-learning activities that kids didn't have time to misbehave. Combined-age Scuba Crews encourage kids to work together instead of squabble, and minor problems can be handled by Scuba Station Leaders or Scuba Crew Leaders.

○ **Stock and maintain a first-aid site.** Keep a good supply of adhesive bandages and first-aid ointment on hand along with phone numbers for local clinics and hospitals. You may also want to keep photocopies of kids' registration forms near your first-aid site. You can use the forms to check for allergies or other health concerns. Be sure to tell your Scuba Crew Leaders of any allergies or special needs, too.

○ **Keep an eye on Scuba Crews.** You may notice that some crew leaders just aren't tuning into their crew members, and you need to reassign a few volunteers to more suitable jobs. Or if a crew leader is struggling with a group that suddenly grew, you'll know to split the crew into two more manageable groups. A "heads-up" attitude will make this VBS experience the best for each child involved.

○ **Prepare SCUBA completion certificates for your "divers."** Photocopy and fill out a certificate (p. 200) for each child. A **SCUBA** completion certificate is also in the Starter Kit, and additional certificates are available from Group Publishing and your local Christian bookstore.

○ **Send the memories home!** We've heard it again and again: "My kids can't stop singing those songs!" Well, when those songs include lyrics such as "We believe in God," "Father, I adore you," and "I will obey you with all my heart," why would you *want* kids to stop singing them? Plan to provide (or sell) *Sing & Play Splash Music* audiocassettes or CDs for the kids at your program. Set up a table, complete with information, outside your Sea Star Finale area. Check out the reduced prices on page 14 of the VBS catalog.

after your Super Cool Undersea Bible Adventure

○ **Collect reusable leftover supplies.** Store the supplies in your church's supply closet or resource room for use in future VBS programs or other children's ministry events. If you borrowed supplies such as box fans, buckets, or cassette players, return them to their owners.

○ **Send your Operation Kid-to-Kid shoes or socks to Shoes for Orphan Souls.** (For more information, see the "Operation Kid-to-Kid" section beginning on p. 43 or visit www.ok2k.org.) The Sea Star Finale Leader may have these from the Day 5 program.

○ **Leave rooms decorated for your next church service.** If outreach was an emphasis during **SCUBA**, you'll be pleased when visitors from your VBS program come for church. They'll feel more comfortable returning to a familiar environment. Also, church members will enjoy getting a glimpse of **SCUBA**.

○ **Follow up with SCUBA visitors.** Mail **SCUBA** follow-up postcards (available from Group Publishing and your local Christian bookstore). Encourage Scuba Crew Leaders to make personal contact with the members of their Scuba Crews within two weeks after VBS. Use the additional follow-up ideas beginning on page 193 in this manual.

○ **Host a Back to SCUBA Party.** This year, Group has made it easy to bring **SCUBA** kids back to church...and get them caught up in all of your children's ministry activities year-round! Our Back to SCUBA Follow-Up Kit contains everything you need for up to three hours of party programming—and you'll get to use your **SCUBA** decorations and music again! The Back to SCUBA Follow-Up Kit is available from Group Publishing or your local Christian bookstore.

○ **Report on your program.** During your next worship service, invite Scuba Station Leaders, Scuba Crew Leaders, and kids who attended **SCUBA** to share their favorite VBS experiences. Encourage kids to display their Bible Point Crafts. You may even want to invite the Sing & Play Splash Leader to lead

Leader Lifeline

It's important to check your registration forms for any mention of food allergies. Let the Dive-In Diner Leader know as soon as possible so that he or she can make alternative snacks if necessary.

Field Test Findings

We highly recommended a "Crew Leader Coordinator" position—a person responsible to help train, support, and guide crew leaders. Since crew leaders are the backbone of your program, it's a great idea to give extra support and time to these awesome volunteers.

Field Test Findings

The church that hosted our field test decided to sell the Sing & Play Splash Music audiocassettes and then use the proceeds to offset their decorating and supply costs. (They quickly sold out and had to start a waiting list.) Not only did children take home the VBS music they were wild about, but the extra dollars helped the church budget. Everyone benefited!

Planning

Here's another reason to go to a SCUBA Splash Party: decoration-sharing! If members of another local church are going to go on a SCUBA, let them know when you'll be taking down your decorations. Most likely, they'll be glad to help in exchange for any decorations that you're willing to part with. It's a great way to work together, help each other, and build community spirit. To find out more about SCUBA Splash Parties, go to www.groupvbs.com.

PLannInG

everyone in singing one or two favorite **SCUBA** songs. You might even host an *Animal Planet*-type show, in which you highlight the adventures (and mis-adventures) of your undersea explorers. (When others see how much fun VBS can be, your recruiting will be a breeze next year! In fact, they may even sign up for *next* year's VBS on the spot!)

Keeping your Focus

If you're planning a Closing Production, remember that this isn't a high-stress performance for kids. We believe the purpose of VBS is *for children to enjoy and experience God's love, not to perform.* Through our field tests, we've watched kids sing praise songs just for the pure joy of singing and worship. We've seen them excitedly experience Bible stories just because God's Word is exciting. That's why we've designed the Closing Production to be easy and stress-free, only requiring a few quick and easy rehearsals.

One VBS Director tells of kids who were dragged, kicking and screaming, to another VBS simply because the emphasis was on prepar-ing for a big "parent-pleasing" performance. "When they came to Bug Safari, the parents wondered what we'd done…their kids *wanted* to come each day! Our focus was on the kids and being sure that this pro-gram was for them. And the kids could really tell!"

We strongly encourage you to invite parents to each day's Sea Star Finale to give them a view of the Bible truths children are discovering!

○ **Present a slide show or video, or post photos from your pro-gram.** Kids (and their parents) love seeing themselves on the "big screen." And colorful photos will bring back memories of a terrific time at **SCUBA**. Set the whole production to music for an even greater effect.

○ **Meet with your entire SCUBA staff to evaluate your pro-gram.** Celebrate a dynamite dive! Make written notes of good ideas that could be used for next year's program. Note any problems that came up and how they were solved. Brainstorm about ways to avoid similar problems in the future. Include notes of how you adapted the **SCUBA** materials to fit your church. Record the names of Scuba Crew Leaders and Scuba Station Leaders who are interested in helping again next year. Post the "We Hope You're Hooked…" handout (p. 202), and allow interested volunteers to sign up for next year's program. (You'll be surprised at the number that will!) Bring the **SCUBA** evaluation forms included in this manual (pp. 207-208), and have staff members fill them out.

○ **Thank your staff members for all their hard work.** Photocopy and fill out an "Our Deepest Tanks!" certificate (p. 199) for Scuba Station Leaders, Scuba Crew Leaders, and other volunteers. Or use the "Thank You" Shell to thank and affirm your volunteers. This adorable shell already comes with a "pearl" of wisdom from God's Word, but you can also add confetti or candy! "Thank You" Shells are available from Group Publishing and your local Christian bookstore. You could even hand out balloons, flowers, or baked goodies to show your appreciation. For more thematic ideas, see page 197.

○ **Fill out the "SCUBA Evaluation."** Tear out this evaluation form (p. 207), and fill it out completely. Send your completed form to Group Publishing—no postage is necessary! You may also want to give a copy of the form to your church pastor, Christian education director, children's minister, or VBS committee. This helps us plan for the future.

Leader Lifeline

VBS is a great time to plant the seeds of God's Word into children's hearts…but those seeds need to be watered! For easy and effective follow-up, check out the Back to SCUBA Follow-Up Kit (available from Group Publishing or your local Christian bookstore). This party-in-a-box is swimming with ways to plug VBS kids into your children's ministry programs all year long! For more information, check out page 196 of this manual!

Planning

WHen anD WHeRe to DiVe In

Any of these options will allow you to have a FIN-tastic time!

If your church has put on VBS programs before, you probably have a good idea of the times and settings that work best in your situation. Use the suggested times and settings listed below to spark creativity as you plan your **S**uper **C**ool **U**ndersea **B**ible **A**dventure!

OPTions foR SCUBa Locations

• **Your church:** Many VBS programs are held in local churches. With this approach, you control the facilities, you have many rooms available, and the station is familiar to church members. Plus visitors who come to **SCUBA** actually visit your church site. (If your church facility isn't large enough, consider teaming up with another local church that might have more room. You'll double your resources and have twice the impact, while showing kids that God's family can do great things when we work together!)

• **A local park:** Kids love being outdoors, and parks draw children who would not normally attend a VBS program. Check with your local parks and recreation department to see about reserving a park or campground for your **SCUBA**. Church, YMCA, and scout camps provide ideal outdoor settings since they usually have electricity available. Consider renting a large tent or canopy to use in your outdoor setting.

• **Inner city:** Turn your **SCUBA** program into an inner city outreach opportunity. Invite kids from your church to join inner city kids in an inner city church or neighborhood setting. Even if you use only portions of the **SCUBA** materials, you'll help needy children and their families understand God's love.

• **A local school:** Since most schools lie dormant for the majority of the summer, consider using their facilities for your program. If public schools are busy with summer classes, check out Christian school facilities in your area.

• **A backyard or home:** Backyard Bible Clubs are a wonderful way to build relationships and a sense of community in your neighborhood. Sing & Play Splash and Sea Star Finale can take place in the backyard, while other Scuba Stations rotate through the dining room, living room, or basement.

With a little creativity, you can welcome a small number of children into your home to hear the good news of God's love!

OPtions for SCUBa Times

- **Weekday mornings:** Many programs are held for five consecutive weekday mornings. Kids have plenty of energy, and the summer sun isn't quite as hot as in the afternoon. For a change of pace, you could even plan to hold a morning program during your students' spring break.

- **Weekday afternoons:** Afternoons may be a new option for many churches, but we've heard from directors who say it's the best. Preschoolers have had naps, older kids are done with morning soccer practice, and everyone is ready for fun!

- **Weekday evenings:** Since many church members work during the day, some churches find it easier to staff an evening program. This could be a special program that you hold for five consecutive evenings, or it could take the place of an existing midweek program. If you hold your **SCUBA** program in the evening, you may want to include families. You can offer separate programming for parents and teenagers or include them in **SCUBA** as full-fledged participants and Scuba Crew Leaders. Church members of all ages will enjoy visiting the stations. Each family can form its own Scuba Crew, or you can mix families and enlist parents as Scuba Crew Leaders. If you invite families, you'll want to provide child-care for children younger than three years old.

- **Midweek clubs:** If your church has a midweek club or another weekly children's program, you may want to use the **SCUBA** materials for five consecutive weeks. If you use **SCUBA** during a regularly scheduled midweek program, you'll probably have Scuba Station Leaders already in place. Just assign Scuba Crews and recruit Scuba Crew Leaders, and you'll be ready to start the adventure!

- **Day camp:** Extend **SCUBA** to a half-day day camp for kids in your community. (Again, consider holding your day camp during spring break.) We've provided extra crafts, plenty of games, and lots of upbeat songs to keep children actively learning Bible truths...and having a great time!

- **Sunday mornings:** Hold **SCUBA** during your normal Sunday school or children's church time. This is a great change of pace for summer for both kids and children's workers. (Plus, it's a wonderful way for families to participate.)

- **Weekend retreat:** Invite children or whole families to participate in a weekend retreat held at your church or a local camp. Schedule Day 1 activities for Saturday morning, Days 2 and 3 for Saturday afternoon (after lunch), Day 4 for Saturday evening (after dinner), and Day 5 for Sunday morning.

• **Ten-day VBS:** Some churches like to do a full two-week program. There's plenty of material in your **SCUBA** leader manuals to do just that. You'll cover each Bible story and Point two days in a row. The first day, kids will go to Deep Bible Adventures but not Chadder's Undersea Bible Adventure. On the second day, kids won't have Deep Bible Adventures, but they *will* attend Chadder's Undersea Bible Adventure. The other manuals contain loads of extra games, songs, and bonus crafts that will allow you to use the same Bible Point and story two days in a row. And kids will have an even easier time remembering these awesome, life-changing Bible truths.

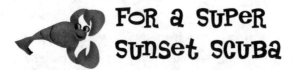

For a Super Sunset Scuba

The following tips will help your evening or intergenerational program go smoothly:

• Start early so young children won't get too tired.

• Consider beginning each session with a simple meal. Recruit a kitchen team to organize potlucks or prepare simple meals such as sandwiches or frozen pizzas. If your church has a lawn or grassy area nearby, you may even want to barbecue. Families will enjoy this casual interaction time, and you'll be able to start your program earlier.

• Make sure children who attend without their families have safe transportation to and from **SCUBA**. Don't allow children to walk home alone in the dark—even if they live nearby.

• Families come in all shapes and sizes. Be sensitive to single-parent families, childless couples, and children who come alone. You may want to assign family members to separate Scuba Crews to avoid drawing attention to family differences.

Have oceans of fun diving into your super cool undersea Bible adventure!

FaciLities: Turning your Church into an underWater Wonder WorLD

Atmosphere and environment enhance learning, so decorations are an integral part of **SCUBA**. They can set the mood for the week and get children excited about God's love. Following, you'll find a listing of suggested decorations for stations and other church areas. Remember, these are options and aren't necessary for the success of your **SCUBA**. If you and others want to go the extra mile, it'll simply enhance the program.

Most decorating items can be found among your church members or can be purchased inexpensively. Have fun! By letting your imagination and creativity go wild, you can create a setting that's swimming with personality. Go for it!

UnDerSea SiGn-In

Your registration area will be kids' first impression of the undersea adventure they're about to enjoy. While you want to keep your table free of clutter, there are plenty of eye-catching ways to show kids that they're in for an amazing undersea adventure.

• **Fishing for fun?** Bright, colorful fish will be a welcome sight as kids enter your **SCUBA** site. Cut simple fish shapes from neon poster board, then use black paint to add eyes, fins, and scales to each fish. Dangle the fish from clear fishing line, and shine a black light on them for an eye-catching effect!

• **A watery world.** To create the illusion of being under the sea, spray old sheets with varying shades of blue and green dye. When the sheets have dried, hang them on the walls, drape them on your table, or place them over any church furniture that's lying around! Or go the extra mile and

LeaDeR LifeLine

VBS directors continue to amaze us with their creativity, hard work, and incredibly imaginative ideas. If you've created life-size coral reefs, fish that really move, or "wowzer" water effects, we'd love to see how you did it! Please send pictures or videocassettes to: VBS Coordinator at Group Publishing, Inc., P.O. Box 481, Loveland, CO 80539. (Sorry, we can't return them.) Or post the pictures on your church's Web site, then share the address on our message board at www.groupvbs.com. This is a great way to share your ideas with others.

Planning

73

FiELD TeST FiNDiNGS

We liked the bubble machine idea and tried it inside. Big mistake! It made tons of kid-pleasing bubbles, but there was sticky bubble "goo" all over the carpet! Our advice is to keep the bubble machine outside, where you can hose off the residue.

LeaDeR LifeLine

Let Chadder Chipmunk welcome your dive buddies! Purchase the Chadder costume pattern (available from Group Publishing or your local Christian bookstore), and ask a seamstress or tailor in your congregation to make the costume.

LeaDeR LifeLine

Use the clip art on the SCUBA Clip Art, Song Lyrics, and Decorating CD to make your decorations sparkle. Simply print out the clip art onto transparency paper, then use an overhead projector to make these dazzling designs larger than life. Project the designs onto bedsheets or butcher paper, trace them, and then color them in.

rent a bubble machine from a party supply store. Have bubbles floating around your registration table to make kids feel like they're really diving underwater!

• **The sounds of the sea.** Remember, you're underwater, so you won't hear waves crashing. For bubbles and burbles of undersea sounds, plug in a CD player and slip in the *SCUBA Skits & Drama* CD (available from Group Publishing or your local Christian bookstore). There you'll find twenty minutes of undersea sounds. Just set your CD player on repeat and enjoy the underwater environment sounds!

• **Have costumed staff on hand.** Have volunteers dressed in scuba gear—flippers, masks, snorkels, or even wet suits—to greet and welcome children each day.

CORaL CORRiDORS

Even your hallways can be eye-catching and exciting. As children travel to their stations, they'll feel as if they're swimming through a colorful coral reef on a real undersea adventure!

• **Egg carton coral.** Start saving those bumpy cardboard egg cartons—then use them to create a colorful coral reef! Soak the egg cartons in a bucket of water for about an hour, then mold and shape them into odd bumpy shapes. Set them in the sun to dry for a few hours. Then add a coat of green, blue, pink, purple, or orange paint. Tape these sheets of "coral" over cardboard boxes to create vibrant coral reefs.

• **Photocopy and cut out the arrows from the back of each of the station leader manuals.** You'll need at least two arrows per station to quickly guide children through your facility. Then photocopy, color, and cut out the station signs from the front of each station leader manual. Hang the posters and arrows so kids can find their way to the correct stations. (You may want to color code your stations and arrows. For example, make the Splish Splash Games Station sign blue, then photocopy arrows on blue paper. Use the blue arrows to point the way to Splish Splash Games.)

• **Who's up there?** Stuff the legs of a wet suit with fiberfill or newspaper. Use electrical tape to attach flippers, then hang the legs from your ceiling. Wrap poster board into tubes to create simple scuba tanks. Kids will look up to see a diver swimming above their heads!

• **Shouldn't you be in school?** Use old wire coat hangers and fishing line to create simple mobiles of small paper fish. Hang the mobiles along your hallway ceiling. Then place an oscillating fan in a corner and watch these schools of fish swim and move together!

Scuba Stations

Specific decorating ideas for each Scuba Station are listed in the individual leader manuals. Plus, you'll find oceans of ideas in the VBS catalog in your Starter Kit can. You can even find great decorating ideas from our field test on the *Dive Deep! Video*. Use the following ideas to reinforce the undersea theme in all of your Scuba Stations.

• **Create a marine scene in each window.** Use blue tempera paint to make waves in the windows. This is a fun and easy way to communicate your theme to those inside and out.

• **Hang posters of real sea critters.** Find posters of fish, octopuses, shells, or crabs. Look through nature magazines for the pictures, and then post them everywhere. You can even purchase Treasure Verse posters, which feature vibrant undersea photos along with each day's Treasure Verse. Adorable Bible Point posters showcase the Bible Memory Buddies and are available from Group Publishing or your local Christian bookstore. (You can also check out our www.groupoutlet.com.)

• **Let dive buddies welcome children at every station.** Add warmth and friendliness to your **SCUBA** by making door-size pictures of the Bible Memory Buddies to place on each station door. Use the clip art on the *SCUBA Clip Art, Song Lyrics, and Decorating* CD to make these dive buddies!

• **Everything but the kitchen "sink."** Think about all the things you might find at the bottom of the ocean. A sunken ship? Ask your congregation members for an old rowboat that you can lay in a corner. A treasure chest?

LeaDeR LifeLine

Be sure to have your Scuba Crew Leaders make poster board or construction paper number signs for each Scuba Crew. Post each number on a different pew or row of chairs in Sing & Play Splash so Scuba Crews know where to sit each day. Encourage your Scuba Crew Leaders to be creative and make their signs look like fish, crabs, or shells.

FieLD TesT FinDinGs

Our field test church posted its signs on five-foot PVC poles, which had each been secured to a small wooden platform. These movable crew signs made it easy to shuffle kids from the back of the sanctuary to the front so that everyone could get a front-row seat during Sing & Play Splash.

PLANNING

Cover an old toy chest with brown paper, dangle some toy jewelry from the opening, and set it near a doorway.

• **Let your imagination swim wild!** These ideas are just a drop in the bucket! Check out local resources—businesses, libraries, universities, or craft and party supply stores—for more ways to turn your facility into a place that's swimming with fun. And don't forget to visit www.groupvbs.com for even more amazing decorating ideas from **SCUBA** Directors just like you!

LeaDeR LifeLine

When you purchase the SCUBA Clip Art, Song Lyrics, and Decorating CD, you are also purchasing the right to reproduce the song lyrics as transparencies or in PowerPoint.

FOR youR InfoRmation...

When you buy a *Sing & Play Splash Music* audiocassette, CD, or *Clip Art* CD you also buy the right to use the twelve **SCUBA** songs. You're welcome to play these songs as often as you like. But the companies that own these songs haven't given you (or us!) the right to duplicate any Sing & Play Splash products. Making your own copies—even to use at VBS—is against the law...a fact many people don't know. If you do want to have a cassette for every child or leader, we've made bulk buying affordable and easy. Check out your **SCUBA** order form for more info.

Bonus Idea!

This great tip comes from churches that have fine-tuned the art of collecting VBS supplies. It just doesn't get any easier!

1. Photocopy the "We're Fishing for Supplies" fish below on colored paper. Designate a different color paper for each station—for example, blue paper for Undersea Crafts and Missions, orange paper for Dive-In Diner, and red paper for Preschool Tide Pool.

2. Fill in the information on each fish. Indicate whether the item needs to be donated (items that will be used up, such as food) or borrowed (items that can be returned, such as a bucket).

3. Cut apart the fish, and post them on a bulletin board in a high-traffic area of your church. (A large fishing net nearby will complete your design!) Make an announcement to inform church members that they can take fish from the board and donate the requested items.

4. As items are delivered to the specified area, sort them by the color of the attached fish. Just before **SCUBA** begins, collect the fish, and sort them into donated and borrowed items.

5. After VBS, simply have station leaders retrieve the borrowed items. Match the items with their fish, and return the items to their owners.

We're Fishing for Supplies!

Item Needed: _____

Donated   Borrowed

SCUBA Director: _____
Phone: _____

Your Name: _____
Phone: _____
Please return this item to me by _____

Please attach this fish to the item and deliver it to _____

by _____ (date).   **Thank you!**

S.C.U.B.A. Daily Supplies

Station	Supplies You'll Use Every Day	Day 1	Day 2
Sing & Play Splash	Bible, microphone, conch shell*, **SCUBA** name badges*, *Sing & Play Splash Music* audiocassette or CD*, cassette or CD player, Bible Point posters, lyrics transparencies (optional), and overhead projector (optional)	Props for Scuba-Do skits (optional), "Who's Who on the Crew?" handout	Props for Scuba-Do skits (optional); five sheets of construction paper or poster board with one of these letters on each sheet: S, C, U, B, A; sheet of construction paper with an arrow drawn on it
Undersea Crafts and Missions	1 sheet of **SCUBA** Surprise Stickers per child* (located inside each child's Bible Book), watercolor markers, Operation Kid-to-Kid Missions Kit*, supplies for Bible Point Crafts* (see the options given each day), Bible Point poster* (optional), *Sing & Play Splash Music* audiocassette or CD* (optional), cassette or CD player (optional), conch shell* or other attention-getting device, wristwatch or clock	**Flying Fish**—1 Flying Fish kit* per child, paint markers, a few paper towels, 1 bottle or cup of water, 1 Alka-Seltzer tablet per child, Day 1 questions (p. 50), finished sample of a Flying Fish, squirt bottle of water, paper towels **Fish-a-Loons**—1 Fish-a-Loon kit* per child, paint markers, child-size scissors, a few paper towels, transparent tape, Day 1 questions (p. 50), a finished sample of a Fish-a-Loon	**Dive Bags**—1 Dive Bag* per child, several colors of fabric paint, permanent markers, sea creature stampers (about 3 designs), paper towels, several small paper plates, Day 2 questions (p. 50), a finished sample of a Dive Bag, Ace Bible Memory Buddy*, sheets or beach towels for kids to work on
Deep Bible Adventures	Bible, *SCUBA Skits & Drama* CD*, CD player, conch shell*	*SCUBA Skits & Drama* CD*: "Mount Carmel Mountaintop Challenge" (track 8); piece of paper to be your "notes"; masking tape; metal or sturdy plastic washtub (12-gallon size); gravel (available at garden centers) to half-fill the washtub; 12 bricks (inexpensive, standard building or paving bricks); garden trowels or large, sturdy spoons; 10 sticks, each about 8-inches long (per rotation); 4 large chocolate bars (1 bar per rotation); newspaper; 3 plastic water pitchers (or half-gallon milk cartons filled with water); plastic siphon (available in automotive or camping stores); 12-inch piece of PVC pipe with a slightly bigger diameter than the siphon tube; old bucket or empty gallon milk container; "hammy" adult helper dressed as a firefighter; CO_2 fire extinguisher (available from fire stations or fire extinguisher providers); helper to assist you in preparing for new rotations of children (optional); photocopy of the "Firefighter's Script" (p. 22); photocopies of the "Day 1 Diving Deeper" card (p. 24) (Make 1 copy for each crew.)	Large box fan; clear wide packing tape or duct tape; 2 10x25-foot rolls of black plastic; 2 cans of tuna in an open plastic container; 10-inch lengths of braided twine (1 per participant); *Dive Deep! Video** for fish-building demonstration; VCR; *SCUBA Skits & Drama* CD*: "Undersea Sounds" (track 7); photocopy of the "Special Effects Assistant Tip Sheet" (p. 32); photocopies of the "Day 2 Diving Deeper" card (1 copy for each crew) (p. 31)

Many VBS directors requested a daily supply list so that they could see what days certain supplies were needed. Check out the chart below to see if there are supplies that can be shared between stations. Dive-In Diner is not included in the chart, due to the specific nature of the food items. (See page 82 for Dive-In Diner supplies.) Also, check with the preschool director to see what supplies he or she will need each day. Be sure to look at supply lists in each Scuba Station leader manual for more detail about supplies needed.

*These items are available from Group Publishing and your local Christian bookstore.

Day 3	Day 4	Day 5
Props for Scuba-Do skits (optional)	Props for Scuba-Do skits (optional)	Props for Scuba-Do skits (optional), black plastic trash bag filled with large balls or crumpled paper
Trusty Timers—1 Trusty Timer Kit* per child, paint markers, paper plates, Surprise Stickers* from kids' Bible Books, 1 child-size scissors, various colors of ½-inch electrical tape, Day 3 questions (p. 51), Operation Kid-to-Kid poster of Alexandra*, finished sample of a Trusty Timer, windup kitchen timer, index cards, pens or pencils **Buzzalong Boats**—1 Buzzalong Boat* per child, paint markers, small handful of modeling clay per child, Day 3 questions (p. 51), Operation Kid-to-Kid poster of Alexandra*, finished sample of a Buzzalong Boat, several tubs of water or a child-sized swimming pool filled with water (placed outside), index cards	**Pearl Diver's Paradise**—1 Pearl Diver Kit* per child, 1 empty 24-ounce water bottle (with lid) per child, paint markers, Surprise Stickers* from kids' Bible Books, marbles or sea glass (optional), glitter (optional), colorful electrical tape, small paper cups, paper towels, Day 4 questions (p. 51), Operation Kid-to-Kid poster of Ishmael*, finished sample of a Pearl Diver Aquarium, buckets or tubs of water (one per Scuba Crew), conch shell* or other attention-getting device **Treasure Books**—1 Treasure Book kit* per child, markers, glue, Surprise Stickers* from kids' Bible Books, glitter glue or other decorative items (optional), Day 4 questions (p. 51), Operation Kid-to-Kid poster of Ishmael*, finished sample of a Treasure Book, index cards	**SCUBA Snapshot Frames**—1 SCUBA Snapshot Frame kit* per child, paint markers, Surprise Stickers* from kids' Bible Books, glitter glue (optional), sandpaper (optional), green mesh netting or tulle (optional), Day 5 questions (p. 52), finished sample of a **SCUBA** Snapshot Frame, index cards, Operation Kid-to-Kid posters* **Share Mail Postcards**— 1 Share Mail Postcard kit* per crew, markers, pencils with erasers, Surprise Stickers* from kids' Bible Books, wet wipes, Day 5 questions (p. 52), finished sample of a Share Mail Postcard, index cards
Individually wrapped Life Savers candies (1 per participant); 2 box fans; extension cords so you can position the fans; helper to turn a fan on and off; 2 spray bottles carefully cleaned and filled with water; helper to turn a fan on and off; life ring or life jacket; *SCUBA Skits & Drama* CD*: "Scared at Sea" (track 11) and "We Can Trust Jesus" (track 12); photocopy of the "Official Fan Club Cue Card"; photocopies of the "Day 3 Diving Deeper" card (1 copy for each crew) (p. 37)	Plastic sword; dramatic volunteer to play the part of the Roman guard; simple Bible-times "guard" costume (such as a robe, sash, and sandals); photocopy of the "Guard's Script" (p. 41); photocopies of the "Day 4 Diving Deeper" card (p. 43) (1 copy for each crew); *Sing & Play Splash Music* CD*: "We Believe in God" (track 3) (optional)	Masking tape; 25-foot length of light nylon rope; 25-foot lengths of clothesline (1 length for each Scuba crew); flashlight for each Scuba Crew (reuse each rotation); yellow, red, and orange tissue paper to tape over the illuminated end of the flashlights; fish-shaped crackers (enough for each participant to have about ⅓ cup); paper cups; *SCUBA Skits & Drama* CD*: "Fish Fry" (track 16) and "Breakfast by the Sea" (track 17); photocopies of the "Day 5 Diving Deeper" card (p. 48) (1 copy for each crew)

PLANNING

Station	Supplies You'll Use Every Day	Day 1	Day 2
SPLISH SPLASH GAMES	Conch shell*, *Sing & Play Splash Music* CD* (optional), CD player (optional)	**You Are True**—1 Ace Bible Memory Buddy* per child **Choose Now!**—1 large bucket half filled with water per crew; 10 whiffle balls per crew; 5 old, white socks (each tied into a ball) per crew; 1 plastic pitcher per pair of children; ⅓ of a Funnoodle per pair of children **Scuba Talk**—1 scuba mask per crew (you may want to have a variety of sizes on hand), dark construction paper, several Ace Bible Memory Buddies* to use as obstacles, 12 Funnoodle sections, bucket, 10 whiffle balls	**The Nineveh Assignment**—1 photocopy of the "Top Secret Assignment" handout (p. 21) for each crew, envelope or bowl for each crew, ⅓ of a Funnoodle per crew, bucket of water with Squirt Bible Memory Buddies* in it, 1 Squirt Bible Memory Buddy* for each child **Top Secret Assignment**—Assignment slips from Splish Splash Games Leader Manual **Runaway Jonah**—1 water-soaked sheet for each crew, 1 spray bottle per crew, bucket of water (to refill spray bottles), Funnoodle sections **Jonah Overboard**—1 plastic foam bowl for each crew member, 1 cotton ball for each crew member, 1 drinking straw for each crew member, small wading pool filled with water
CHADDER'S UNDERSEA BIBLE ADVENTURE	Bible; *Chadder's Undersea Bible Adventure* video*; TV and VCR (or DVD player); **SCUBA** Bible Books and Dive Logs* (one per child); Bible Book from the Starter Kit* (for your example); Bible highlighter for each child; clock or watch with a second hand; conch shell* or other attention-getting device; chalkboard and chalk, white board and dry-erase marker, or poster board and marker; fine-tip markers or pencils; Treasure Verse posters* (optional); cassette or CD player; *Sing & Play Splash Music* CD* (optional)	Kid-friendly comic book	*SCUBA Skits & Drama* CD* ("Whale Sounds," track 6) and CD player
Sea Star Finale	Bible, CD player, *Sing & Play Splash Music* CD*, conch shell*, set of Bible Point posters*	5 sheets of construction paper or poster board, each with one of the following letters on it: S, C, U, B, A (The Sing & Play Splash Leader should have these.); Day 1 Treasure Verse (p. 54); 1 muffin tin (the kind that holds a half-dozen muffins) per Scuba Crew; pitchers of water; about 1 teaspoon of white vinegar per Scuba Crew; about half of a 1-ounce square of dark, unsweetened baker's chocolate per Scuba Crew; about half of a 1-ounce square of dark, sweetened Hershey's chocolate per Scuba Crew; 1 teaspoon of sugar per Scuba Crew; 1 teaspoon of salt per Scuba Crew; table; bedsheet or tablecloth	*SCUBA Skits & Drama* CD*: "The Choice Is Right, Jonah, Part 1" (track 9); "The Choice Is Right, Jonah, Part 2" (track 10); Day 2 Treasure Verse (p. 55); 3 large, colorful beach towels or sheets; spray bottle filled with water (You can get this from the Deep Bible Adventures leader.); plastic hoop; 2 different noisemakers (such as bells, whistles, and pots and pans); party horn; masking tape or safety pins; photocopies of "Door #1," "Door #2," and "Door #3" signs (pp. 30-32); photocopy of "Nineveh" sign (p. 33); photocopies of "Behind the Door" instructions (p. 34); at least 10 five-foot-long green, yellow, or black streamers

Day 3	Day 4	Day 5
Stop the Storm—3 spray bottles filled with water for each crew, Funnoodle sections (to mark off your playing boundaries) **Sharks and Turtles**—1 large bucket of water for each crew, 1 Tank Bible Memory Buddy* for each person, Funnoodles (to use as boundary lines), swimming flippers (2 per crew), 1 5-ounce paper cup per crew **Treasure Hunt Mix-Up**—Box or bag filled with simple prizes or candy, sheet of paper with the wrong directions to the "treasure," sheet of paper with the correct directions for finding the "treasure"	**Dive Danger**—Funnoodles (to designate one area as The Ship) **Give It All You've Got!**—Pair of large gloves; bag of jelly bean candies poured into two bowls; diving mask smeared with petroleum jelly; masking tape; 3 jump-ropes; chair; 4 paper wads; large, plastic cup; ⅓ sections of Funnoodles (4 sections); photocopies of the "Station Instruction" cards (p. 31), taped around the room with the specified items placed below each card **Find the Pearl**—Pearl Bible Memory Buddies* (one per child), 1 bucket of water per crew, shaving cream, table tennis balls (about 2 per crew)	**Stuck on You!**—Masking tape, scuba masks (in a variety of sizes), dark construction paper, red construction paper **Candy Capers**—Individually wrapped candy, basket, box **Fish Net Friends**—Starla Bible Memory Buddies* (one per child), 5 buckets of water
No additional supplies needed.	Special memento or picture from home, poster-board cross (large enough so that all the kids can place a heart sticker on it), small desk lamp, tape	No additional supplies needed.
Day 3 Treasure Verse (p. 56), four 6-foot-long yellow streamers, 2 spray bottles filled with water	*SCUBA Skits and Drama* CD*: "Sadness and Joy, Part 1" (track 13); "Sadness and Joy, Part 2" (track 14); "Sadness and Joy, Part 3" (track 15); Day 4 Treasure Verse (p. 57); roll of black plastic (the Deep Bible Adventures Leader might have this); one 2-foot-long red streamer for each Scuba Crew; Roman soldier sword (from Deep Bible Adventures Leader); white sheet or robe (white choir robes work great!); volunteers to be Jesus, Jesus' followers, and the Roman soldier (the Roman soldier should be the same one who helps during Deep Bible Adventures); simple Bible-times costumes for your volunteers; photocopies of the "Sadness and Joy" script (pp. 44, 46) for your volunteers	Day 5 Treasure Verse (p. 58); 5 sheets of construction paper with one of these letters on each sheet—S, C, U, B, A—used in the Day 1 Finale; 5 sheets of construction paper with the numbers 1 through 5 written in large print—one number per sheet; transparent tape; flashlight; fish nets from Undersea Crafts and Missions and Preschool Tide Pool, filled with shoes and socks kids have collected throughout the week

PLANNING

81

DiVe-In DineR

FOOD SUPPLIES

Item	Required Amount	Total Number of Participants	Total Required Amount
Day 1			
unfrosted cupcakes	1 per participant	X _____	= _____
whipped topping	1 tablespoon per participant	X _____	= _____
candy corn candies	about 5 per participant	X _____	= _____
water or juice	2 quarts for every 10 participants	X _____	= _____
Day 2			
sliced bread	1 slice per participant	X _____	= _____
jelly (in squeeze bottles)	about 1 squeeze bottle per Service Crew		= _____
corn flakes	¼ cup per participant	X _____	= _____
chocolate chips	1 chip per participant	X _____	= _____
Goldfish crackers	¼ cup per participant	X _____	= _____
water or juice	2 quarts for every 10 participants	X _____	= _____
Day 3			
apples	¼ apple per participant	X _____	= _____
unsliced processed cheese	¼ slice per participant	X _____	= _____
white frosting	about 1 tablepoon per participant	X _____	= _____
graham crackers	1 square per participant	X _____	= _____
water or juice	2 quarts for every 10 participants	X _____	= _____
Day 4			
hamburger buns	1 per participant	X _____	= _____
softened margarine	1 tub per Service Crew		= _____
honey	1 squeeze bottle per Service Crew		= _____
large marshmallows	1 per participant	X _____	= _____
water or juice	2 quarts for every 10 participants	X _____	= _____
Day 5			
cheddar cheese	3 1-inch cubes per participant	X _____	= _____
red and green seedless grapes	3 grapes per participant	X _____	= _____
water or juice	2 quarts for every 10 participants	X _____	= _____

SeRVinG SUPPLieS

Item	Required Amount	Total Number of Participants	Total Required Amount
paper plates	4 per participant	X _____	= ____ paper plates
paper cups	5 per participant	X _____	= ____ paper cups
napkins	5 per participant	X _____	= ____ napkins
pitchers	2 for every 10 participants	X _____	= ____ pitchers
toothpicks	4 per participant	X _____	= ____ toothpicks

DiVe–In DiNeR SeRViCe CReW SUPPLieS

Item	Required Amount	Total Number of Service Crews (¼ total Scuba Crews)	Total Required Amount
paper plates	1 per preschool Service Crew	X _____	= _____
heart-shaped cookie cutters	2 per Service Crew	X _____	= _____
1 bottle of blue food coloring			
paring knives	2 per Service Crew	X _____	= _____
plastic knives	4 per Service Crew	X _____	= _____
baby wipes	1 per participant	X _____	= _____

OtHeR SUPPLieS

- ○ a conch shell or other attention-getting signal*
- ○ antibacterial soap, hand gel, or individually wrapped hand wipes
- ○ two or three rolls of paper towels
- ○ an assortment of serving bowls, plates, trays, and utensils
- ○ trash cans or trash bags
- ○ *Sing & Play Splash Music* audiocassette or CD (optional)*
- ○ audiocassette or CD player (optional)

*Available from Group Publishing and your local Christian bookstore.

DAiLy SCHeDuLeS

FieLD TeST FinDinGS

We discovered that it's a good idea to arrange your Scuba Crews so that you have at least one experienced adult crew leader in each lettered group. Adults can offer encouragement, leadership, or helpful advice to younger crew leaders.

FieLD TeST FinDinGS

It always happens on Day 2: Someone looks at the schedule and protests "This is the same schedule as yesterday!" Actually, it's not. The elementary kids do rotate in the same order, but one group will have Dive-In Diner Service instead of Splish Splash Games. Since preschoolers have Dive-In Diner Service on Day 1, there's no need for the schedule to change until Day 3.

Each day when kids come to **SCUBA**, they visit seven Scuba Stations. All Scuba Crews visit Sing & Play Splash, Dive-In Diner, and Sea Star Finale together. In between these activities, the remaining stations run simultaneously. Station leaders repeat their activities four times, with a different group of Scuba Crews each time. When it's time for groups to move to a new station, walk through **SCUBA** and blow the conch shell (or use some other attention-getting device). This helps kids, crew leaders, and station leaders stay on schedule.

After you've assigned kids to Scuba Crews, you should assign Scuba Crews to groups. Each group consists of one-fourth of the elementary-age Scuba Crews at **SCUBA**. To eliminate confusion with Scuba Crew numbers, use letters, colors, or sea-creature names to label these four groups.

For example, if you have thirty-five kids, you will end up with seven Scuba Crews of five kids. You will put all seven Scuba Crews into one large group. The large group will travel to the stations together. (See sample schedule on p. 25.)

If you have sixty kids, you will end up with twelve Scuba Crews of five kids. You will then assign the crews to larger groups in this way:

A—crews 1-3   C—crews 7-9
B—crews 4-6   D—crews 10-12

If you have 150 kids, you will end up with thirty Scuba Crews of five kids. You will then assign the crews to larger groups in this way:

A—crews 1-7   C—crews 16-22
B—crews 8-15   D—crews 23-30

If you have more than 150 kids, set up double stations for Splish Splash Games, Deep Bible Adventures, Undersea Crafts and Missions, and Chadder's Undersea Bible Adventure. For more information on running double stations, see the diagram on page 27.

You'll notice on the "Daily Schedule and Announcements" pages (pp. 89-98) that groups visit the stations in a different order each day. This schedule shift provides welcome variety for kids and allows a different group to perform Dive-In Diner Service each day. Dive-In Diner Service is extremely important to the crews, who get a chance to share God's love.

PLANNING

Preschool children will keep the same schedule each day but will perform Dive-In Diner Service on Day 1. Preschoolers will leave their room and join older kids for Sing & Play Splash and Sea Star Finale. All other preschool activities take place in or near the Preschool Tide Pool room.

Use the sample morning and evening schedules (pp. 86-87) to plan your VBS times. Each day before **SCUBA**, fill in the appropriate day's schedule with times and announcements. Then photocopy both sides of the schedule and distribute the schedule. (To avoid confusion, you might want to photocopy each day's schedule on a different color of paper.) Don't forget to give copies to the Scuba Crew Leaders!

FiELD TesT FinDinGS

Our crew leaders asked for more "talk-starters" on their daily schedules, so they could really get to know the kids in their crews. So we've made these schedules two-sided: The daily schedule is on the front, and a few fun jokes and activities for crews are on the back! There's even room for you to add your own creative ideas!

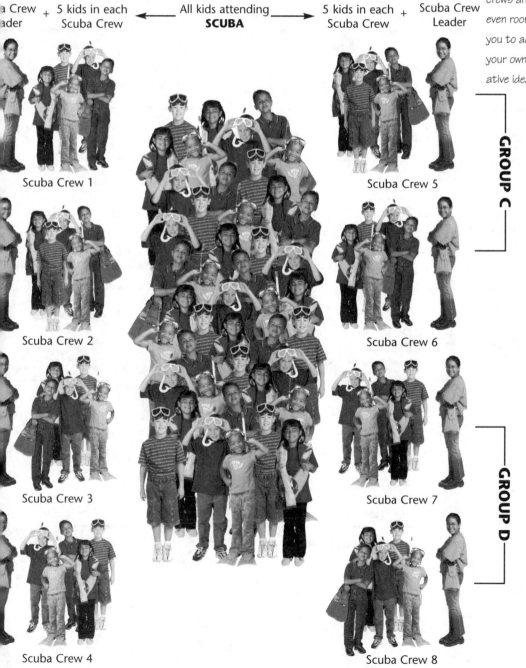

a Crew + 5 kids in each ⟵ All kids attending ⟶ 5 kids in each + Scuba Crew
ader   Scuba Crew   **SCUBA**   Scuba Crew   Leader

Scuba Crew 1

Scuba Crew 2

Scuba Crew 3

Scuba Crew 4

Scuba Crew 5

Scuba Crew 6

Scuba Crew 7

Scuba Crew 8

GROUP C

GROUP D

PLanning

Sample

Morning Schedule (8:30-11:30)

DAILY SCHEDULE

TIME	GROUP A Crews 1–5	GROUP B Crews 6-10	GROUP C Crews 11-15	GROUP D Crews 16–20	PRESCHOOL
8:30-8:55	Sing & Play Splash	Sing & Play Splash	Sing & Play Splash	Sing & Play Splash	Preschool Tide Pool
Allow five minutes to dive to your next Scuba Station.					
9:00-9:20	Deep Bible Adventures	Undersea Crafts and Missions	Splish Splash Games	Chadder's Undersea Bible Adventure	Dive-In Diner Service
Allow five minutes to dive to your next Scuba Station.					
9:25-9:45	Undersea Crafts and Missions	Splish Splash Games	Chadder's Undersea Bible Adventure	Deep Bible Adventures	Preschool Tide Pool
Allow five minutes to dive to your next Scuba Station.					
9:50-10:10	Dive-In Diner	Dive-In Diner	Dive-In Diner	Dive-In Diner	Chadder's Undersea Bible Adventure
Allow five minutes to dive to your next Scuba Station.					
10:15-10:35	Splish Splash Games	Chadder's Undersea Bible Adventure	Deep Bible Adventures	Undersea Crafts and Missions	Preschool Tide Pool
Allow five minutes to dive to your next Scuba Station.					
10:40-11:00	Chadder's Undersea Bible Adventure	Deep Bible Adventures	Undersea Crafts and Missions	Splish Splash Games	Preschool Tide Pool
Allow five minutes to dive to your next Scuba Station.					
11:05-11:30	Sea Star Finale	Sea Star Finale	Sea Star Finale	Sea Star Finale	Sea Star Finale

Planning

Sample

S.C.U.B.A.

Evening Schedule (6:30-9:10)*

DAILY SCHEDULE

TIME	GROUP A Crews 1–5	GROUP B Crews 6-10	GROUP C Crews 11-15	GROUP D Crews 16–20	PRESCHOOL
6:30-6:45	Sing & Play Splash	Sing & Play Splash	Sing & Play Splash	Sing & Play Splash	Preschool Tide Pool
Allow five minutes to dive to your next Scuba Station.					
6:50-7:10	Deep Bible Adventures	Undersea Crafts and Missions	Splish Splash Games	Chadder's Undersea Bible Adventure	Dive-In Diner Service
Allow five minutes to dive to your next Scuba Station.					
7:15-7:35	Undersea Crafts and Missions	Splish Splash Games	Chadder's Undersea Bible Adventure	Deep Bible Adventures	Preschool Tide Pool
Allow five minutes to dive to your next Scuba Station.					
7:40-7:55	Dive-In Diner	Dive-In Diner	Dive-In Diner	Dive-In Diner	Chadder's Undersea Bible Adventure
Allow five minutes to dive to your next Scuba Station.					
8:00-8:20	Splish Splash Games	Chadder's Undersea Bible Adventure	Deep Bible Adventures	Undersea Crafts and Missions	Preschool Tide Pool
Allow five minutes to dive to your next Scuba Station.					
8:25-8:45	Chadder's Undersea Bible Adventure	Deep Bible Adventures	Undersea Crafts and Missions	Splish Splash Games	Preschool Tide Pool
Allow five minutes to dive to your next Scuba Station.					
8:50-9:10	Sea Star Finale	Sea Star Finale	Sea Star Finale	Sea Star Finale	Sea Star Finale

*Kids will need at *least* twenty minutes to complete each **SCUBA** Station. If you need to end your program promptly at 9 p.m., shorten your "dive" time to two or three minutes between each **SCUBA** Station.

PLANNING

Fish Jokes

Fishing for a few laughs? Try a few of these fish jokes when you make your closing announcements. (We'll warn you; these are real groaners...but kids loved 'em!)

What fish is the most valuable?
A goldfish

Why did the dolphin cross the ocean?
To get to the other tide

What fish can do an operation?
A sturgeon

What do fish use to help them hear?
A herring aid

If fish lived on land, what country would they live in?
Finland

Why are fish so smart?
Because they stay in schools

What is a whale's favorite game?
Swallow the Leader

Why is it so easy to weigh a fish?
They have their own scales.

What happens when you cross a shark with a cow?
I don't know...but I wouldn't want to milk it!

Planning

DAILY SCHEDULE AND ANNOUNCEMENTS

Believe in God.

"But you are the only true God" (Jeremiah 10:10a).

DAY 1 SCHEDULE

Time	Group A Crews_____	Group B Crews_____	Group C Crews_____	Group D Crews_____	Preschool
	Sing & Play Splash	Sing & Play Splash	Sing & Play Splash	Sing & Play Splash	Preschool Tide Pool
Allow five minutes to dive to your next Scuba Station.					
	Deep Bible Adventures	Undersea Crafts and Missions	Splish Splash Games	Chadder's Undersea Bible Adventure	Dive-In Diner Service
Allow five minutes to dive to your next Scuba Station.					
	Undersea Crafts and Missions	Splish Splash Games	Chadder's Undersea Bible Adventure	Deep Bible Adventures	Preschool Tide Pool
Allow five minutes to dive to your next Scuba Station.					
	Dive-In Diner	Dive-In Diner	Dive-In Diner	Dive-In Diner	Chadder's Undersea Bible Adventure
Allow five minutes to dive to your next Scuba Station.					
	Splish Splash Games	Chadder's Undersea Bible Adventure	Deep Bible Adventures	Undersea Crafts and Missions	Preschool Tide Pool
Allow five minutes to dive to your next Scuba Station.					
	Chadder's Undersea Bible Adventure	Deep Bible Adventures	Undersea Crafts and Missions	Splish Splash Games	Preschool Tide Pool
Allow five minutes to dive to your next Scuba Station.					
	Sea Star Finale	Sea Star Finale	Sea Star Finale	Sea Star Finale	Sea Star Finale

TODAY'S ANNOUNCEMENTS:

A flying fish can build up tremendous speed underwater by beating its tail up to fifty times in one second!

Just for "Fin"

a sea of stuff for crews to do!

WHAT GAME DO FISH LIKE PLAYING THE MOST?

Name That Tuna!

Get to know your Scuba Crew members. Tell your name, then name an object that starts with the first letter of your name, that you could take on a dive. For example, "My name is Lisa, and I could take a life preserver!"

As you walk from station to station, walk single file...but switch the order each time you travel!

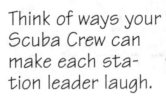

Think of ways your Scuba Crew can make each station leader laugh.

HOW DO FISH GET TO SCHOOL?

On the octobus

90

DAILY SCHEDULE AND ANNOUNCEMENTS S.C.U.B.A.

Obey God.

"Here is what it means to love God.
It means that we obey his commands" (1 John 5:3).

DAY 2 SCHEDULE

Time	Group A Crews_____	Group B Crews_____	Group C Crews_____	Group D Crews_____	Preschool
	Sing & Play Splash	Sing & Play Splash	Sing & Play Splash	Sing & Play Splash	Sing & Play Splash
	Allow five minutes to dive to your next Scuba Station.				
	Deep Bible Adventures	Undersea Crafts and Missions	Dive-In Diner Service	Chadder's Undersea Bible Adventure	Preschool Tide Pool
	Allow five minutes to dive to your next Scuba Station.				
	Undersea Crafts and Missions	Splish Splash Games	Chadder's Undersea Bible Adventure	Deep Bible Adventures	Preschool Tide Pool
	Allow five minutes to dive to your next Scuba Station.				
	Dive-In Diner	Dive-In Diner	Dive-In Diner	Dive-In Diner	Chadder's Undersea Bible Adventure
	Allow five minutes to dive to your next Scuba Station.				
	Splish Splash Games	Chadder's Undersea Bible Adventure	Deep Bible Adventures	Undersea Crafts and Missions	Preschool Tide Pool
	Allow five minutes to dive to your next Scuba Station.				
	Chadder's Undersea Bible Adventure	Deep Bible Adventures	Undersea Crafts and Missions	Splish Splash Games	Preschool Tide Pool
	Allow five minutes to dive to your next Scuba Station.				
	Sea Star Finale	Sea Star Finale	Sea Star Finale	Sea Star Finale	Sea Star Finale

Today's announcements:

The call of the blue whale chimes in at a whopping 188 decibels. That's louder than a jet engine!

Copyright © Group Publishing, Inc., P.O. Box 481, Loveland, CO 80539. www.groupvbs.com

Planning

JuSt foR "Fin"

a sea of stuff foR CReWS to Do!

Which crew member can make the best fish face?

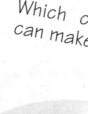

WHat game SHOW DO fiSH LiKe to WatCH?

Whale of fortune!

How many famous fish can your crew think of? (Such as Charlie the Tuna, Sebastian the crab, SpongeBob SquarePants...)

WHY DiDn't anyone PLaY WitH tHe LoBSteR?

He was too SHeLLfiSH.

See if you can think of an ocean creature for every letter of the alphabet! Hmmmm...Alba core, Barracuda, Cod...

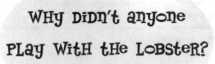

PLannIng

DAILY SCHEDULE AND announcements

Trust God.
"Trust in the Lord with all your heart.
Do not depend on your own understanding" (Proverbs 3:5).

DAY 3 SCHEDULE

Time	Group B Crews_____	Group C Crews_____	Group D Crews_____	Group A Crews_____	Preschool
	Sing & Play Splash	Sing & Play Splash	Sing & Play Splash	Sing & Play Splash	Sing & Play Splash
	Allow five minutes to dive to your next Scuba Station.				
	Deep Bible Adventures	Undersea Crafts and Missions	Dive-In Diner Service	Chadder's Undersea Bible Adventure	Preschool Tide Pool
	Allow five minutes to dive to your next Scuba Station.				
	Undersea Crafts and Missions	Splish Splash Games	Chadder's Undersea Bible Adventure	Deep Bible Adventures	Preschool Tide Pool
	Allow five minutes to dive to your next Scuba Station.				
	Dive-In Diner	Dive-In Diner	Dive-In Diner	Dive-In Diner	Chadder's Undersea Bible Adventure
	Allow five minutes to dive to your next Scuba Station.				
	Splish Splash Games	Chadder's Undersea Bible Adventure	Deep Bible Adventures	Undersea Crafts and Missions	Preschool Tide Pool
	Allow five minutes to dive to your next Scuba Station.				
	Chadder's Undersea Bible Adventure	Deep Bible Adventures	Undersea Crafts and Missions	Splish Splash Games	Preschool Tide Pool
	Allow five minutes to dive to your next Scuba Station.				
	Sea Star Finale	Sea Star Finale	Sea Star Finale	Sea Star Finale	Sea Star Finale

Today's announcements:

Sea turtles can stay underwater for as long as two hours...without breathing!

Planning

Just for "Fin"

a sea of stuff for crews to do!

WHAT DO YOU GET WHEN YOU CROSS A SHARK WITH A PARROT?

an animal that talks your head off!

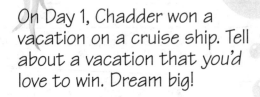

On Day 1, Chadder won a vacation on a cruise ship. Tell about a vacation that you'd love to win. Dream big!

What movie character would you love to have as your best friend? Why?

Who on your crew…

- has a birthday during the summer?
- owns the most pets?
- likes a strange food?
- has been to the ocean?
- ate pancakes for breakfast?

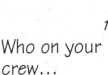

Who is your favorite person in the whole world? Why?

WHAT DO YOU GET WHEN YOU CROSS A FISH WITH AN ELEPHANT?

swimming trunks

DaILY SCHEDULE
anD announcements

Love God.

"Love the Lord your God with all your heart and with
all your soul. Love him with all your strength" (Deuteronomy 6:5).

DaY 4 SCHEDULE

Time	Group C Crews_____	Group D Crews_____	Group A Crews_____	Group B Crews_____	Preschool
	Sing & Play Splash	Sing & Play Splash	Sing & Play Splash	Sing & Play Splash	Sing & Play Splash
	Allow five minutes to dive to your next Scuba Station.				
	Deep Bible Adventures	Undersea Crafts and Missions	Dive-In Diner Service	Chadder's Undersea Bible Adventure	Preschool Tide Pool
	Allow five minutes to dive to your next Scuba Station.				
	Undersea Crafts and Missions	Splish Splash Games	Chadder's Undersea Bible Adventure	Deep Bible Adventures	Preschool Tide Pool
	Allow five minutes to dive to your next Scuba Station.				
	Dive-In Diner	Dive-In Diner	Dive-In Diner	Dive-In Diner	Chadder's Undersea Bible Adventure
	Allow five minutes to dive to your next Scuba Station.				
	Splish Splash Games	Chadder's Undersea Bible Adventure	Deep Bible Adventures	Undersea Crafts and Missions	Preschool Tide Pool
	Allow five minutes to dive to your next Scuba Station.				
	Chadder's Undersea Bible Adventure	Deep Bible Adventures	Undersea Crafts and Missions	Splish Splash Games	Preschool Tide Pool
	Allow five minutes to dive to your next Scuba Station.				
	Sea Star Finale	Sea Star Finale	Sea Star Finale	Sea Star Finale	Sea Star Finale

TODAY'S announcements:

Not all pearls are white. In fact,
pearls can be gold, purple, or even black!

JUSt foR "Fin"

a sea of stuff foR CReWS to DO!

Say this fast ten times...
"A noisy nose annoys an oyster."

Kids, do you know your Scuba
Crew Leader's...
- favorite color?
- least favorite food?
- strange talents?
- middle name?
- favorite Bible verse?

No? Then find out!

I Spy!
As you walk to your Scuba Stations, look for the following:
- nine blue objects
- things that start with the letter B
- someone on a different crew pretending to swim
- five people wearing hats
- a crew leader who is smiling

PLANNING

DAILY SCHEDULE
AND ANNOUNCEMENTS

Share God's love.
"Go into all the world. Preach the good news to everyone" (Mark 16:15).

DAY 5 SCHEDULE

Time	Group D Crews_____	Group A Crews_____	Group B Crews_____	Group C Crews_____	Preschool
	Sing & Play Splash	Sing & Play Splash	Sing & Play Splash	Sing & Play Splash	Sing & Play Splash
	Allow five minutes to dive to your next Scuba Station.				
	Deep Bible Adventures	Undersea Crafts and Missions	Dive-In Diner Service	Chadder's Undersea Bible Adventure	Preschool Tide Pool
	Allow five minutes to dive to your next Scuba Station.				
	Undersea Crafts and Missions	Splish Splash Games	Chadder's Undersea Bible Adventure	Deep Bible Adventures	Preschool Tide Pool
	Allow five minutes to dive to your next Scuba Station.				
	Dive-In Diner	Dive-In Diner	Dive-In Diner	Dive-In Diner	Chadder's Undersea Bible Adventure
	Allow five minutes to dive to your next Scuba Station.				
	Splish Splash Games	Chadder's Undersea Bible Adventure	Deep Bible Adventures	Undersea Crafts and Missions	Preschool Tide Pool
	Allow five minutes to dive to your next Scuba Station.				
	Chadder's Undersea Bible Adventure	Deep Bible Adventures	Undersea Crafts and Missions	Splish Splash Games	Preschool Tide Pool
	Allow five minutes to dive to your next Scuba Station.				
	Sea Star Finale	Sea Star Finale	Sea Star Finale	Sea Star Finale	Sea Star Finale

TODAY'S ANNOUNCEMENTS:

If you cut a sea star in half,
it will grow into two completely new sea stars!

Planning

Just foR "Fin"

a sea of stuff foR CREWS to Do!

Make up a song about **SCUBA**, to the tune of "Row, Row, Row Your Boat."

WHat Do you Get WHen you GRaDuate fRom SCUBA?

a Deep-Loma!

What has been the most fun at **SCUBA**?

Who made you laugh the most?

Why should other kids come to **SCUBA**?

Tell your station leaders "Tanks a lot!" (They're always fishing for compliments!)

WHat Do WHaLes eat?

FISH anD SHIPS!

Give all the members of another Scuba Crew a high five. Can you give high fives to everyone at **SCUBA**?

ReCRuiting

With these easy ideas, getting all your volunteers will be a snap!

Does Recruiting Make you Crabby?

You love VBS, right? You love watching kids' faces light up as they worship. You love preparing awesome Bible adventures for kids to take part in. You actually dream of wild, elaborate decorations for your VBS theme. And you'll be the first to admit that VBS crafts are right up your alley. But you get downright "crabby" so to speak, when it comes to recruiting. "Where will I find leaders for all these kids?" It's true that finding all the right volunteers to pull off a successful VBS program *can* be a challenge.

That's why we're here to help! You see, recruiting doesn't *have* to be a headache. It can actually be a fun, energizing opportunity to connect with people who have a passion for children's ministry...people just like you! We're here to help you fish for all the Scuba Station Leaders and Scuba Crew Leaders you need for your **SCUBA** VBS. (You might even find additional registration staff, photographers, decorating specialists, and maybe a co-director!) So swim through these pages and discover just how fun—and effective—your recruiting efforts can be!

Wow! Take a Look at all the other Ways Group Helps you Recruit Volunteers!

This year recruiting can be even easier! That's because we've provided you with two bonus tools to help you catch all the volunteers you need for a great undersea adventure. The *Dive Deep! Recruitment, Overview, and Pass-Along Training Video* includes three brief "commercials" that will have everyone signing up to help with **SCUBA**. You can also sign up for a free **SCUBA** Recruitment e-mail service. (Think of this as "e-cruitment"!) This service will send you several e-mail letters, which *you* can send to potential volunteers, detailing what positions are available, job descriptions, and more! Plus, these e-mail letters are specifically timed to *your* **SCUBA** dive dates! For more information, check out *your* **SCUBA** catalog or visit www.groupvbs.com.

SCUBa Station LeaDeRS

Scuba Station Leaders are the backbone of your **S**uper **C**ool **U**ndersea **B**ible **A**dventure. These are the people who teach and show God's love to the kids who attend your program. Kids look forward to seeing the station leaders each day, and so do you! You need at least eight volunteers—one leader for each of the following stations:

- Sing & Play Splash
- Undersea Crafts and Missions
- Splish Splash Games
- Dive-In Diner
- Deep Bible Adventures
- Chadder's Undersea Bible Adventure
- Sea Star Finale
- Preschool Tide Pool

If you're expecting more than 150 kids to attend **SCUBA**, you may want to double up on station leaders. Purchase an additional leader manual for each station, and run two sessions of each station simultaneously. This will help keep station group sizes manageable (fewer than thirty kids per session). Or have two station leaders team teach a large group of kids in a larger classroom.

If you have fewer than forty children, your job is even easier! Form Scuba Crews, then have all the Scuba Crews travel together in one group. (See the schedule and setup on p. 25.) This way, station leaders only need to teach their stations one time. Or station leaders may want to teach more than one station—making your recruiting efforts a snap!

Station leaders should be adults or mature older teenagers. You'll find a specific job description for each station leader in the following pages. In general, you should look for station leaders who are

- dependable church members or regular attendees,
- enthusiastic about working with children,
- excited about serving at **SCUBA**,
- patient and kind,
- good communicators,
- comfortable speaking in front of groups of thirty or more, and
- gifted in their station areas.

FieLD TeST FinDinGS

Our station leaders who took the team teaching approach were glad they did. They reduced their planning time and shared the task of bringing in supplies and setting up. Not only was it easier for them to manage fewer kids in each session, but they simply liked having a "dive buddy" to work with. (Plus, we've found that adults love the program as much as the kids!)

LeaDeR LifeLine

If you have enough volunteers, choose two people to team teach each station regardless of the size of your program. Station leaders benefit from a lighter load and an encouraging partner. Preschool Tide Pool especially benefits from an extra set of helping hands!

LeaDeR LifeLine

If you want to appoint an assistant director, ask the Sing & Play Splash Leader or the Sea Star Finale Leader. Because these two leaders present their material only once each day, they'll be free to help you handle last-minute details. (These two stations can even be led by the same person.)

FieLD TeSt FinDinGS

Talk about easy recruiting! After our field test, several station leaders volunteered to lead their areas next year. Other churches have reported similar results, with a high volunteer return rate. One director of a VBS of six hundred kids said that she delighted in sitting back and watching last year's volunteers recruit this year's!

In more traditional VBS models, volunteers prepare and teach everything from games and Bible lessons to crafts and more. That's why your volunteers will *love* being station leaders: because they can lead out of their gifts, interests, and abilities. Plus, each Scuba Station leader manual is easy to follow, providing lists of easy-to-collect supplies and field-tested activities.

Use the details in the job descriptions (pp. 107-114) to help you enlist leaders for the stations. Give each leader a copy of his or her job description, and offer to address any questions or concerns that may arise. Invite Scuba Station Leaders and Scuba Crew Leaders to your scheduled leader training.

List the names, addresses, and phone numbers of your station leaders in the chart on page 103 so that you're able to quickly access the information.

SCUBA Station Leaders

STATION	LEADER'S NAME	ADDRESS	PHONE NUMBER	E-MAIL ADDRESS	OTHER NOTES
SING & PLAY SPLASH					
UNDERSEA CRAFTS AND MISSIONS					
SPLISH SPLASH GAMES					
DIVE-IN DINER					
DEEP BIBLE ADVENTURES					
CHADDER'S UNDERSEA BIBLE ADVENTURE					
SEA STAR FINALE					
PRESCHOOL TIDE POOL					

RECRUITING

Although we were blessed with many, many wonderful Scuba Crew Leaders, there were some who simply didn't "get it." They sat back and expected the station leaders to take charge, rather than jumping in themselves and working with their crew members. As a result, some kids didn't get as much out of the program. It's crucial that you take time to connect face to face with each crew leader and help him or her better understand his or her vital role in the success of your **SCUBA**.

LeaDeR LifeLine

If crew leaders can't attend the leader training meeting, encourage them to watch the *Dive Deep! Recruitment, Overview, and Training Video* and review their Crew Leader's Pocket Guide. To allow plenty of time for crew leaders to understand their roles, you might distribute the Crew Leader's Pocket Guides several weeks before **SCUBA**. Your job will be much easier if crew leaders read and understand this information well before the dive begins.

SCUBA CReW LeaDeRS

After you've enlisted Scuba Station Leaders, you'll need a group of Scuba Crew Leaders. The Scuba Crew Leader is an important part of each Scuba Crew. Anyone in your church who loves the Lord and loves children can be a Scuba Crew Leader! You'll need one Scuba Crew Leader for every five elementary-age children.

Scuba Crew Leaders don't have to prepare anything; they just come each day, guide their crew members through activities, help facilitate discussions, and generally join in the **SCUBA** fun. Their week will go more smoothly if you have a brief orientation meeting with your Scuba Crew Leaders or invite them to your leader training meeting. The *Dive Deep! Video* has special training tips just for them. It gives them helpful hints on leading discussions and solving any problems that might arise among their crews. We've also included photocopiable handouts that orient Scuba Crew Leaders with the teaching style at **SCUBA** and give them some ideas for capitalizing on extra time. You can find these handouts in the leader training section of this manual (pp. 125-140).

The following guidelines will help you find top-notch Scuba Crew Leaders.

A Scuba Crew Leader is

- a friend and a helper.
- responsible for drawing kids into discussions, as much as possible.
- someone who offers kids choices.
- someone who asks questions.
- someone who encourages kids.
- someone who helps and encourages station leaders.

A Scuba Crew Leader isn't

- the boss or the teacher.
- responsible for making sure everyone gives a "right" answer.
- someone who makes all the decisions.
- someone who gives all the answers.
- someone who yells at kids or puts them down.
- someone who tags along as an adult supervisor.

Photocopy the "Are You Ready to Dive In? Join a Super Cool Undersea Bible Adventure (**SCUBA**)...and Find Out!" sign (p. 117), and post it in your church lobby. You'll be pleasantly surprised at how many Scuba Crew Leaders join your team!

HOW DO I BEGIN RECRUITING?

Get ready to dive into recruiting!

First, take a deep breath. Now…pray. Remember, God knows each person in your church and each child who will attend your **SCUBA**. So ask God to open the eyes, hearts, and minds of those who will be just the right "fit" for your program.

Shine the news!

Next, get the word out! (This is the fun part!) Let folks know that this is more than "your grandfather's VBS." Prayerfully determine the number of children you'd like to reach with **SCUBA**…and don't be afraid to think big! Then share your vision in a creative way. For example, if your goal is to have one hundred kids attend **SCUBA**, you might cover a bulletin board with wavy, blue paper, then add one hundred paper fish swimming toward a coral reef. The reef might have a sign with the **SCUBA** logo on it and an arrow. Add the heading, "We Want Our Church to be Swimming With 100 Kids!" or "We're Giving a Whole New Meaning to Vacation Bible 'School'…of Fish!" Leave this bulletin board up for a few weeks to get everyone bubbling with excitement about what's coming.

Then tell how people can make this vision a reality. Using the bulletin board idea, you might simply add the words, "And *You* Can Help Make That Happen!" to the bottom of your bulletin board. Surround your board with job descriptions—people will be amazed at the fun and creative

Get everyone hooked on your vision!

LEADER LifeLine

A multisensory, multimedia approach could net many additional volunteers. Set out some of the sample Dive-In Diner treats near your sign-up area. Have a TV/VCR nearby, and play the *Dive Deep! Video* or the *Sing & Play Splash Music Video*. If you've used a Group VBS in the past, videotape a few volunteers or kids, telling what they liked best about it. You'll attract a crowd of potential volunteers!

We Want Our Church to be Swimming With 100 Kids!

Scuba

RECRUITING

ways they can get involved with this program! If you've used a Group VBS pro-gram before, you might even print out some great testimonials on brightly col-ored paper. Post these next to the job descriptions as a way to show *everyone* that VBS can be a blast!

You don't need to nag people, but keep your vision out in front of people at all times. Show a clip from the *Dive Deep! Video* in church (or for Bible stud-ies, senior citizens, or even college groups) every couple of weeks. Rather than making a negative plea for help ("I know nobody really wants to help, but..."), state your needs simply. You might say, "Our goal is to reach one hundred chil-dren with God's love at **SCUBA**. Right now we have enough volunteers to reach fifty kids. How can you help?" Visually remind people of your goal. If you use the fish bulletin board, you might use the clip art on the *SCUBA Clip Art, Song Lyrics, and Decorating* CD to add schools of fish throughout the church bulletin. (Maybe they're all headed to your volunteer sign-up area!)

Come out of your shell and meet people face to face!

Experienced VBS directors will tell you that there's no substitute for the personal touch. (Plus, it's harder for people to turn you down face to face!) If you truly think someone would be a dynamite Scuba Crew Leader, tell him or her! If, after the youth Christmas drama, you see a teenager who would be a great help in Deep Bible Adventures, let him or her know! One director tells us that he goes through the church telephone direc-tory line by line, prayerfully considering *each* person. It has been a super way to involve those who don't naturally come to mind! (With Group's free **SCUBA** Recruitment e-mail service, you can even e-mail job descriptions or letters to those who might be excellent **SCUBA** staff members!)

Your volunteers are as precious as gold. (Of course, you knew that!) So be sure to treat each one with thoughtfulness and respect. If someone volunteers for a position that you don't feel is a good "fit," gently recommend another place where he or she might better serve. In our field tests, we've had Scuba Crew Leaders who would have been much better assis-tant station leaders, preschool crew leaders, or other helpers. Check out pages 118-122 for a list of other ways to use people's gifts and abilities to ensure that **SCUBA** is a positive experience for everyone!

Remember, your volunteers are priceless gems!

S.C.U.B.A.
SUPER COOL UNDERSEA BIBLE ADVENTURE

JOB DESCRIPTION

SING & PLAY SPLASH LEADER

Qualifications

You'll be a successful Sing & Play Splash Leader if you

- ○ love the Lord and love children,
- ○ have experience leading songs or singing with children,
- ○ can motivate and energize kids, and
- ○ are comfortable speaking in front of large groups.

Responsibilities

As a Sing & Play Splash Leader, you'll be responsible for

- ○ attending scheduled leader training,
- ○ repeating the daily Bible Point as you teach,
- ○ learning the music and motions for twelve **SCUBA** songs,
- ○ teaching kids the words and motions to several songs each day,
- ○ leading singing for the entire VBS,
- ○ assisting with Sea Star Finale programs each day, and
- ○ assisting the **SCUBA** Director as needed.

Join the excitement of a SUPER COOL UNDERSEA BIBLE ADVENTURE!

Related Interests

You'll enjoy leading Sing & Play Splash if you enjoy any of the following activities:

- ○ playing a musical instrument,
- ○ directing or singing,
- ○ leading worship, and
- ○ acting or drama.

Recruiting

SUPER COOL UNDERSEA BIBLE ADVENTURE

JOB DESCRIPTION

UNDERSEA CRAFTS AND MISSIONS LEADER

Qualifications

You'll be a successful Undersea Crafts and Missions Leader if you

- ○ love the Lord and love children,
- ○ are creative and fun-loving,
- ○ can give clear directions to children, and
- ○ show patience while working with lots of children.

Responsibilities

As an Undersea Crafts and Missions Leader, you'll be responsible for

- ○ attending scheduled leader training meetings,
- ○ collecting necessary supplies,
- ○ preparing sample Bible Point Crafts before **SCUBA**,
- ○ explaining and encouraging children to carry out Operation Kid-to-Kid,
- ○ repeating the daily Bible Point as you teach,
- ○ helping children create one-of-a-kind crafts,
- ○ leading four sessions of Undersea Crafts and Missions each day, and
- ○ assisting with Sea Star Finale as needed.

Join the excitement of a super cool undersea Bible adventure!

ReCRuitinG

Related Interests

You'll enjoy leading Undersea Crafts and Missions if you enjoy any of the following activities:

- ○ missions projects,
- ○ watching kids have a great time,
- ○ arts and crafts, and
- ○ working with your hands.

S.C.U.B.A.
SUPER COOL UNDERSEA BIBLE ADVENTURE

JOB DESCRIPTION

SPLiSH SPLaSH Games LeaDeR

Qualifications

You'll be a successful Splish Splash Games Leader if you

○ love the Lord and love children;

○ enjoy playing games;

○ are positive, active, and energetic; and

○ can organize and motivate children.

Responsibilities

As a Splish Splash Games Leader, you'll be responsible for

○ attending scheduled leader training,

○ repeating the daily Bible Point as you teach,

○ collecting necessary supplies for Splish Splash Games,

○ clearly explaining each game,

○ handing out Bible Memory Buddies each day,

○ leading three sessions of Splish Splash Games each day,

○ assisting with Dive-In Diner Service each day, and

○ assisting with Sea Star Finale as needed.

Join the excitement of a Super Cool Undersea Bible Adventure!

Related Interests

You'll enjoy leading Splish Splash Games if you enjoy any of the following activities:

○ team sports,

○ outdoor recreational activities, and

○ encouraging others to do their best.

Recruiting

S.C.U.B.A.
SUPER COOL UNDERSEA BIBLE ADVENTURE
JOB DESCRIPTION

DiVe-In DineR LeADeR

Qualifications

You'll be a successful Dive-In Diner Leader if you

- ○ love the Lord and love children,
- ○ enjoy cooking and food preparation,
- ○ believe children can accomplish big tasks,
- ○ can give clear directions to children, and
- ○ accept and encourage children's abilities.

Responsibilities

As a Dive-In Diner Leader, you'll be responsible for

- ○ attending scheduled leader training,
- ○ repeating the daily Bible Point as you teach,
- ○ coordinating food supplies for each day's snack,
- ○ setting up assembly lines to help kids prepare each day's snack,
- ○ serving snacks to the entire **SCUBA**,
- ○ cleaning up the Dive-In Diner area after snacks are served, and
- ○ assisting with Sea Star Finale as needed.

Join tHe eXcitement of a
SUPeR CooL UnDeRSea BiBLe aDventuRe!

Related Interests

You'll enjoy leading Dive-In Diner if you enjoy any of the following activities:

- ○ preparing and serving food,
- ○ maintaining a clean environment,
- ○ working in a kitchen or restaurant, and
- ○ organizing and supervising teams of people.

ReCRuiting

Deep Bible Adventures Leader

S.C.U.B.A.
SUPER COOL UNDERSEA BIBLE ADVENTURE
JOB DESCRIPTION

Qualifications

You'll be a successful Deep Bible Adventures Leader if you

- ○ love the Lord and love children;
- ○ have a flair for drama and can play a role convincingly;
- ○ relish a fast-paced, exciting atmosphere;
- ○ believe in hands-on discovery as a learning technique; and
- ○ feel comfortable facilitating group discussions.

Responsibilities

As a Deep Bible Adventures Leader, you'll be responsible for

- ○ attending scheduled leader training,
- ○ repeating the daily Bible Point as you teach,
- ○ collecting necessary supplies,
- ○ recruiting three volunteers to perform simple roles as Bible characters,
- ○ setting up props for Deep Bible Adventures,
- ○ leading four sessions of Deep Bible Adventures each day, and
- ○ assisting with Sea Star Finale as needed.

Join the excitement of a SUPER COOL UNDERSEA BIBLE ADVENTURE!

Related Interests

You'll enjoy leading Deep Bible Adventures if you enjoy any of the following activities:

- ○ storytelling,
- ○ acting or drama,
- ○ leading discussions, and
- ○ surprising others.

RECRUITING

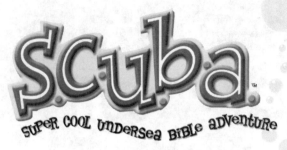

S.C.U.B.A.
SUPER COOL UNDERSEA BIBLE ADVENTURE

JOB DESCRIPTION

CHADDER'S UNDERSEA BIBLE ADVENTURE LEADER

Qualifications

You'll be a successful Chadder's Undersea Bible Adventure Leader if you

- ○ love the Lord and love children,
- ○ have an interest in Bible study skills,
- ○ know how to operate your church's TV and VCR,
- ○ understand that videos can be effective learning tools for today's kids,
- ○ enjoy facilitating group discussions, and
- ○ ask questions to help kids connect the Bible Point they've learned in the *Chadder's Undersea Bible Adventure* video to their everyday lives.

Join the excitement of a super cool undersea Bible adventure!

Responsibilities

As a Chadder's Undersea Bible Adventure Leader, you'll be responsible for

- ○ attending scheduled leader training,
- ○ repeating the daily Bible Point as you teach,
- ○ setting up a TV and VCR,
- ○ cuing the *Chadder's Undersea Bible Adventure* video to each day's segment,
- ○ helping Scuba Crew Leaders facilitate group discussions,
- ○ leading four sessions of Chadder's Undersea Bible Adventure each day,
- ○ showing the *Chadder's Undersea Bible Adventure* video segment to the preschoolers each day, and
- ○ assisting with Sea Star Finale as needed.

Related Interests

You'll enjoy leading Chadder's Undersea Bible Adventure if you enjoy any of the following activities:

- ○ watching movies,
- ○ acting or drama,
- ○ leading discussions, and
- ○ operating electronic equipment.

RECRUITING

S.C.U.B.A.
SUPER COOL UNDERSEA BIBLE ADVENTURE
JOB DESCRIPTION

SEA STAR FINALE LEADER

Qualifications

You'll be a successful Sea Star Finale Leader if you

- ○ love the Lord and love children,
- ○ enjoy being in front of people,
- ○ are an expressive storyteller,
- ○ like to laugh and have a good sense of humor, and
- ○ can encourage and affirm kids' participation in each day's Sea Star Finale.

Responsibilities

As a Sea Star Finale Leader, you'll be responsible for

- ○ attending scheduled leader training,
- ○ repeating the daily Bible Point as you teach,
- ○ collecting necessary supplies,
- ○ setting up props for each day's Sea Star Finale,
- ○ practicing each day's Sea Star Finale script ahead of time,
- ○ recruiting and training other station leaders to assist you,
- ○ leading Sea Star Finale for the entire **SCUBA** each day, and
- ○ assisting the director as needed.

Join the excitement of a SUPER COOL UNDERSEA BIBLE ADVENTURE!

Related Interests

You'll enjoy leading Sea Star Finale if you enjoy any of the following activities:

- ○ public speaking,
- ○ acting or drama,
- ○ storytelling,
- ○ making people laugh, and
- ○ supervising teams of people.

RECRUITING

SCUBA
SUPER COOL UNDERSEA BIBLE ADVENTURE
JOB DESCRIPTION

PRESCHOOL TIDE POOL DIRECTOR

Qualifications

You'll be a successful Preschool Tide Pool Director if you

- ⭕ love the Lord and love children;
- ⭕ get down on the floor and interact with children at their eye level;
- ⭕ use simple language that preschoolers can understand; and
- ⭕ stock your room with blocks, dress-up clothes, modeling dough, and other age-appropriate toys and supplies.

Responsibilities

As a Preschool Tide Pool Director, you'll be responsible for

- ⭕ attending scheduled leader training,
- ⭕ repeating the daily Bible Point as you teach,
- ⭕ collecting necessary supplies,
- ⭕ leading a team of Scuba Crew Leaders for preschoolers,
- ⭕ telling the daily Bible story in a fun and involving way,
- ⭕ supervising preschoolers during outdoor activities, and
- ⭕ leading preschoolers in singing.

Join the excitement of a
SUPER COOL UNDERSEA BIBLE ADVENTURE!

Related Interests

You'll enjoy leading Preschool Tide Pool if you enjoy any of the following activities:

- ⭕ playing with young children,
- ⭕ storytelling,
- ⭕ singing, and
- ⭕ being outdoors.

RECRUITING

aRe you ReaDy to DiVe In?

Join a Super Cool Undersea Bible Adventure (SCUBA)...and Find Out!

QuaLificatioNs

- Be at least fourteen years old.
- Love the Lord.
- Love children.
- Like to have fun.
- Have some experience working with children.

RespoNsiBiLities

- Attend a leader training meeting.
- Attend **SCUBA** each day.
- Participate in fun activities while shepherding a group of three to five elementary-age kids.
- Arrive twenty minutes early to greet crew members each day.

If you'Re inteRested, SigN BeLoW oR See _____ toDay!

SCUBA Director

NAME, PHONE NUMBER, AND E-MAIL ADDRESS

_____
_____
_____
_____
_____
_____
_____
_____
_____

NAME, PHONE NUMBER, AND E-MAIL ADDRESS

_____
_____
_____
_____
_____
_____
_____
_____
_____

ReCRuitiNg

Recruiting Scuba Crew Leaders for Preschoolers

Your youngest divers need Scuba Crew Leaders too! Like Scuba Crew Leaders for the elementary-age kids, Scuba Crew Leaders for preschoolers don't need to prepare anything in advance. In fact, their job is even easier! Instead of *leading* Scuba Crews, Scuba Crew Leaders for preschoolers help their Scuba Crews follow directions given by the Preschool Tide Pool Director.

Scuba Crew Leaders for preschoolers play with children, help them complete art projects, and keep them together when they leave the room. To ensure adequate supervision for the preschoolers who attend your **SCUBA**, you need one Scuba Crew Leader for every five preschool-age children.

What kind of person would make a good Scuba Crew Leader for preschoolers?

A Scuba Crew Leader for preschoolers is

- a friend and a helper.
- someone who helps children complete activities.
- someone who gets down on the floor to interact with children.
- someone who encourages children.

A Scuba Crew Leader for preschoolers isn't

- the boss or the teacher.
- someone who completes children's activities for them.
- someone who supervises children from a distance.
- someone who yells at children or puts them down.

Photocopy the "Are You Ready to Dive In? Join Preschool Tide Pool...and Find Out!" handout (p. 117), and post it in your church lobby. You'll be pleasantly surprised at how many Scuba Crew Leaders for preschoolers join your team!

aRe you ReaDy to DiVe In?

Join Preschool Tide Pool... and Find Out!

QuaLifications
- Be at least fourteen years old.
- Love the Lord.
- Love children.
- Like to have fun.
- Have some experience working with children.

ResPoNsiBiLities
- Attend a leader training meeting.
- Attend **SCUBA** each day.
- Participate in fun activities while shepherding a group of three to five preschool-age children.
- Arrive twenty minutes early to greet the children in your crew.

If you'Re inteResteD, sign BeLow oR see _____today!

SCUBA Director

NAME, PHONE NUMBER, AND E-MAIL ADDRESS

_____

_____

_____

_____

_____

_____

_____

_____

NAME, PHONE NUMBER, AND E-MAIL ADDRESS

_____

_____

_____

_____

_____

_____

_____

_____

RecRUiting

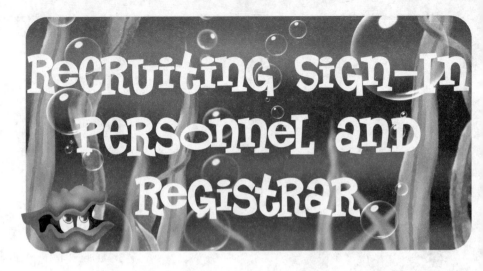

ReCRuiting Sign-In PeRsonnel and RegistRar

FieLD TeST FinDingS

This may seem obvious, but be sure your registration team members really do read the registration section in this Director Manual. We find that our host church directors who follow these instructions to the letter have great success.

LeaDeR LifeLine

A crew of registration "experts" will make the first day feel like a breeze for everyone else. We highly recommend recruiting a small crew of volunteers devoted to registration. You'll love handing that responsibility over to someone else, freeing you up to attend to other details. Teamwork is the way to go!

LeaDeR LifeLine

You might consider enlisting a few middle-schoolers to act as guides who will lead children inside and help them find their Scuba Crews. This simple step will speak volumes to parents (and kids) who are new to the church. It's a great way to get everyone off to a good start...and a wonderful way to give responsibility to middle-schoolers!

It's important to have staff near the registration tables to greet, welcome, and direct children. You'll also need at least one official registrar to make sure registration goes smoothly.

For your registrar, look for someone who

- pays close attention to details,
- is organized,
- is familiar with many kids in your church (this helps when forming Scuba Crews and provides kids with a familiar face on Day 1),
- understands the "combined-age" concept, and
- meets deadlines with a cheerful spirit.

Allow the registrar to read through the registration section on page 151 of this **SCUBA** Director Manual several weeks before **SCUBA** begins. Be sure that all registration forms and phone registrations are given to the registrar.

For sign-in volunteers, look for individuals who

- are friendly and outgoing,
- are comfortable interacting with children, and
- want to help with **SCUBA** but can't commit much time.

You can have different sign-in greeters each day—kids will love the surprise! Encourage your greeters to dress up in **SCUBA** staff T-shirts or diving "gear." Greeters can direct children to Preschool Tide Pool or help kids find their Scuba Crew Leaders. We've even heard from churches that recruited volunteers to say goodbye to the kids as they left each day! Wow! What an awesome way to affirm and bless each child!

RECRUITING

RecRuiting a Scuba Photographer

SCUBA will be a memorable event—one you'll want to capture on film. With today's speedy photo processing, you can make photos a fun part of your **SCUBA** program. (You may even want the photographer to act as a National Geographic-type photojournalist!)

Here's how:

1. Enlist a staff photographer. This person could be

- a parent,
- a church member,
- a friend or acquaintance from your community,
- the Sing & Play Splash Leader,
- the Sea Star Finale Leader,
- your pastor or another church staff person, or
- you.

Your photographer should be familiar with the camera or video equipment he or she will be using.

2. Decide whether you want to shoot slides, prints, or video. The following ideas will help you decide how to incorporate photography into your VBS.

- **Sea Star Finale slide show**—Have your photographer visit each station and take slide photographs of kids in action. Take the slide film to be processed. On the last day of Sea Star Finale, show slides you've taken during the week. If your photographer is fast and if you have one-hour slide processing available, you can even have more than one slide show during the week.

- **SCUBA photo frames**—During Dive-In Diner, have your photographer take two print photos of each participant (including Scuba Crew Leaders) and three print photos of each Scuba Crew. (It may take two or three days to complete this project, so start early!) Have the print

LeaDeR LifeLine

We've enjoyed visiting many church Web sites to see photos of their Group VBS programs. Posting your pictures on your church's Web site is a simple way to create excitement for your entire church! If you post photos, be sure to let us know at www.groupvbs.com.

film processed, and then put the photos in cardboard photo frames to sell or give away as souvenirs. Souvenir photo frames are available from Group Publishing or your local Christian bookstore. Check with your Undersea Crafts and Missions Leader to see if he or she is planning to have kids make **SCUBA** Snapshot Frames as a craft.

- **SCUBA Adventure Show**—Have your photographer videotape kids as they visit the stations each day. Encourage the photographer to interview kids about the things they're doing and what they like best. After your program, have the photographer edit the video to create a *SCUBA Adventure Show*! Host a video night when you show the video to kids, parents, and church members.

- **SCUBA photo display**—Have your photographer take print photographs of kids in action. Then display the photographs on a poster or bulletin board in your church lobby. This is a great way to give church members a peek into **SCUBA**. And extra photos make great outreach tools as an excuse to visit new families who sent their children to **SCUBA**.

3. Meet with your photographer before SCUBA. Talk about the number and kinds of photos you want. Decide who will have the film processed and who will select the photos or slides you'll use.

4. Watch kids' eyes light up as they see themselves in living color!

In addition to Scuba Station Leaders, Scuba Crew Leaders, a photographer, and registration staff, you may want to enlist the following staff members:

- **co-director or Crew Leader Director**—Pulling off a successful VBS takes a lot of attention to detail. That's why you'll benefit from another creative brain and an additional set of helping hands. A Crew Leader Director is responsible for training, communicating with, and checking in with each Scuba Crew Leader (daily during **SCUBA**). Handing this responsibility off to one person is a great way to see that it's done well!

• **publicity coordinator**—This person is responsible for coordinating publicity before and during your **SCUBA**. This might include selecting publicity supplies, planning outreach publicity campaigns, inviting local TV or newspaper reporters, contacting church and community members, or arranging for community news releases. (TV coverage on Day 5 would be a super way to tell your community about Operation Kid-to-Kid!) The publicity section of this manual will help your publicity coordinator plan a great publicity campaign using the **SCUBA** publicity supplies available from Group Publishing and your local Christian bookstore.

Want to Make an even Bigger Splash?

Wouldn't you love to have Gill (that adorable yellow fish on your **SCUBA** logo) come to your neighborhood? Check out www.groupvbs.com to see how your creative publicity ideas could bring Gill to your church!

• **family resource coordinator**—This person is responsible for collecting the completed order forms and money for family resources (such as *Sing & Play Splash Music* audiocassettes or *Chadder's Undersea Bible Adventure* videos), placing the order, and then distributing the items when they arrive. You may want to direct this person to the "Follow Up" section of this manual (pp. 193-198).

• **transportation coordinator**—This person is responsible for coordinating transportation to and from **SCUBA**. This might include organizing car pools, planning van or bus routes, or actually picking up children and transporting them to your facility.

• **child-care coordinator**—This person is responsible for providing or coordinating child care for the **SCUBA** staff. If possible, child care should be provided for all children (age three and younger) of Scuba Station Leaders and Scuba Crew Leaders.

• **extra registration workers**—You'll need a team of four to five registration workers to ensure smooth, speedy check-in on Day 1. Registration workers check in kids who have preregistered and make sure walk-in participants complete registration forms. With your guidance, registration workers also assign walk-in participants to Scuba Crews. Plan to meet with the registration team *before* registration to go over the registration information on pages 151-171.

LeadeR LifeLine

We've received many letters from VBS directors who entered a VBS float in a local parade. Consider creating a float that's decorated as an ocean of adorable fish and sea creatures. Have kids and adults, decked out in dive gear, out swimming with the fish! Or let kids dress up as enormous friendly fish "swimming" in the parade. What a fun way to alert the community about your SCUBA!

RecRuiting

• **music accompanist**—If you want to use live music during Sing & Play Splash, enlist a pianist, guitarist, or even a drummer to help lead singing. Some churches have pulled together a VBS praise band, composed of high-schoolers! (Be sure your accompanist listens to the *Sing & Play Splash Music* CD or audiocassette to hear the speed and beat of the music that worked so well in our field test.)

When your staff is complete, you're ready to dive into a real adventure!

Staff Training

THESE PRICELESS IDEAS WILL GET YOUR VOLUNTEERS READY TO DIVE INTO SCUBA!

USinG tHe DiVe DeeP! ViDeo

We know *you're* excited about **SCUBA**. The *Dive Deep! Video* can help you get others in your church excited too. The video is divided into the following segments: recruitment, promotional, overview, and pass-along training.

• **The Recruitment section** makes it easy to hook all of your **SCUBA** volunteers! This section contains three short "commercials" that you can show before adult Sunday school classes, during announcement time at worship services, or any time people are gathered. You might even set up a TV and VCR near your volunteer sign-in area and leave these commercials playing. With these additional recruiting tools, you'll look like a pro!

• **The promotional clip** gives a brief introduction to Group's **SCUBA**. In this brief segment, you'll discover what makes **SCUBA** different from other programs. Your church leaders, your Christian education board, and your congregation will see that this VBS program results in deeper Bible learning, not just games and crafts. Show the promotional clip in your children's church or Sunday school classes to get kids excited about discovering God's love. (This is a great way to get most of your kids preregistered, too.) This short "teaser" will get everyone geared up for your underwater adventure!

• **The overview portion** is a great tool for helping volunteers, parents, or other church members understand how **SCUBA** works. (After all, this VBS doesn't look like the Bible school programs many of us grew up with!) Use this portion to give volunteers and parents a better understanding of Scuba Crews, crew rotations, Scuba Stations, and more.

• **The pass-along training portion** will get your entire staff ready for action. Not only will your station leaders see kids successfully completing the activities described in their station leader manuals, but crew leaders will get to peek at great crew leaders. Your staff will see kids in a real **SCUBA** program enjoying Splish Splash Games, serving and tasting Dive-In Diner treats, creating spectacular Bible Point Crafts, and discovering Bible truths in new and meaningful ways. This segment is filled with practical, helpful tips that will make your staff the best it can be!

Through interviews with real staff members from our field test, your volunteers can learn how to work with their Scuba Crews, discover what's expected of them, and see the impact they can have on the kids at **SCUBA**.

LeaDeR LifeLine

The *Dive Deep! Video* really does make your job easy. Your staff will love seeing a real **SCUBA** in progress, and they'll be reassured that their activities really will be a success. This is a simple way to recruit, train, and prepare your staff.

FieLD TeST FinDinGs

We filmed a group of Scuba Crew Leaders moments after each day's program. This format captured the crew leaders' thoughts and feelings right away and gave us excellent insight as to what activities and experiences had risen to the top. You may want to gather a group of Scuba Crew Leaders each day and ask them to give advice to your future VBS volunteers. Compile these interviews with VBS footage to create a promotional video for your 2004 program. You'll be amazed at how these real-life "explorers" will help next year's staff.

Staff Training Meeting

You'll need the following supplies.

Things you can find around your home:

- cassette or CD player

Things you can find around your church:

- name tags
- TV and VCR
- scissors
- napkins
- small paper plates
- markers
- tape

Things you'll find in your Starter Kit:

- *Sing & Play Splash Music* audio-cassette or CD
- *Dive Deep! Recruiting, Overview, and Pass-Along Training Video*
- **SCUBA** leader manuals

Things you'll need to collect or purchase:

- *SCUBA Clip Art, Song Lyrics, and Decorating* CD*
- conch shell* or another attention-getting signal
- Bible Memory Buddies*
- *Sing & Play Splash Music Video* or DVD (optional)
- **SCUBA** staff T-shirts* (optional)
- Scuba Crew leader hats* (optional)
- photocopies of the "For Scuba Crew Leaders Only" handouts (pp. 135-138) and "For Preschool Scuba Crew Leaders Only" handouts (pp. 139-140)
- Bible Point posters*
- colorful poster board (1 large sheet per Scuba Crew Leader)
- 5 sheets of white poster board or foam core (for backing the Bible Point Posters)
- paint markers
- about 3 seedless grapes per person (pre-washed and placed in a bowl)
- 3 cubes of cheddar cheese per person
- 3 toothpicks per person
- 1 paper plate per person

*These items are available from Group Publishing and your local Christian bookstore.

Leader Lifeline

Your Sing & Play Splash Leader will need a set of Bible Point posters to use every day. You can use the same set for this training meeting.

Leader Lifeline

The Sing & Play Splash Music Video lets volunteers see Sing & Play Splash fun in action. We've added the song lyrics to each video song to make it even easier to follow along. This video (available from Group Publishing and your local Christian bookstore) is a super way to add enthusiasm, build confidence, and teach all twelve **SCUBA** songs.

LeaDeR LifeLine

Before your meeting, watch the Dive Deep! Video. Note the places where you'll stop the video. If your VCR has a counter, you may even want to jot down the counter number for each stopping place in the margin of this manual.

LeaDeR LifeLine

A giant inflatable Gill (that adorable yellow fish on your **SCUBA** logo) is available from Group Publishing or your local Christian bookstore.

LeaDeR LifeLine

Not only do Crew Leader's Pocket Guides save you time and energy, they also give important information in a concise, easy-to-read format. Your crew leaders will appreciate such a practical, handy guidebook!

Before the meeting, set up a TV and a VCR in your meeting room. Insert the *Dive Deep! Video*. Set chairs facing the TV.

Decorate your meeting room with paper fish, green crepe paper "sea weed," blue fabric "waves" on the walls, and clear balloon "bubbles." Hang inflatable fish from the ceiling, and throw gray or brown blankets over chairs and tables to make undersea rocks. Place adorable plush sea creatures such as crabs, octopuses, and sea horses in corners and on tables. To make your meeting room even "fishier," try some of the decorating ideas beginning on page 73 and in the VBS catalog. You may even get some clever ideas from the *Dive Deep! Video*. You can log onto www.groupoutlet.com for economical decorating resources.

Provide a Crew Leader's Pocket Guide for each of your Scuba Crew Leaders. (Crew Leader's Pocket Guides for elementary *and* preschool crew leaders are available from Group Publishing or your local Christian bookstore.) Or create an informative "Leader Lifeline" packet for each of your Scuba Crew Leaders to keep. Include the following:

• photocopies of the "For Scuba Crew Leaders Only" handouts (pp. 135-138),

• sample daily schedule (p. 86),

• list of station leader names (p. 103),

• age-level information sheets (on p. 30 of this manual and p. 19 of the Preschool Tide Pool Director Manual), and

• "Helping Children Follow Jesus" handout (p. 181 of this Director Manual).

Distribute the Pocket Guides (or packets) to your Scuba Crew Leaders as they enter the room.

Set a sheet of colorful poster board and a pair of scissors under each chair.

Place name tags and markers near your entryway. Tape each Bible Point poster to a sheet of white poster board or foam core. (This makes posters stiff so that they're easier to hold up for your staff to see.) Place a roll of tape and the posters where you can reach them easily.

Play the *Sing & Play Splash Music* audiocassette or CD as volunteers arrive. (This sets the mood and gives everyone a chance to preview the awesome music they'll be hearing all week.) Greet each Scuba Crew Leader or Scuba Station Leader with a warm smile. Encourage each volunteer to write his or her name on a name tag before sitting down. Be sure to thank everyone for coming to this meeting and for helping with **SCUBA**.

Let's get started!

When everyone has arrived, gradually turn down the volume on the cassette or CD player, and then stop the music. Blow your conch shell, or use another attention-getting signal. Say: **Let's get ready to dive into our Super Cool Undersea Bible Adventure! My name is** [name]**, and I'll be your SCUBA Director. It's great to have each one of you on our SCUBA staff.**

Just as real scuba divers have to go through training and practice, my goal is to give you a taste of what's going to happen at our Super Cool Undersea Bible Adventure. You'll leave here prepared to be the best staff ever. First, we'll spend some time focusing on the kids who will attend our SCUBA. After all, those kids are the entire reason for the program! Then we'll use our *Dive Deep! Video* to guide us through some activities and discussion about your roles on the dive. I'll give you some helpful tips to make you the best crew leaders and station leaders around. Let's start our training time with a prayer.

Pray: **Dear God, thank you for allowing us to serve you with VBS. Thank you for each person here and the gifts and abilities he or she brings to our children. Be with us as we prepare our hearts and minds for an important week, where kids will dive deeper into relationship with you. Guide our time together. In Jesus' name, amen.**

Say: **Think of a fun, memorable experience you've had in water. Maybe you went to the ocean with your family or learned to swim in the lake near your grandmother's cabin. Now, turn to a friend and tell about your favorite water memory!**

Play "Deeper With God" while staff members share. (This song will allow enough time for sharing, while giving staff members a

LeaDeR LifeLine

The information contained in the Crew Leader's Pocket Guide and "For Scuba Crew Leaders Only" handouts will be incredibly helpful to your staff. Be sure to provide this information and stress the importance of reading them before SCUBA begins. Scuba Crew Leaders will likely find that many of their questions are answered here.

Leader LifeLine

If you're providing attention-getting signals for your station leaders, this would be a good time to distribute them. You can use conch shells, available from Group Publishing and your local Christian bookstore, or any other noisemakers of your choice.

sampling of the great music they'll be hearing at **SCUBA**!) When the song ends, turn off the CD player, and blow your conch shell.

Say: **This is my conch shell. I'll use it whenever I need to get your attention. At SCUBA we'll use attention-getting signals to let kids and crew leaders know when it's time to stop talking and pay attention. I'll also use the conch shell each day of our SCUBA to let you know when it's time to send kids to their next station. Station leaders, you may want to use your own conch shells during SCUBA. It's a lot easier and nicer than lots of "shushing." Each day is bubbling with activities, so you won't want to lose a minute. Now let's hear what you talked about.** Let a few people share what they talked about in their pairs.

Say: **Water is great because it refreshes us, cools us, and even cleans us! Turn to your friend again and discuss this question:**

• How can this Super Cool Undersea Bible Adventure be memorable for the kids who attend?

Play "I Wanna Go Deep" while partners share. When the song ends, turn off the CD, and blow your conch shell.

Say: **You'll find that we use pair shares and group discussions a lot at SCUBA. That gives everyone, even shy or quiet kids, a chance to talk. Now I'd like to hear some of the things you talked about concerning how SCUBA can be memorable for the kids who attend.**

Let a few people share what they discussed.

Say: **At this Super Cool Undersea Bible Adventure, we hope kids are refreshed as they understand that God loves them, that their hearts are cooled and calmed as they trust God, and that their hearts are cleansed by God's forgiveness. This "water" experience could be life-changing for the kids who come to SCUBA!**

Then say: **Each day at SCUBA, kids will discover one important truth about our relationship with God. We call this the Bible Point. Station leaders, you'll say the Point many times each day. That's because repetition is an important way for kids to learn. Crew leaders, you'll join your kids in shouting "OK!" each time you hear the Point. Your enthusiastic participation will speak volumes to kids. You'll also do the dive sign for "OK." It goes like this.** Demonstrate the sign for "OK," according to the margin illustration.

At SCUBA, kids dive deeper into a relationship with God. Find three

people and form a small group. When your group is together, quickly brainstorm some things that today's kids are already "deep into." What's important to them? What do they talk about when parents aren't listening? You'll have about one minute to think of as many things as you can. I'll blow the conch shell when it's time to stop.

CD **track 2** Play "Jump, Shout & Sing" while groups are working. After one minute, blow the conch shell to call time. Let each group share a few of its ideas aloud.

Say: **Kids are into so many things today—clothes, toys, video games, movies—that it's hard to keep up. But at SCUBA, we want them to be deep into God! One way to reach into the hearts and minds of kids is through relationship. That's why at SCUBA, kids will form small mixed-age groups called Scuba Crews. Scuba Crews are a great way for kids to build and nurture friendships as they learn. Right now we're going to make a sign for each Scuba Crew on our SCUBA. These signs will help kids find their crews each day.**

Lead the group in counting off, then give Scuba Crew Leaders five minutes to write their numbers as large as possible on the sheets of poster board under their chairs. Encourage them to cut the signs into large sea-creature-shapes, such as crabs, angelfish, sea horses, or seashells. Then let Scuba Crew Leaders decorate the signs with paint markers. (Paint markers actually work better than regular markers on neon poster board, since the color is so opaque.) Station leaders may want to work on decorating their door signs during this time.

After five minutes, blow the conch shell to regain everyone's attention. Say: **Each crew sign represents about five children who will dive into God's love at SCUBA. Gather with a few people nearby—people you haven't worked with yet—and form a circle. Put your signs in the middle of your circle, and pray for the kids who will be in those crews.**

Allow about two minutes for groups to gather and pray. Then say: **Amen. Have one of your group members bring your stack of signs up front while the rest of you return to your seats.**

When everyone has returned to his or her seat, say: **Now let's dive into *your* roles at SCUBA. Whatever your role here, you'll work with kids who are in crews. To help you be the coolest leaders in town, let's check out the *Dive Deep! Video* and get an overview of what you can expect during SCUBA.**

FiELD TeST FinDinGS

We discovered that it's crucial to get your staff prepared to work with mixed-age groups of kids. Crew leaders who approached the multi-age concept with a positive, can-do attitude had a wonderful experience. (Many were secretly surprised that it worked as well as it did!) They were better prepared to help kids work as a team or family.

LeaDeR LifeLine

You may want to get super creative and name each crew after a sea creature. Here are a few to get you started: Anemones, Angelfish, Dolphins, Flying Fish, Lobsters, Mollusks, Mussels, Octopuses, Sea Horses, Sea Squirts, Sea Turtles, Sea Urchins, Sharks, Shells, Sponges, Sea Stars, and Whales.

VIDEO Start the video, and show the promotional segment. When that segment ends, stop the tape, and answer any questions about the overall format.

Play the training portion of the video until you hear the announcer say, "And kids are always diving into new adventures, which means there's not time to get bored...or get into trouble!" Stop the video, and say: **This VBS *will* keep the kids—and you—on the go!** Tape up the Bible Point poster of Ace. **Ace is a flying fish kids meet on Day 1. He helps them remember to believe in God. Today he'll remind us that as you "fly" through VBS, don't forget to take the time and get to know the kids. We'll provide some great "crew time" opportunities, like this game I want you to play next.**

Hey, here's where we get to play a game!

Have participants form groups of five or six, then give each group an Ace Bible Memory Buddy. Ask groups to sit in tight circles so that group members can see one another.

Explain that individuals will take turns holding Ace, then saying their name, two true things about themselves, and one thing that they *wish* were true. For example, someone might say, "My name is Melody. I love to eat broccoli. I have three dogs. My husband is a firefighter." (Remind players that their "wish" doesn't have to be the last item mentioned!)

CD track 3 Play "We Believe in God" from the *Sing & Play Splash Music* CD as some conversation-boosting background music during this game.

As each person shares, the group members will decide which item is true and which is a wish. Then have the "sharer" hand Ace to the next person who will share.

After about five minutes, blow your conch shell to call time. Ask:

• **How did you know which things were true and which things weren't true?** (I had to guess; the untrue things seemed too weird; I didn't know.)

• **Why do people sometimes believe in things that aren't true or real?** (Because people have lied to them so they think those things are real; because they don't know the truth.)

Read aloud Jeremiah 10:10a: **"But you are the only true God."**

• **How do you know that God is real?** (The Bible says so; I trust God; God answered my prayers, and I saw that he is real.)

LEADER LifeLine

If your entire staff made it to the meeting, pat yourself on the back. Now you have extra hands to create the preschool signs. Preschoolers join crews that have colorful sea creature names rather than numbers— Blue Dolphins, Red Seashells, Green Sea Turtles, or Yellow Sea Stars, for example. Find the Bible Memory Buddies clip art on page 145 of this Director Manual or from the *SCUBA Clip Art, Song Lyrics, and Decorating CD*. Create large copies of the Bible Memory Buddies on colored paper. Have volunteers glue each sea creature to a sheet of poster board to create a preschool crew sign.

GReen Sea TuRtLes

• **Why is God the only one we can believe in?** (Because the Bible says so; because there can be only one God—the others are fake.)

Say: **Games like this give you insight not only to a child's life, but also to his or her spiritual understanding. That's why debriefing times are so important! Make eye contact with kids; circle up so you can see and hear each child. Take the time to make the most of these important, life application moments.**

ViDeo

Collect the Ace Bible Memory Buddies, then continue the video. Stop the tape when you hear Squirt say, "So swim a little closer if you're a preschool crew leader!" Post your picture of Squirt, then say: **Squirt is our Bible Memory Buddy who reminds kids to obey God. Whales work together and send messages to each other underwater. Those messages help other whales find food, family, and safe waters. At SCUBA, we need to help one another, too! We're all a team—crew leaders helping station leaders and vice versa. Even though crew leaders won't prepare anything, they have the great responsibility of making sure kids get the most out of every station. Let's practice working together to make a snack.**

Demonstrate how to make the Bunch-o'-Believers snack, using the following instructions. Then form groups of five, and let each group make snacks for about ten minutes. Play the *Sing & Play Splash Music* CD while participants work.

Yum, it's time to eat a snack!

1. Place a grape "head" on one end of a toothpick. Hand it to another staff member.

2. When you receive the grape and toothpick, place a cheese cube "body" underneath the head.

3. Set three "people" on one plate. You'll need one plate per **SCUBA** staff member.

After ten minutes, blow your conch shell. Have each participant take a snack and return to his or her seat. Ask:

• **What was fun about working together?** (We made a good snack; it was fun to get to know new people.)

FieLD TeSt FiNDiNGS

Some crew leaders complained that they didn't have time to sit down with their crew members and get to know them. Yet during Dive-In Diner, these same crew leaders sat in the shade while their kids played Tag! We encouraged crew leaders to use the Dive-In Diner time as "crew time." You may want to write a question on the daily schedule for them to discuss or announce a few suggestions during morning devotions or your "huddle and prayer." (We've even provided some ideas on page 94!) In our field test, the crews that had crew time during Dive-In Diner formed closer bonds among their members than those who didn't.

• **What was challenging about working together?** (Not eating all the snacks; making sure there were enough; keeping up—they were really fast!)

• **As staff members, how can you help one another during SCUBA?** (Helping to make sure the kids are paying attention; keeping our eyes open to see if the leaders need anything.)

Say: **We want kids to get a lot out of this time at SCUBA, so it's important that we support one another. Crew leaders, tune into the station leaders to see how you can help them. Station leaders, watch your crew leaders to see if you need to slow down or explain something more clearly. Now let's see what other tips we can gather from our video!**

ViDeo Play the *Dive Deep! Video* until you hear the announcer say, "Your church will partner with Shoes for Orphan Souls to provide new shoes and socks to orphans around the world." Stop the video, and put up the Tank poster.

Say: **Tank the sea turtle helps kids discover that they can trust God. Sea turtles like Tank trust their sturdy shells to keep them safe. But kids won't hide in their shells during** *this* **VBS! The kids at SCUBA will reach around the world to help orphans discover God's love! That's because we'll take part in Operation Kid-to-Kid, an international giving project.**

Tell me more about Operation Kid-to-Kid!

On Day 2, kids—both elementary *and* **preschoolers—will hear how they can bring in a brand-new pair of shoes or socks for needy orphans around the world.** (You might have children just bring socks, or allow kids to choose which items they'll bring. Be sure to change your explanation to match *your* Kid-to-Kid focus.) **Kids will take home a letter, explaining the project to parents. Be aware that some kids in your crew may not be able to bring in any items. Crew leaders, you may want to bring in a new pair of shoes so every child in your crew can contribute to Operation Kid-to-Kid. This is a tangible, practical way for kids to make a difference in the lives of other children across the globe.**

ViDeo Play the *Dive Deep! Video* until you hear the announcer say, "Take the time to circle up and tune in!" Then stop the video, and put up the poster of Pearl the oyster. Say: **Pearl the oyster reminds kids**

to love God. That's because oysters like Pearl make priceless treasures that remind us of God's treasure—Jesus! Pearl can also remind *you* to circle up...sort of like a tight little clam shell! Let's see why crew circles are so important.

Form two large groups, and have members of each group form new crews. Ask the crews in Group A to stay in their rows, while the crews in Group B form knee-to-knee circles. Ask members of both groups to discuss the following questions:

• **What are you most looking forward to this week?**

• **What are you most apprehensive about this week?**

After a few minutes, let each crew member from Group A partner with a crew member from Group B. Ask partners to talk about what they learned from their discussion "lines" and "circles." After pairs have had a minute or two to share, ask for responses from the large group.

Say: **Pearl is a good reminder to circle up. Just as she makes a treasure inside her shell, God can allow beautiful, priceless conversation and discovery to take place within those crew circles! Discussion circles are important because they help kids focus *in* on what's being said, while they allow crew leaders to make excellent eye contact. Station leaders, remember to wait until all crews are circled up before starting your discussion time.**

Crew leaders, some station leaders may ask you to actually ask the questions. In some stations, such as Undersea Crafts and Missions or Dive-In Diner, you'll receive slips of paper with questions on them. As kids are working on making snacks or crafts, it's important that you refer to the questions and make sure each child has the chance to answer them.

VIDEO
Let your staff return to their seats. Continue the *Dive Deep! Video* until it ends. Stop the video, and tape up the poster of Starla. Say: **This is Starla—a cute little sea star! Starla reminds kids to reach out and share God's love. By taking the time to staff our SCUBA, you're shining God's love to the children who will come to our VBS! Let's take a minute and think of some practical ways we can show God's love during SCUBA. And let's stretch our arms while we do!**

Have participants form a line, stretching their arms out between each other. Each person should have his or her arms outstretched, but should not be touching another person. (You may need your line to wind around the room, like an eel!) Hold up a Starla Bible Memory Buddy. Say: **I'll pass Starla down the line. When she**

FIELD TEST FINDINGS

Although most parents took their children to purchase shoes or socks for Operation Kid-to-Kid, there were a few families who couldn't afford any donation. Our wonderful crew leaders took it upon themselves to provide a donation for each crew member! They all hit the discount stores together on Thursday evening, then "smuggled" a pair of shoes or socks to those children who hadn't contributed to Operation Kid-to-Kid. It meant so much for each child to feel as if he or she had made a difference in the life of an orphan!

LEADER LIFELINE

It's a good idea to give Scuba Crew Leaders some idea as to what they can expect **SCUBA** to be like. After all, this isn't the VBS that many of us grew up with! Let crew leaders know that a little extra noise and movement is OK—that's how kids learn and explore awesome Bible truths. Remind them that even though kids aren't sitting in quiet rows with their hands folded, kids will be taking God's Word to heart.

FIELD TEST FINDINGS

The director at one field test made a great statement. She told her staff, "You need to treat these kids as more precious than gold." Isn't that the truth? What a great concept to pass along to people who will be ministering at your VBS!

Oooh, this will be fun!

comes to you, you might have to reach out to get her! Hold Starla and tell one way you can share God's love with kids at SCUBA. Then reach out and pass her down the line.

cd track 11 Quietly play "Come to the Water" while participants share their ideas. When Starla reaches the end of the line, have participants remain standing, but have them join hands and form a circle.

Say: **The song I just played has lyrics that say, "Come to the water...refresh your soul." It's my prayer that kids come to the waters of our SCUBA VBS and leave refreshed with God's love. Remember that God can use you to reach the heart of a child and show that child the face of God. Let's close our time in prayer.**

Pray: **Dear God, we thank you for VBS and for all the children you will bring to our church. We pray for wisdom as we get to know these precious treasures you've entrusted to us. Help us to guide each child into a deeper relationship with you. We pray that your love will touch children's hearts and lives, changing them forever. In Jesus' name, amen.**

While your **SCUBA** crew is assembled, it's a good idea to take care of lots of "housekeeping" items. You might want to use the clip art on page 145 (or on the *SCUBA Clip Art, Song Lyrics, and Decorating* CD) to create a "**SCUBA** Basics" handout. Be sure to include the following:

• Tell your staff what time to arrive on the first day and where to meet. If you're planning to have staff devotions, let your staff know so that they can arrive early. Be sure they know meeting times and places each day after that as well.

• Distribute a map that shows where each station will be located.

• Give a complete list of names and phone numbers of crew leaders, station leaders, registration staff, and the VBS director(s).

• Inform station leaders and crew leaders of procedures you'll follow if there's a fire or another emergency.

WHAT'S A SCUBA CREW LEADER?

If you've been asked to be a Scuba Crew Leader, you've met two important qualifications: You love the Lord, and you love kids.

During **SCUBA**, you'll visit different Scuba Stations with a group of three to five kids. **You're not in charge of preparing or teaching activities; you just get to be there and help kids enjoy them as you shepherd the members of your Scuba Crew.**

The following guidelines will help you be an awesome Scuba Crew Leader.

A Scuba Crew Leader is

• a friend and a helper.

• someone who knows and calls kids by name.

• someone who offers kids choices.

• someone who asks questions.

• someone who encourages kids.

A Scuba Crew Leader isn't

• the boss or the teacher.

• someone who makes all the decisions.

• someone who gives all the answers.

• someone who yells at kids or puts them down.

When talking with kids,

say,

• Let's keep moving so we can do as many fun activities as possible.

• Listen carefully so you'll know what to do next.

• Stay with the Scuba Crew; we need your help in this activity!

• That's a unique way of doing things! How did you think of that? Let's try it this way.

• It's important that we all follow the instructions and work together as a team.

• Please move over here so you can see better.

• Let's all sit in a circle so we can see and hear one another better.

don't say,

• Stop talking and get back to work.

• Be quiet and listen!

• Don't run around the room.

• You're doing it wrong!

• Don't do that!

• Stay out of that area!

Most of the time, things will go smoothly for your crew, but every once in a while, you may run into a dilemma. Here's some advice on how to handle different challenges.

If My Crew Won't Stay Together

Encourage your Scuba Guide to come up with creative ways to travel. Or work with your Coach to come up with cheers to say as you travel.

If Older Kids Are Unhappy Being Grouped With Mixed Ages

Highlight their helping role. Encourage them to help younger kids with crafts and other activities. Acknowledge them by telling younger kids, "[Name of older child] is really good at that. Why don't you ask him [or her] to help?"

If I Have a Clique in My Crew

Cliques can make the Scuba Crew experience unhappy for the outsiders. Encourage friendships between all crew members by pairing kids with partners they don't know very well during games and crafts.

If a Crew Member Won't Participate

Help shy children feel welcome by calling them by name and asking them questions directly. Respond to their questions with a smile and a statement such as "That's really interesting!" Also try giving children special jobs. For example, assign them the task of finding a place for your crew to sit at each station.

If someone doesn't want to participate in Splish Splash Games, that's OK. **SCUBA** can be tiring! Let children rest until they're ready to participate.

If People in My Crew Don't Get Along

Quietly take the children aside. Tell them you've noticed that they're not getting along. Let them know that although they don't have to be best friends, they do have to be together all week, so things will be a lot more fun if they can at least be kind to one another. (Use the daily Bible Points for these teachable moments!)

If I Have an Overly Active Child

Pair this child with yourself during partner activities, and suggest that he or she sit with you during quiet times. Try to make sitting still a game by saying, "Let's see how long you can sit still without interrupting. I'm timing you. Ready? Go!"

If the child is really uncontrollable, ask your director if you could have an Assistant Scuba Crew Leader to help.

WHO'S WHO IN THE SCUBA CREW?

During their first Sing & Play Splash session, kids will choose Scuba Crew jobs. Each child will have one of the jobs listed in the chart below.

- If your crew has fewer than five kids, some kids may have more than one job.

- If your crew has more than five kids, let kids share jobs.

- If children can't agree on who should perform each job, tell them that everyone will get a chance to do all the jobs. Assign kids jobs for Day 1; then rotate jobs each day so that by the end of the week, all children in the crew have had an opportunity to do each job.

Kids are excited about having special jobs. Encourage them to fulfill their roles, and provide lots of opportunities for them to do so.

READER		• likes to read • reads Bible passages aloud
SCUBA GUIDE		• chooses action ideas for traveling between stations (swimming, bobbing, shuffling, skipping, hopping, galloping, marching, and so on) • serves as line leader to guide crew through daily schedule
MATERIALS MANAGER		• likes to distribute and collect supplies • carries Scuba Crew bag • distributes and collects Bible Point Craft materials • distributes **SCUBA** Bible Books
COACH		• likes to smile and make people happy • makes sure people use kind words and actions • leads group in cheering for others during Splish Splash Games
PRAYER PERSON		• likes to pray and isn't afraid to pray aloud • makes sure the crew takes time to pray each day • leads or opens prayer times

WHAT DO SCUBA CREW LEADERS DO AT EACH STATION?

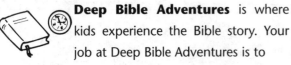

Sing & Play Splash is where kids worship by singing upbeat action songs. Your job at Sing & Play Splash is to

- arrive a few minutes early;
- greet your crew members in your designated seating area;
- follow the motions and sing out loud; and
- remember that if you get involved, the kids will too!

Deep Bible Adventures is where kids experience the Bible story. Your job at Deep Bible Adventures is to

- line up with your crew outside the door at the "Diving Dock,"
- listen carefully to hear how crew leaders should help out that day,
- keep your crew together until you receive other directions, and
- encourage crew members to participate.

Undersea Crafts and Missions is where kids make Bible Point Crafts and learn about Operation Kid-to-Kid™. Your job at Undersea Crafts and Missions is to

- listen carefully to the instructions because you will most likely need to repeat them for some members of your crew,
- help kids make their crafts (*when* they need help),
- ask the daily questions you've been given as kids work, and
- help clean up your area before leaving.

Splish Splash Games is where kids play team-building games. Kids also receive special Bible Memory Buddies to place in their Dive Bags each day. Your job at Splish Splash Games is to

- listen carefully to the instructions so you can help your crew members follow them,

- perform any tasks the games leader assigns to you, and
- participate in each activity and cheer on your crew members as they participate.

Dive-In Diner is where crews come for a tasty snack. (One day of VBS, your crew will help make Dive-In Diner treats for the entire VBS!) Your job at Dive-In Diner is to

- gather your crew in a designated area,
- quiet kids and help them focus on the Dive-In Diner Leader as he or she explains the snack,
- talk with kids about their experiences at VBS that day, and
- help kids clean up your area before leaving.

Chadder's Undersea Bible Adventure is where children watch *Chadder's Undersea Bible Adventure* video. Each child reads and marks verses in Scripture passages contained in the **SCUBA** Bible Book. Your job at Chadder's Undersea Bible Adventure is to

- encourage kids to sit still and watch the video,
- lead your crew in participating in the activities before and after the video,
- lead kids in discussion when it's called for, and
- help kids find and mark Bible verses.

Sea Star Finale is an exciting review of the day's lesson. Your role at Sea Star Finale is to

- lead kids to your assigned seating area,
- participate in singing and other activities,
- remind your crew to participate without being rowdy or disruptive,
- make sure each child leaves with his or her craft, and
- collect kids' name badges as they leave and store them in your crew bag.

WHAT'S A SCUBA CREW LEADER FOR PRESCHOOLERS?

If you've been asked to be a Scuba Crew Leader for preschoolers, you've met two important qualifications: You love the Lord, and you love children.

During **SCUBA**, you'll visit different Scuba Stations with a group of three to five children. **You're not in charge of preparing or teaching activities; you just get to be there and help children enjoy them as you shepherd your Scuba Crew.**

The following guidelines will help you be the most awesome Scuba Crew Leader.

A Scuba Crew Leader for preschoolers is

• a friend and helper.
• someone who helps children complete activities.
• someone who gets down on the floor to interact with children.
• someone who encourages kids.

A Scuba Crew Leader for preschoolers isn't

• the boss or the teacher.
• someone who completes children's activities for them.
• someone who supervises children from a distance.
• someone who yells at kids or puts them down.

During **SCUBA**, you'll shepherd a group of up to five preschool children. Your role is to love, encourage, and enjoy the children in your crew. If you've never worked with preschoolers before, the following tips will help you.

• Learn the names of the children in your crew. Call children by name often.

• You'll have three-, four-, and five-year-olds in your Scuba Crew. You'll probably notice big differences in motor skills (such as cutting and coloring) between older and younger children. Help children work at their own pace, and encourage five-year-olds to help younger children when possible.

• Look into preschoolers' eyes when you speak to them. You may need to kneel or sit on the floor to do this.

• Empower children by offering them choices. Ask, "Would you like to make a craft or play with blocks?" Don't ask, "What do you want to do?" or children may decide they want to do activities that are unavailable or inappropriate.

AS A SCUBA CREW LEADER FOR PRESCHOOLERS, YOU'LL BE EXPECTED TO

• arrive at least ten minutes early each day. Report to the Preschool Tide Pool area (Day 1) or the Sing & Play Splash area (Days 2 through 5), and be ready to greet children who arrive early. Your welcoming presence will bring smiles to anxious faces! (Plus, the Preschool Tide Pool Director may have some special instructions for you.)

• greet each child by name and with a warm smile. Help children put on their name badges each day.

• keep track of your crew members' Tide Pool Bible Books. Put these in a Scuba Crew bag, and keep the bag in a convenient place in your classroom or church at the end of the day.

• sit with the children in your crew during group activities.

• accompany children to Scuba Discovery Stations and Splash and Dash Playtime activities. Read the instructions at each station, and help children complete the activities. Distribute supplies from the Bible Books as needed.

• repeat the daily Bible Point often. The more children hear or say the Bible Point, the more likely they are to remember it and apply it to their lives.

• always check to make sure all children are accounted for before leaving the Preschool Tide Pool room! Be sure children hold hands or a rope as you travel.

(Never grab, pinch, or pull children as you travel. If a child lags behind, remind him or her to stay with the crew. You may want to walk behind your crew so that you can keep all the children in view and avoid traveling too fast.)

• report any potential discipline problems to the Preschool Tide Pool Director. He or she will help you handle problems appropriately.

• sit with your crew during Sea Star Finale. Help children participate in each day's show.

• collect children's name badges after each day's Sea Star Finale.

• help children collect their Bible Activity Pages and Bible Point Crafts at the end of each day so that children can take them home.

• release children only to a designated parent or caregiver. If an unfamiliar adult comes to pick up a child, refer the adult to the Preschool Tide Pool Director.

• assist the Preschool Tide Pool Director with cleanup and preparation for your next meeting.

Thanks for joining the SCUBA!

PUBLICITY

THIS STUFF WiLL *REALLY* GET YOUR COMMUNITY GLOWING ABOUT SCUBA!

PROMOTING Scuba in YOUR CHURCH and Community

You've planned, prepared, recruited, and trained. You've assembled an awesome team for your **S**uper **C**ool **U**ndersea **B**ible **A**dventure. Now it's time to promote your program. Use the publicity items described below to give parents and kids in your church and community a sneak peek at the oceans of fun that awaits them at **SCUBA**!

In this section of your **SCUBA** Director Manual, you'll find the following resources:

• **SCUBA clip art**—Use the photocopiable clip art on page 145 to create your own custom promotional materials. You can make your own letterhead, memos, transparencies, and more.

• **SCUBA bulletin inserts**—Distribute information to everyone who attends your church. Just tear out the bulletin inserts on page 146, type in your church's information, photocopy the inserts, and slip the copies into your church bulletins. To help you conserve paper, we've included two bulletin inserts on a single page.

• **Invitation to parents**—Fill in your church's information, then photocopy and mail the parent letter on page 147. If you want to personalize the letter, make any desired changes, and then transfer the letter to your church's letterhead. You can mail the letter to parents in your church or your community.

• **News release**—Adapt the news release on page 148 to fit your church's program. Then submit typed, double-spaced copies to local newspapers, radio stations, and TV stations. A local newspaper may do a story on

your church, especially if you do a bang-up job of decorating! Your extra efforts can generate excitement beyond your church walls.

- **Community flier**—Photocopy the flier on page 149, and post copies in local libraries, restaurants, grocery stores, self-service laundries, parks, recreation centers, banks, shopping malls, and schools. Be sure to get permission before posting the fliers. You may also want to check with church members who own businesses in your community. They may be willing to post fliers at their businesses, and they may even suggest additional business owners you can contact.

- **Publicity Skit**—Ask for volunteers to perform this publicity skit (p. 150) for your church congregation. The skit will give the congregation a preview of the fun and excitement they can be a part of at **SCUBA**.

The following items are also available to help you publicize your VBS. Refer to your **SCUBA** catalog for illustrations and prices.

- *Dive Deep! Recruitment, Overview, and Pass-Along Training Video*—You may have already previewed this video when you examined your **SCUBA** Starter Kit. In addition to being a great leader training resource, the *Dive Deep! Video* provides you with a "teaser" to show your congregation. This two-minute video clip gives church members a sneak peek at Bible Point Crafts, scrumptious Dive-In Diner treats, and exciting Bible learning that will take place at **SCUBA**.

- **SCUBA T-shirts**—Invite **SCUBA** team members to wear their staff T-shirts to church events in the weeks preceding your program.

You may also want to purchase a few iron-on transfers ahead of time and encourage children to wear them on T-shirts at school or in their neighborhoods.

- *Sing & Play Splash Music* **audiocassette or CD**—Get kids excited about **SCUBA**! Play **SCUBA** songs in your Sunday school classes or your other children's ministry programs.

- **SCUBA invitation postcards**—Send personalized invitations to all the families in your church and your community. Just fill in the time, date, and location of your **SCUBA** program, and drop these postcards in the mail or hand them out at children's ministry events. These colorful postcards are available in packages of fifty.

- **SCUBA posters**—Hang these attractive posters on church or community bulletin boards to publicize your program. Be sure to include the name and phone number of someone to contact for more information.

If you're hanging a poster in your church, surround it with photographs from last year's program. When parents and kids remember the fun they had last year, they'll be eager to come back for even more Bible-learning fun at **SCUBA**.

• **Giant outdoor theme banner**—Announce **SCUBA** to your entire neighborhood by hanging this durable, weatherproof banner outside your church. If parents are looking for summer activities for their kids, they'll know right away that your church has a program to meet their needs.

• **SCUBA doorknob danglers**—Hand-deliver information about SCUBA to families in your community with these bright, lively doorknob danglers.

Choose the items you think will work best in your church and community. Then promote your **S**uper **C**ool **U**ndersea **B**ible **A**dventure until you're ready to dive in!

Dear Parents:

Make sure your kids will have oceans of fun this summer on a **S**uper **C**ool **U**ndersea **B**ible **A**dventure. You'll find plenty of action at this address:

_____

_____

Each day your children will be a part of fun Bible learning they can see, hear, touch, and even taste! Bible Point Crafts, team-building games, lively Bible songs, and tasty treats are just a few of the **SCUBA** activities that help kids dive into Bible adventures about Bible people who went deeper with their faith. As they learn about God's love, children will also enjoy hands-on Bible adventures and daily video visits from Chadder Chipmunk™. Your kids will even participate in a hands-on missions project called Operation Kid-to-Kid™ that involves nearly a million other children across North America!

SCUBA is great fun for children of all ages; even teenagers will enjoy signing on as Scuba Crew Leaders who help younger children. And parents, grandparents, and friends are invited to join us each day at _____ because that's when we'll be having Sea Star Finale—a daily celebration of God's love you won't want to miss.

So mark these dates on your calendar:_____. The dive starts at _____ and will end at _____. Call this number _____ to register your children for this awesome Bible-learning adventure!

Sincerely,

Your **SCUBA** Director

Permission to photocopy this handout from **SCUBA** Director Manual granted for local church use.
Copyright © Group Publishing, Inc., P.O. Box 481, Loveland, CO 80539. www.groupvbs.com

NeWS ReLease

*Adapt the information in this news release to fit your church's **SCUBA** program. Then submit typed, double-spaced copies to your local newspapers, radio stations, and TV stations. You may want to check with them for any other specific requirements regarding news releases.*

[Name of Church] Invites Children to Dive Into God's Love at **SCUBA**—a Super Cool Undersea Bible Adventure.

"This year our church is bubbling with excitement as we dive into a Super Cool Undersea Bible Adventure," says [your church pastor's name]. "On this adventure, kids won't find any boring reminders of tedious schoolwork. Our **SCUBA** program will provide fun, memorable Bible-learning activities for kids of all ages. Each day kids will sing catchy songs, play teamwork-building games, nibble tasty treats from Dive-In Diner, experience electrifying Bible adventures, and create Bible Point Crafts they'll take home and play with all summer long."

"**SCUBA** is an exciting way for kids to learn about Bible people who went deeper in their faith," says [your pastor's name]. "We'll be studying Elijah, Jonah, and stories about Jesus and his followers. Plus, kids will join nearly a million children in North America and take part in a hands-on mission project that will reach needy children around the world. We'll conclude each day with a festive Sea Star Finale that gets everyone involved in celebrating what they've learned. Family members and friends are encouraged to join us daily for this special time at [time of Sea Star Finale]. We hope **SCUBA** will help our community dive deeper into God's love."

SCUBA begins at [VBS starting date] and continues through [VBS ending date]. "Divers" will meet at [name of church and church address] each day from [VBS starting time] until [VBS ending time]. For information, call [church phone number].

LOOK WHO'S MAKING a SPLASH in YOUR neIGHBORHOOD!

Join us as we dive into a Super Cool Undersea Bible Adventure! You'll enjoy Bible Point Crafts and exciting games, experience thrilling Bible stories, sample tasty snacks, and hear unforgettable music. Plus, you'll meet lots of new friends!

_____
(church name)

_____
(Dive dates)

_____
The Dive Begins at:

_____
The Dive ends at:

For more information, call:

_____
(church phone number)

Publicity Skit

Setting: The home of Jack and Jill, a married couple

Props: Newspaper, chair, wet suit, diving mask, snorkel, flippers, and a crumpled **SCUBA** bulletin

Have a few volunteers perform this skit before a worship service, during your announcements, at a midweek program, or during children's church or Sunday school.

(Jill is sitting in a chair, reading the newspaper. She's holding the newspaper at eye-level, so she doesn't see Jack enter.)

Jill: *(Speaking loudly, as if to Jack)* Oh, it looks like macaroni and cheese is on sale this week. Buy one, get one free! And I think I've got a coupon.

(Jack enters quietly, decked out in his diving gear. He walks slowly toward Jill, walking backward, since he's wearing flippers. She continues reading her newspaper.)

Jill: And hamburger, too. We can grill burgers when the Stewarts come over on Friday. OK, Jack? Jack?

(Jill puts her paper down, sees Jack, and screams. She throws the newspaper high in the air, jumps up, and cowers behind the chair.)

Jill: Wh-wh-who are you! And what did you do with Jack? *(Yells.)* Jack! Jack! *(She picks up the newspaper and starts hitting Jack with it.)*

(Jack takes the snorkel from his mouth, so he can talk.)

Jack: Jill...it's me!

Jill: *(Stops hitting him and looks closer.)* Jack? What in the world are you doing in *that*? Trying to give me a heart attack? Now go get ready for VBS—we've got to leave in five minutes!

Jack: I *am* ready for VBS. Remember, we're doing **SCUBA**—a *Super Cool...Undersea...Bible...Adventure.* That's **SCUBA**!

Jill: But it's not a *real* scuba dive! You can't go like that.

Jack: *(Clumsily pulls a crumpled bulletin from his sleeve, uncrumples it, and "reads.")* They said to be ready to *dive* into Bible adventures, experience oceans of fun games and crafts, and that this VBS would be *swimming* with unforgettable treasures from God's Word. So I'm ready to dive in!

Jill: *(Pauses.)* So you're wearing *that* to church?

Jack: I want to be ready for **SCUBA**!

Jill: *(Sighs.)* OK, but I think I'd better drive. *You're* wearing flippers.

(Jack and Jill exit, Jack moving awkwardly in his flippers.)

Jack: But can I have a tuna sandwich before we leave. For some reason, I'm in the mood for fish...

*Have your pastor or **SCUBA** Director come up to give the details of the times and dates of your **SCUBA** and how to register or sign up to volunteer.*

Registration

These pages are just swimming with ways to welcome your scuba crews!

Make an Unforgettable Impression

SCUBA is a fun place for kids to dive into God's love. Once kids sample the activities at each station, they'll want to explore with you all week long. But you can start generating excitement and enthusiasm for **SCUBA** before the adventure begins!

> Believe me!
> Follow these registration instructions exactly.
> I guarantee it works!

The excitement starts with preregistration. About a month before your scheduled **SCUBA**, begin preregistering children in your church. Preregistration is simple: Just make copies of the "**SCUBA** Registration Form" (p. 169), and have parents fill them out. Or slip **SCUBA** registration cards into your church bulletins. (These registration cards are available on the *SCUBA Clip Art, Song Lyrics, and Decorating* CD.) Save the completed registration forms; you'll use them to assign Scuba Crews (described on p. 156).

To pique kids' (and parents') interest in preregistration, try incorporating some of the following activities:

• **Show the *Dive Deep!* promotional video clip in your church worship service and Sunday school sessions.** This video clip gives everyone in your church a chance to preview **SCUBA** and see what an impact Group's VBS can have.

• **Have kids in your children's ministry programs design their own SCUBA posters.** Distribute large sheets of poster board, and encourage kids to draw posters about the strange (but not scary) creatures they might swim into undersea. Kids can even get creative and design their own imaginative sea creatures.

• **Have Sunday school classes work together to turn their rooms into a wonderful, watery world.** Provide rolls of blue bulletin board paper (available at most school- and teacher-supply stores). Let kids draw or stamp

Field Test Findings

"Registration is always so hard! How can I make it easier?" Our best tip to you: Follow these instructions *exactly* as they're written. We've heard from VBS directors from across North America who were skeptical. But when they followed these simple step-by-step instructions, it worked! Remember, we've made the mistakes during our field tests...so you don't have to!

brightly colored fish, crabs, sea horses, sea stars, and whales on the blue background. Kids can use glitter glue to make a sparkly, sandy ocean floor at the bottom of the paper. Cover walls with your sea mural for instant ocean! You'll be amazed at how creative kids will be!

• **Chart your preregistration in eye-catching ways.** Decorate a wall or bulletin board with some thematic décor. Each time someone preregisters, add another decoration. Here are some variations you can dive into:

• Create an ocean scene, and add a sea creature such as a crab, fish, or sea horse each time someone preregisters.

• Drape a fishing net on the bulletin board, then add a paper fish inside the net for each preregistered child.

• Cover a bulletin board with blue cellophane. When a child preregisters, inflate a small, clear balloon to make a bubble. Tape the bubbles to your ocean-y blue background!

• Make an enormous colorful fish without any scales on it. Each time a child preregisters, tape an aluminum foil scale to the fish's side.

When it's time for **SCUBA** to begin, you'll have a wonderful wall decoration to show that kids are swimming to your VBS.

The excitement continues as kids arrive at **SCUBA**. At registration remember that some families from your community are coming into contact with your church for the first time. You don't want their first impression to be of long, boring registration lines. To make an unforgettable impression, try the following ideas:

• **Prepare a large "Welcome, Divers!" sign, and post it behind your registration table.** Ask an artistic person in your church to write, "Welcome, Divers! The **S**uper **C**ool **U**ndersea **B**ible **A**dventure Begins Here" in large block letters on a large sheet of poster board or butcher paper. Decorate the sign with paints, markers, fish stickers, and bubbles for a garden-like appearance.

• **Set up the SCUBA Starter Kit can as a display on your registration table.** Set the can on top of a blue sheet covered with Bible Memory Buddies. You may want to fill the can with Goldfish crackers or gummy fish (or "jellyfish" beans) for kids to enjoy as they register.

• **Play the *Sing & Play Splash Music* audiocassette or CD.** The fun, upbeat music will provide a festive atmosphere.

• **Distribute sample Dive-In Diner treats.** You can use a snack from the Dive-In Diner Leader Manual, or you can come up with your own. Be sure to include drinks, especially if the weather's hot.

LeaDeR LifeLine

Clever VBS directors have told numerous success stories of letting middle-schoolers and high-schoolers work on decorations. One director had a group of fifth- and sixth-graders work on decorations during a lock-in the week before VBS began. Aside from setting a spectacular stage for VBS, it was a great way to involve older kids and help them be an important part of the program.

LeaDeR LifeLine

Many churches use preregistration time as a simple fundraising time. Ask adults to "sponsor" one or more children who will attend VBS. (Post the total number of children you're expecting at VBS so that people have an idea of the number of kids you need to sponsor.) The sponsorship fee can be monetary or a food donation for Dive-In Diner. Each time someone sponsors a child, tape a paper fish to the wall near your registration area. We've heard of churches funding their entire VBS program through these easy donations!

Field Test Findings

Tub Tints were a fun surprise—especially to adults who no longer have small children. Just a few of these colorful tablets turned water a deep blue, without the worry of stains!

eXtRa IDea!

If you want to start your dive with a big splash, consider planning an all-church Scuba Social. Decorate your fellowship hall, church lawn, or a nearby park, and set up one or more of the following "stations."

• Set out a wading pool filled with water, then use Tub Tints to make the water an ocean blue. (Tub Tints are found in the children's bath aisle at most discount stores.) Drop in small plastic sea creatures, shells, or sea stars. (Better yet, drop in the Bible Memory Buddies!) Cut a piece of dark paper to fit inside a diving mask to create a thematic blindfold. Let participants slip on a mask, then feel inside the water for a scuba surprise!

• Set a bucket of water at one end of a playing area, and an empty bucket with several cups at the other end. Have participants wear flippers and see how quickly they can transfer the water from one bucket to the other...cup by cup!

• Set out large, round sugar cookies, blue frosting, fish-shaped candies, and tubes of decorator's frosting. Let participants use the sweets to turn their cupcakes into fishbowls swimming with sea creatures.

• Paint clothespins red to create crab claws. Scatter paper fish across a lawn or playing area, and let participants snap up as many fish as they can!

• Blow up colorful balloons and tie a string to each one. Set out construction paper, tissue paper, markers, and tape. Let participants create bobbing balloon fish!

Be sure to have at least one person videotaping your party. You can use the edited footage for further promotion—this year or in years to come!

Get Ready foR oceans of fun!

Setting up Scuba Crews

One week before **SCUBA** begins, assign preregistered kids to Scuba Crews. Participating in Scuba Crews is an important part of kids' **SCUBA** experience, so use care and consideration when making Scuba Crew assignments. Follow the guidelines given in the planning section of this manual under "One Week Before **SCUBA**" (p. 63). If you don't know very many of the kids who will attend **SCUBA**, ask Sunday school teachers or other Christian education workers to help you assign kids to crews.

Step One: Inventory Your Registrations

• When you're ready to assign crews, make nine copies of the "Age-Level Roster" form (p. 166). Label the forms with grades K, 1, 2, 3, 4, and 5; do the same using "3-year-olds," "4-year-olds," and "5-year-olds" (for 5-year-olds who have not yet attended kindergarten). List the names of preregistered kids on the appropriate age-level rosters.

• Count how many kids have preregistered for your **SCUBA**, and divide them into two groups: elementary-age children and preschool-age children. Elementary-age children have completed kindergarten, fifth grade, or any grade in between. Be sure to check forms carefully; some families may have registered more than one child on one form. If children who have completed sixth grade want to participate in your program, that's OK; keep in mind, though, that most of the **SCUBA** activities are designed for slightly younger kids. **SCUBA** is designed to use young people in grades six and higher in leadership roles, so encourage mature sixth-graders to serve as Assistant Scuba Crew Leaders. For other ideas about how upper-elementary kids can participate in **SCUBA**, see page 33.

Step Two: Determine How Many Scuba Crews You'll Have

• Each Scuba Crew will have no more than five kids and one adult or teenage Scuba Crew Leader. (Preschool crews may have a high school leader.)

Leader LifeLine

Prayerfully consider the responsibility of setting up Scuba Crews. These small groups have a powerful impact on children, helping them form special relationships and memories.

Leader LifeLine

We've heard from directors who place all 5-year-olds in one group of Scuba Crews and have them rotate together through the elementary program. This may seem like a nifty way to include pre-kindergartners, but be aware that the elementary program is designed for children who have completed kindergarten. Plus, these little ones will miss out on the wonderful relationship-building opportunities of being in a mixed-age group in Preschool Tide Pool. Don't rob kids of this awesome experience!

FiELD TesT FiNDiNGS

When we used sixth-graders as assistant crew leaders, we learned that, depending on interests and maturity level, some were interested in doing the crafts, games, and snacks as participants rather than being crew leaders. Use your best judgment as each situation arises. Be flexible so you can provide the best possible experience for "tweenagers."

LeaDeR LifeLine

Ask volunteers to help create a complete Scuba Crew bag for each Scuba Crew. Place the following items inside each Crew Bag:

- permanent marker,
- 5 name badges,
- five 1-yard lengths of string, and
- 5 SCUBA Bible Books or Tide Pool Bible Books.

(You'll also need five Bible highlighters in each elementary bag.) You may want to staple a list of the crew members' names to the bags so that they can see who will be in their crews. On Day 1, simply give Scuba Crew Leaders their bags...and they'll be ready for the adventure to begin!

Divide the total number of preregistered elementary-age kids by five to discover how many elementary Scuba Crews you'll have. Do the same with preschool preregistrations. Use the line below to help you determine this.

If you want to encourage kids to bring their friends to **SCUBA**, you may want to place only three or four kids in each crew. This will allow you to add to your crews.

Once you've determined the number of preschool and elementary crews you'll need, check to see that you've recruited enough Scuba Crew Leaders. Remember that you'll need a Scuba Crew Leader for every crew, plus a few extra leaders on hand on Day 1.

Number of (elementary or preschool) kids _____/ at five kids per crew = Number of Scuba Crews_____.

STeP THRee: assiGN SCUBa CReWS

- Photocopy the "Scuba Crew Roster" form (p. 167). You'll need one form for every four Scuba Crews.

- Assign a Scuba Crew Leader to each Scuba Crew. It's helpful to indicate whether the leader is an adult (A), a teenager (T), or a junior higher (J).

- Set up preschool Scuba Crews.

Gather the age-level rosters for ages three, four, and five. Beginning with the three-year-old age-level roster, assign one child from each preschool age-level roster to each preschool Scuba Crew. Since each crew has five spaces, you'll have more than one representative of some age levels in each crew. Remember, it's helpful to have a mixture of preschool ages in each crew so that crew leaders can work with three-year-olds, while five-year-olds may be a bit more self-sufficient. Be sure to check off the names on the age-level rosters as you assign them to crews.

- Set up elementary Scuba Crews.

Gather the elementary age-level rosters. Beginning with the kindergarten age-level roster, assign one child from each age-level roster to each Scuba Crew. Since each crew has only five spaces, you won't be able to have every age level in every crew. Check off the names on the age-level rosters as you assign them to crews. Refer to the following examples for ways to spread age levels evenly among your Scuba Crews.

You aren't *required* to group children in combined-age Scuba Crews, but we strongly recommend it because it works so well. Children, young and old alike, help one another throughout their time together. Plus you'll minimize discipline problems because the diversity frees children from the need to compete with peers of the same age. For more information on the benefits of combining ages, see page 31.

If you have an equal number of children in each grade level,

• fill one-third of your crews with kids who have completed kindergarten and grades two through five.

• fill one-third of your crews with kids who have completed grades one through five.

• fill one-third of your crews with kids who have completed kindergarten through grade four.

If you have an abundance of younger children,

• group kindergartners, second-graders, third-graders, and fifth-graders together. Assign two kindergartners to each crew if necessary. Remind Scuba Crew Leaders to encourage the fifth-graders to help younger children. Fifth-graders might even be named Assistant Scuba Crew Leaders.

• group kids in grades one through four together. Assign two first-graders to each crew if necessary.

If you have an abundance of older children,

• group kindergartners, first-graders, second-graders, and fourth-graders together. Assign two fourth graders to each crew if necessary.

• group grades two through five together. Assign two fifth-graders to each crew if necessary.

If you have fewer than five kids per Scuba Crew,

• vary the age-level mix, if possible, so you'll have open spaces in your program at every age level. These spaces can be filled by kids who haven't preregistered.

Step Four: Complete the Master List

• Double-check to make sure you've assigned each participant to a Scuba Crew. Then write kids' Scuba Crew numbers on their registration forms next to their names.

Field Test Findings

Our Scuba Crew Leaders are always amazed at how well kids work together in a multi-age setting! Most kids truly enjoy being with children of other ages, and your discipline problems will practically disappear. However, if some children insist on being with same-age friends, put pairs of friends in the same Scuba Crew. This allows children to be with their buddies, while giving them wonderful opportunities to interact with kids of other ages and abilities.

Leader LifeLine

It's a good idea to keep gender in mind when assigning children to Scuba Crews. If at all possible, be sure to include more than one child of each gender. Even though SCUBA activities are designed to help kids work together, kids will feel at ease more quickly if there are a few members of their own gender in the group.

• Alphabetize the registration forms, and then transfer kids' names and crew numbers to the "Alphabetical Master List" (p. 168). Put a P in the crew-number space next to each preschooler's name.

• Give the preschool registration forms, age-level rosters, and Scuba Crew rosters to the Preschool Tide Pool Director.

Bring the "Age-Level Roster" lists, "Scuba Crew Roster" lists, and "Alphabetical Master List" with you to registration!

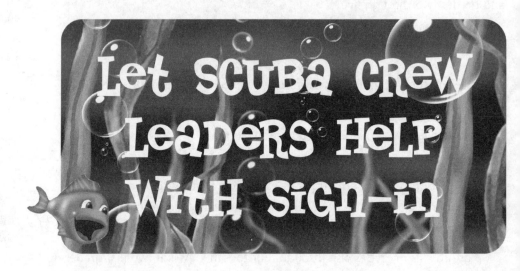

Let SCUBA CREW Leaders Help With Sign-in

Scuba Crew Leaders can help you breeze through registration. They meet and greet kids and help keep kids busy while others are standing in line. Read on to find out how Scuba Crew Leaders help make registration a snap.

FieLD TesT FinDinGS

We had Scuba Crew Leaders make their crew posters during the training session (see pp. 125-140). Not only did this save time on the first day of VBS, but it also got the crew leaders thinking (and praying) about their crews before VBS had even started.

SCUBA CREW LeaDeR ReGiStRation SuPPLies

Each Scuba Crew Leader will need the following supplies:
• permanent marker,
• colorful washable markers,
• 1 sheet of poster board,
• 1 Scuba Crew bag,
• copy of the "Scuba Crew Roster" for his or her crew, and
• masking tape.

Each child will need a **SCUBA** Bible Book and a name badge strung on one yard of string. Give these items to the Scuba Crew Leaders, and have them store the items in their Scuba Crew bags.

SCUBa CReW LeaDeR ReGiStRaTion PROCeDUReS

- Give each Scuba Crew Leader a **SCUBA** crew leader hat to wear. This helps station leaders and kids recognize crew leaders.

- When Scuba Crew Leaders arrive, they'll write their Scuba Crew numbers on sheets of poster board and then hang the crew-number posters *where they can be seen easily* in the Sing & Play Splash area. It helps if leaders hang the posters in numerical order.

- After children complete the registration process, they'll meet their Scuba Crew Leaders by their crew-number posters in Sing & Play Splash.

- Scuba Crew Leaders will greet kids and welcome them to **SCUBA**. Leaders will use permanent markers to write kids' names and crew numbers on their name badges. If additional kids have been assigned to Scuba Crews during registration, Scuba Crew Leaders will update their copies of the "Scuba Crew Roster."

- Scuba Crews will work on decorating their crew-number posters while they wait for others to arrive. This is a fun time for Scuba Crew Leaders and crew members to get acquainted.

ReGiStRaTion SUPPLieS

For registration, you'll need the following supplies:

- entry decorations such as paper fish, plastic ivy "seaweed," Bible Point posters, and stuffed toy fish;
- 3 tables;
- 4 signs:
  - ✔ "Preregistered—kindergarten through fifth grade,"
  - ✔ "Walk-in registration—kindergarten through fifth grade,"
  - ✔ two "Preschool registration" signs with arrows pointing to Preschool Tide Pool;

FIELD TEST FINDINGS

Our field test host church did an amazing job of preparing for registration. Registration helpers were visible everywhere, with clipboards containing all the information for preregistered kids. Parents could breeze in, find out where their children went, and get everyone "delivered" easily. This extra-mile preparation spoke volumes to the parents—many of whom expected chaos on that first day of VBS. (Needless to say, they were pleasantly surprised!) Remember, parents are hesitant to drop off their children if everything looks chaotic. More than ever, they'll expect a safe environment in which to place their children.

LEADER LIFELINE

You may want to give each Scuba Crew Leader a few extra name badges and one-yard lengths of string for walk-in registrants who may join their crews.

- 2 copies of each completed elementary "Scuba Crew Roster" (p. 167);
- 1 copy of each completed preschool "Scuba Crew Roster" (p. 167);
- 3 copies of each completed elementary "Age-Level Roster" (p. 166);
- 2 copies of each completed preschool "Age-Level Roster" (p. 166);
- 2 copies of the completed "Alphabetical Master List" (p. 168);
- plenty of pens and pencils;
- at least 5 volunteers, including the registrar;
- chairs for your volunteers; and
- blank copies of the "**SCUBA** Registration Form" (p. 169).

Registration Setup

Before registration, set up two tables in your church's foyer or entry area. If weather permits, you may want to set up your tables outside to allow more room. (It's a good idea to place these tables far apart to avoid a bottleneck.) Put the "Preregistered—kindergarten through fifth grade" sign above one table. Put the "Walk-in registration—kindergarten through fifth grade" sign above the other table. Set up chairs for your volunteers at each table. Be sure to place your signs high enough for everyone to clearly see them.

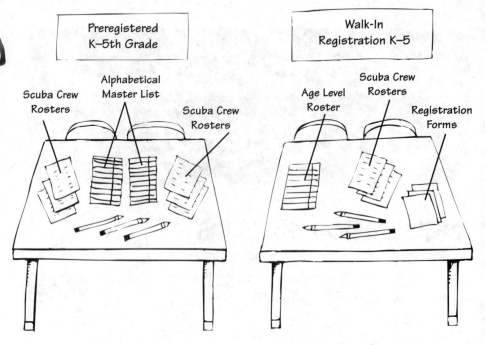

Preregistered K–5th Grade

Scuba Crew Rosters

Alphabetical Master List

Scuba Crew Rosters

Walk-In Registration K–5

Age Level Roster

Scuba Crew Rosters

Registration Forms

PReReGiSteReD TaBLe

On the table below the preregistered sign, place

- 1 copy of the completed "Alphabetical Master List" (p. 168),
- 1 copy of each completed "Scuba Crew Roster" (p. 167), and
- several pencils.

WaLK-In ReGiStRation TaBLe

On the table below the walk-in registration sign, place

- 1 copy of each completed elementary "Age-Level Roster" (p. 166),
- 1 copy of each completed "Scuba Crew Roster" (p. 167),
- blank copies of the "Registration Form" (p. 169), and
- several pens or pencils.

Take tHe eXPReSS Lane!

Consider an "Express Preregistered Check-In" system. Have a couple of volunteers stand at the entryway, holding copies of the "Alphabetical Master List." (If lines get long, your volunteers can start asking children who are standing in the middle of the Preregistered line.) Kids who are preregistered can tell the "express checkers" their names and have the checkers look at the list to see which Scuba Crews kids are in. Or if you're low on volunteers, enlarge your "Alphabetical Master List," and post several copies of it near your registration area. Kids (and parents) can check the list to find which Scuba Crews they're in and then simply find their crew numbers and Scuba Crew Leaders.

PReSCHooL ReGiStRation TaBLe

Set up a table (or several if you have more than twenty-five preschoolers) outside your Preschool Tide Pool area. Put the two "Preschool registration" signs (with arrows pointing to Preschool Tide Pool) near your main registration area.

On the preschool registration table(s), place

- 1 copy of each completed preschool "Age-Level Roster" (p. 166),
- 1 copy of each preschool "Scuba Crew Roster" (p. 167),
- blank copies of the "Registration Form" (p. 169), and
- several pencils.

ReGistRation: HeRe tHey Come!

LeaDeR LifeLine

It's important that you have a completed registration form for each child, not just one for each family! When families place all their children on one form, it can be difficult to find information that's specific to each child.

FieLD Test FinDiNGS

We discovered that it was parents (not so much the children) who had the biggest objection to mixed-age groups. Our director patiently explained the benefits of combined-age learning over and over and over. To save your time (and sanity), it's a good idea to have copies of the parent letters (pp. 170-171 of this manual) on hand to help explain why you've set up your program in this nontraditional, yet beneficial, way.

1. Arrange for your registration workers (including Scuba Crew Leaders) to arrive at least thirty minutes *before* registration is scheduled to begin.

2. Cut apart the individual "Scuba Crew Roster" lists from the third set of "Scuba Crew Roster" lists you copied. As Scuba Crew Leaders arrive, give each a copy of his or her crew roster.

3. Send elementary Scuba Crew Leaders to the Sing & Play Splash area and preschool Scuba Crew Leaders to Preschool Tide Pool. Explain that as kids arrive, they'll find their Scuba Crew numbers at the registration tables and then join their crew leaders and other Scuba Crew members in Sing & Play Splash or Preschool Tide Pool.

4. Assign two workers to the preregistration table, two workers to the walk-in table, and at least one worker to the preschool table.

5. Go over the registration instructions for each area (preregistered, walk-in registration, and preschool). Answer any questions workers have, and offer the following helpful hints:

- Kindly insist that each participant fill out a complete registration form, including all pertinent health and emergency information. *This is very important!*

- If families have both preschool and elementary children, encourage them to go to the preschool area first. This will keep preschoolers from getting fidgety as they wait for their parents to register their older siblings.

- Walk-in registration will naturally take more time. As families are filling out their registration forms, scan the Scuba Crew rosters for openings. This will help you complete Scuba Crew assignments quickly.

After you've answered all the questions, have registration workers and Scuba Crew Leaders take their places. You're ready to welcome kids to **SCUBA!**

ImpoRtant!

It's important that you know at all times who is in each Scuba Crew. In an emergency or if a parent needs to pick up a child midprogram, you'll want an accurate "map" of where everyone is.

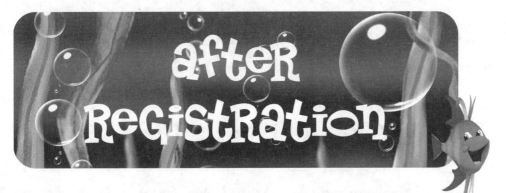

afteR RegistRation

After registration on Day 1, shout out a loud, "OK!" Your biggest job is done! Read on to find out how you can ensure that Days 2 through 5 are successful.

- **Leave your registration tables in place.** You'll want to continue welcoming children as they arrive on Days 2 through 5, as well as registering any newcomers. Tape the "Alphabetical Master List" to the table, and set out several pencils or pens. To chart attendance, let children (or parents) check each day's box as they come to **SCUBA**.

- **Check in with Scuba Station Leaders and Scuba Crew Leaders.** Even if you've taken care of the details ahead of time, unforeseen glitches can mar your adventure. After you've gone through one day's activities, meet with your staff to evaluate how things went. Station leaders may find that they need additional supplies or alternative room assignments. Inexperienced Scuba Crew Leaders may be having trouble handling unruly children in their Scuba Crews. If this is the case, you may need to reassign some children to different crews or rearrange your groups so that Scuba Crews with inexperienced leaders visit stations with crews that have experienced leaders.

- **Update your "Alphabetical Master List" and "Scuba Crew Rosters" as needed.** Be sure to check with the volunteers at the walk-in table. Kids who completed walk-in registration on Day 1 can be added to the "Alphabetical Master List" for speedier check-in through the rest of the week. If you've rearranged your Scuba Crews, make sure each Scuba Crew receives an updated "Scuba Crew Roster."

You did it! Now sit back and enjoy the adventure!

FieLD TesT FinDinGs

It really is important to touch base with Scuba Crew Leaders after the first day (or even after each day!). We made a few "tweaks" in Scuba Crews, such as pairing up a less-experienced crew leader with a veteran leader. By catching problems or miscommunications early on, everyone enjoyed a smoother program.

RegistRation

SCUBa Registration Instructions

Photocopy these instructions, and place copies in all registration areas. Have registration workers highlight their areas of responsibility.

PRESCHOOL: PREREGISTERED AND WALK-IN

Preschool registration will take place_____.

1. Greet family members or caregivers with a warm smile. Thank them for bringing their children to **SCUBA**.

2. Ask for each child's name and age (three, four, or five years old). Greet each child by name, and thank him or her for coming.

If a child has completed kindergarten or is older than six, send the family to the elementary preregistered line.

3. Have parents or caregivers complete registration forms for unregistered children.

4. Locate each registered child's name on the "Alphabetical Master List," and place a check mark on the Day 1 box to indicate that he or she is present.

5. If a child is a walk-in, scan the preschool "Scuba Crew Roster" lists to find an appropriate Scuba Crew to place him or her in. Add the child's name to the "Scuba Crew Roster" list as well as to the "Alphabetical Master List."

6. Point out the child's Scuba Crew Leader, and have a Preschool Tide Pool volunteer guide the child to the Scuba Crew Leader.

7. Tell the family members or caregivers that they can pick up their preschoolers in the Sea Star Finale area each day. Assure them that an adult or teenage Scuba Crew Leader will stay with children until the family members or caregivers arrive.

ELEMENTARY: PREREGISTERED

Elementary registration will take place_____.

1. Greet family members or caregivers with a warm smile. Thank them for bringing their children to **SCUBA**.

2. Ask for each child's name and the grade he or she last completed (kindergarten through fifth grade). Greet each child by name, and thank him or her for coming.

If a child has not yet attended kindergarten, send the family to Preschool Tide Pool for registration.

3. Locate each child's name on the "Alphabetical Master List," or if a child's name isn't on the list, send the family to the walk-in table to complete a new registration form.

4. Put a check mark by each child's name to indicate that he or she is present at **SCUBA**. Then tell the child his or her Scuba Crew number and crew leader's name.

5. Direct children to the Sing & Play Splash area, and explain that crew leaders are waiting there with name badges. Tell children to look for the large signs with their crew numbers on them.

6. Tell the family members or caregivers what time they can pick up their children each day. Encourage them to come early and participate in Sea Star Finale.

REGISTRATION

eLementaRy: WaLK-In RegistRation

Elementary registration will take place_____.

1. Greet family members or caregivers with a warm smile. Thank them for bringing their children to **SCUBA**.

2. Ask for each child's name and the grade he or she last completed (kindergarten through fifth grade). Greet each child by name, and thank him or her for coming.

If a child has not yet attended kindergarten, send the family to Preschool Tide Pool for registration.

3. Add each child's name to the appropriate "Age-Level Roster." Have the child's parent or caregiver complete a registration form.

4. While parents fill out registration forms, assign each child to a Scuba Crew. Refer to the "Scuba Crew Rosters" to see which crews have openings. Look for a Scuba Crew *without* a member in that child's grade. *If you have questions about assigning children to Scuba Crews, see your director!*

5. Write each child's Scuba Crew number on his or her completed registration form. (Later you'll need to add the new name and Scuba Crew assignment to the "Alphabetical Master List.")

6. Direct children to the Sing & Play Splash area, and explain that crew leaders are waiting there with name badges. Tell children to look for the large signs with their crew numbers on them.

7. Tell the family members or caregivers what time they can pick up their children each day. Encourage them to come early and participate in Sea Star Finale.

AGE-LEVEL ROSTER

GRADE: _____

REGISTRATION

SCUBA CREW ROSTER

SCUBA CREW NUMBER: _____

SCUBA CREW LEADER: _____

SCUBA CREW MEMBERS

1. _____
2. _____
3. _____
4. _____
5. _____

SCUBA CREW NUMBER: _____

SCUBA CREW LEADER: _____

SCUBA CREW MEMBERS

1. _____
2. _____
3. _____
4. _____
5. _____

SCUBA CREW NUMBER: _____

SCUBA CREW LEADER: _____

SCUBA CREW MEMBERS

1. _____
2. _____
3. _____
4. _____
5. _____

SCUBA CREW NUMBER: _____

SCUBA CREW LEADER: _____

SCUBA CREW MEMBERS

1. _____
2. _____
3. _____
4. _____
5. _____

Registration

ALPHABETICAL MASTER LIST

Name	SCUBA CREW NUMBER	Day 1	Day 2	Day 3	Day 4	Day 5
_____	_____	○	○	○	○	○
_____	_____	○	○	○	○	○
_____	_____	○	○	○	○	○
_____	_____	○	○	○	○	○
_____	_____	○	○	○	○	○
_____	_____	○	○	○	○	○
_____	_____	○	○	○	○	○
_____	_____	○	○	○	○	○
_____	_____	○	○	○	○	○
_____	_____	○	○	○	○	○
_____	_____	○	○	○	○	○
_____	_____	○	○	○	○	○
_____	_____	○	○	○	○	○
_____	_____	○	○	○	○	○
_____	_____	○	○	○	○	○
_____	_____	○	○	○	○	○
_____	_____	○	○	○	○	○
_____	_____	○	○	○	○	○

Registration

SCUBA REGISTRATION FORM

(one per child)

Name: _____

Street address: _____

City: _____ State: _____ ZIP: _____

Home telephone: (___) _____

Home e-mail address: _____ Age: _____

Date of birth: _____

Last school grade completed: _____

In case of emergency, contact: _____

Mother: _____

Father: _____

Other: _____

Allergies or other medical conditions: _____

Home church: _____

Scuba Crew number (for church use only): _____

Name of a special friend your child might like to be with: _____

Registration

Dear Parents:

We're so glad you've signed up your child for a busy week on our **S**uper **C**ool **U**ndersea **B**ible **A**dventure. This VBS program is a wonderful way to help your child dive into a deeper relationship with God.

You'll notice that things at **SCUBA** are…well, a little different than you might be used to. For one thing, elementary kids will be in mixed-age groups with other children who have finished kindergarten through grade 5. These small groups, called Scuba Crews, are led by adults or teens who love children and love the Lord. Scuba Crews are an important part of **SCUBA**! But you still might have some doubts…

My child won't come if he can't be with his friends. While it's true that your child might not get to be with his or her very best friend, your child *will* have wonderful opportunities to make new friends and interact with a new group of children. Most of us assume that age-graded classes are the best way to go, simply because that has been our only experience. However, studies indicate that children choose to play with children of other ages. Studies show that children learn as much—or more—when they're linked with kids of different ages. In fact, one study observed that children naturally chose to play with other children their age only 6 percent of the time. They played with children who were at least one year older or younger than they were 55 percent of the time. Encourage your child to try something different—he or she might be surprised! (And remember, it's only for a few days.)

My child won't like being with little kids. Parents are continually surprised that, after a few days of VBS, their older children *love* this newfound role! Suddenly, they're the "cool" big kids with younger children looking up to them. And while your child is helping younger kids with simple tasks like reading and writing, he or she is having the chance to serve and demonstrate Christ's love! It's a meaningful way to discover—and practice—the joy of service.

My child will get trampled by those bigger kids. SCUBA is carefully designed for groups of multi-age children. That means games are noncompetitive, team-building activities (brilliantly disguised as wildly fun games) in which your child's abilities will shine. In fact, many games are designed to *highlight* the importance of smaller kids. It's more likely that your younger child will be loved, affirmed, and doted upon by his or her older crew mates.

You'll have to water down the Bible lessons so everyone can learn. Since **SCUBA** doesn't rely on more traditional teaching methods (like fill-in-the-blank puzzles or word searches), kids *experience* Bible stories in powerful, life-changing ways. And that's something kids of *all* ages will enjoy…and remember. Then, crew leaders gather with kids for small-group discussion. These are questions that apply to every child but may touch each child at a different level. For example, on Day 3 as we learn about Jesus calming a storm, a crew leader might ask, "When is it hard to trust God?" A younger child might respond, "When I have a bad dream at night," while an older child with more experience with life's challenges may say, "When my friends want to do something I know is wrong." Each child is exploring his or her relationship to God in an age-appropriate way.

Millions of children have experienced this multi-age approach with Group's VBS, with surprise and delight at the outcome. Children's ministry experts agree that combining ages has numerous benefits: teaching children to work together, experiencing what it means to be a family, and serving others in love. However, the most important factor in making this program a success is your attitude. If your child has doubts, reassure him or her that this is a wonderful opportunity to try something new. Your support will speak volumes to the children we're serving.

We look forward to ministering to your child at **SCUBA**.

SCUBA Director

Dear Parents:

We're so glad you've signed your child up for a busy week at **SCUBA**. This VBS program is a wonderful way to help your little one dive deeper into a relationship with God.

You'll notice that things at **SCUBA** are…well, a little different than you might be used to. For one thing, preschoolers will be in mixed-age groups with other young children, ages 3- through 5-years-old. These small groups, called Scuba Crews, are led by adults or teens who love children and love the Lord. Scuba Crews are an important part of **SCUBA**! But you still might have some doubts…

My 5-year-old will be bored with all these little kids. Five-year-olds play an important role in their Scuba Crews. Pre-kindergarteners now become the "big kids" who can cut with more accuracy, glue more easily, and (gasp) even write their names! Younger children will *love* being with your child and will show their affection generously. All this admiration is wonderful for your child's self-esteem and allows him or her to serve younger children in hands-on, practical ways.

My 3-year-old will get hurt by those older kids. Actually, younger children will be loved, served, and doted on by their older crew mates. Plus, in a mixed-age small group, a crew leader has much more time to spend one-on-one with your child. And you can be sure that **SCUBA** activities are all specially designed just for mixed-age groups, so younger children won't be in over their heads.

My child won't come if she can't be with her friend. While it's true that your child may not be able to be with her very best friend, she will have the opportunity to make many new friends. Studies show that children learn as much—or more—when they're linked with kids of different ages. In fact, one study observed that children naturally chose to play with other children their age only 6 percent of the time. They played with children who were at least one year older or younger than they were 55 percent of the time. If your child really needs the security of a familiar face, we can most likely pair him or her with one special friend.

Millions of children have experienced this multi-age approach with Group's VBS, with surprise and delight at the outcome. Children's ministry experts agree that combining ages has numerous benefits: teaching children to work together, experiencing what it means to be a family, and serving others in love. However, the most important factor in making this program a success is your attitude. If your child has doubts, reassure him or her that this is a wonderful opportunity to try something new. Your support will speak volumes to the children we're serving.

We look forward to ministering to your child at **SCUBA**.

Preschool Tide Pool Director

Leader Lifelines

FOLLOW THESE trusty tips...OR YOU'LL BE ALL WET!

DAILY STAFF DEVOTIONS

Plan to meet with your Scuba Station Leaders and Scuba Crew Leaders for fifteen to twenty minutes before your program begins each day. Use this time to give announcements, address questions or concerns, and pray together. Ministering to children is rewarding but hard work, so you may also want to refresh your staff daily with an encouraging devotional. The following devotions tie into the **SCUBA** daily Bible Points and help your staff understand the importance of these Points in the lives of children.

LeaDeR LifeLine

Due to last-minute details, it can be tough to set aside time to meet *before* VBS. You may want to use these devotions after each day's program as a reflection and encouragement to your staff. (You may need to provide child care in order for some of your staff to attend.)

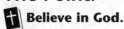 **The Point**

Day 1
HeaRinG VoiCes

The Point:
✝ **Believe in God.**

Supplies: a Bible and conch shell (or other attention-getting device)

Greet your staff, and welcome them to the first day of **SCUBA**! Say: **Our kids are beginning their Super Cool Undersea Bible Adventure by learning how awesome it is to ✝ believe in God. They'll discover our God is the only true God.**

Today, many things clamor for our kids' attention and belief. These things are distractions that make it hard for kids to believe in Jesus. Ask:

• **What are our children encouraged to believe in today?** (Music celebrities; sports figures; money; that all religions are OK.)

Then say: **For thirty seconds, I want everyone to choose one of the distractions you discussed and shout that distraction until I blow this shell. You'll repeat your word again and again. Ready? Go!** As participants shout out repeatedly, read today's Treasure Verse in a normal voice from a Bible: *"But you are the only true God"* (Jeremiah 10:10a).

After thirty seconds, use your conch shell to silence the shouting. Ask:

• **Could anyone hear what I was saying while the shouting was** going on? What was I trying to say? (I couldn't tell; I knew you were reading the Bible, but that was all.)

• **How was this experience similar to real life for our kids?** (Everything competes with God's Word; the truth of the Bible is muffled by other things.)

Say: **Kids experience this kind of confusion daily. God is always speaking the truth—that he is "the only true God." But there are other voices, too. These voices can easily drown out the truth that God is real.**

Tell your staff that today's Bible story is how Elijah had a "showdown" with the prophets of Baal. Say: **Elijah faced 450 prophets who didn't believe in God. It was one to 450! Elijah boldly proclaimed that God was the only true God...then he called on God to prove it to the people.** Ask:

• **How might our VBS kids feel like Elijah at times?** (They're outnumbered; they're afraid they're the only ones who believe in God.)

• **At SCUBA today, how can you be like Elijah?** (I can share God's truth with the kids; I can help them see that God is real; I can pray for the kids.)

Ask the staff members to spend thirty seconds in silent prayer, reflecting on the importance of bringing the truth to children—that God is real and we can believe in him. Then close by praying: **Dear Lord, we thank you that you are the only true God. Please help us to be bold in our faith today as we encourage children to believe in you. In Jesus' name, amen.**

 **The Point**

Day 2
BLOW against the FLOW!

The Point:
 **Obey God.**

Supplies: 2 or 3 balloons for each person, several permanent markers, an electric fan, a CD player, the *Sing & Play Splash Music* CD

Say: **Today kids will discover how important it is to**  **obey God, as they learn how Jonah *disobeyed* God. As Christians, many times we want to obey God, but it just seems too hard. Let's see what that's like.**

Form groups of two to four people. Give each group a handful of balloons and a permanent marker. Ask the staff to think of ways that kids need to obey

The Point

LeaDeR
LifeLine

If some staff members are uncomfortable on the floor, distribute paper plates and allow individuals to fan the balloons.

God. Some examples might include being kind to others who aren't kind to us, telling others about God, or praying. Then explain that group members will inflate their balloons, tie them off, and label each one with a way that kids can obey God.

Play "I Will Obey You" from the *Sing & Play Splash Music* CD while groups work. After three minutes, have participants take their balloons to the back of the room and set them on the floor. Say: **It's time to be a kid again! Get down on the floor and blow your balloons toward the front of the room.** After thirty seconds, turn the fan on high. Encourage your staff members to continue trying to move the balloons "against the flow." After thirty seconds, turn off the fan.

Gather in a circle, then ask:

• **How did it feel to "blow against the flow?"** (It was hard; frustrating; it was a challenge; I got tired.)

• **How was this like trying to obey God?** (God's ways are different than the world's ways; God asks us to do things that are challenging.)

• **How have people encouraged you to follow God?** (They've prayed for me; helped me see God's great plans; taught me more about who God is and how much he loves me.)

Say: **Obeying God can be hard. Some children don't know or understand God's ways. Others want to obey, but have friends or family members who make that difficult. Today, you can be someone who encourages kids to**  **obey God.**

† The Point

Have each staff member hold a balloon. Begin the following prayer: **Dear God, thank you for loving us and loving each child here at SCUBA. Help kids obey you as they...** Go around the circle and let each person read what is written on his or her balloon. When everyone has prayed, say: **In Jesus' name, amen.**

Day 3
Calmer Seas

The Point:

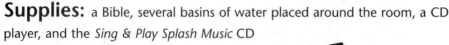 **Trust God.**

Supplies: a Bible, several basins of water placed around the room, a CD player, and the *Sing & Play Splash Music* CD

Say: **Today kids will explore what it means to** 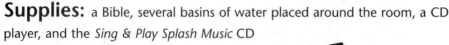 **trust God. It's easy to** **trust God when everything is going well and the sun is shining! But it's harder to trust God when something difficult or scary is happening.**

Have someone read today's Bible story from Matthew 8:23-27. Then ask:

• **What sort of relationship did the disciples have with Jesus?** (They were his followers; they loved him; he taught them; they were together all the time.)

Say: **Turn to a partner and share your response to the following question. You'll have thirty seconds each.** Ask:

• **How is that like or unlike your relationship with God?** (It's similar because I love God; it's different because I don't always see God the way they did.)

After one minute, say: **Although we love and follow God, we may struggle with trusting him. The disciples were afraid...and Jesus was right there in the boat!** Read aloud today's Treasure Verse, Proverbs 3:5: **"Trust in the Lord with all your heart. Do not depend on your own understanding."**

Say: **Confessing our fears and turning them over to God helps us come closer to God and** **trust God more completely.** Have the group spread out around the room and sit down. Say: **Think of your deepest fear; the thing that makes it hardest for you to trust God.** Explain that, while the music plays, individuals each may go to a basin of water and use their finger to write that fear in the water. **Watch the water move. As you form the letters, the water will stir and then calm. Use this time to give this fear to God, asking him to calm and quiet your heart. Then step away and let someone else have a turn.**

Quietly play the song "Come to the Water" from the *Sing & Play Splash Music* CD. (You may need to repeat the song if staff members still haven't had a turn going to the basin.)

 The Point

 The Point

Leader Lifeline

Be sure to have at least one basin for every four staff members.

When everyone has had an opportunity at the basins, ask small groups of four or five people to gather around each basin.

Say: **During our closing prayer time, let's focus our attention on the kids who come to SCUBA, and the fears they may be struggling with. If God brings a child to your mind, please feel free to pray aloud or silently.** Let the small groups have five minutes to pray together. (You may want to softly play "Come to the Water" again.) As the prayer time winds down, close by praying: **Dear Lord, you encouraged the disciples to be people of faith. You wanted them to trust you with even their worst fears. Please help us to teach the kids that you are trustworthy. In Jesus' name, amen.**

Day 4
a Perfect Heart

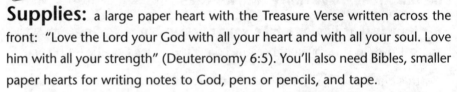

The Point:
 Love God.

Supplies: a large paper heart with the Treasure Verse written across the front: "Love the Lord your God with all your heart and with all your soul. Love him with all your strength" (Deuteronomy 6:5). You'll also need Bibles, smaller paper hearts for writing notes to God, pens or pencils, and tape.

Welcome your staff to another great day of **SCUBA!** Say: **Today is an important day at SCUBA. Kids will discover that God gave his most precious treasure—Jesus—for each of us. In return, God asks us to love him with all our heart, soul, and strength! We have a great opportunity to help kids grow in their love for God today!**

Today's Bible story shows just how much Jesus loves us. Form groups of three, and have one person be the Reader, who will read aloud Luke 23:32-43. Then have trios discuss the following questions:

• In what ways did Jesus demonstrate love during his crucifixion? (He underwent tremendous pain for us; he forgave the soldiers; he offered paradise to the other criminal.)

• How does our love for God differ from his love for us? (God was willing to give everything; God's love was completely selfless; God *is* love—we aren't; we can never love God as fully as he loves us.)

Hold up the large paper heart which has the Treasure Verse written across the front. Read the verse aloud: "Love the Lord your God with all your heart and with all your soul. Love him with all your strength" (Deuteronomy 6:5). Say: **Think about your own heart of love for God.** Ask:

• **How do you withhold love from God?** (I forget to pray and spend time with him; I disobey his commands, even though I know I shouldn't; I talk during worship time.) As people share, tear off parts of the heart. Ask:

• **What about the kids at SCUBA? What parts of their lives might they be keeping from Jesus?** (Their friendships; their language; their time.) Continue to tear from the heart as people share.

Hold up what is left of the paper heart. Say: **This paper heart looks torn and incomplete! Only a small part is left for God.**

Distribute small paper hearts to each person. Ask staff members to write "love notes" to Jesus. Encourage individuals to commit their entire hearts and lives to living for—and loving—God. Then play "Father, I Adore You," and ask staff members to come forward and tape their hearts to the wall, in the shape of a cross.

Close your time by leading the staff in a prayer. Pray: **Lord Jesus, we thank you for the love you've shown to each of us and to the children at SCUBA. Thank you for giving your most precious treasure— Jesus—for each of us. We love you, God. We want to give all of our love back to you! Please help us guide the kids into a deeper relationship of love *with* you. In Jesus' name, amen.**

Day 5
Food and Fellowship

The Point:

✝ **Share God's love.**

Supplies: simple snack foods (muffins, cookies, nuts, juice boxes), paper plates for serving, a Bible, conch shell (or other attention-getting device)

Greet your staff and thank them for sharing themselves throughout this week at **SCUBA**. Say: **Thanks to you, many kids have taken their relationship with God to a deeper level. Today they'll learn the importance of ✝ sharing God's love with others. I've brought some tasty, nourishing food to share with *you* today!**

Ask for a volunteer to open in prayer and bless the food you are about to share. Then welcome everyone to take some food and find a seat. As people are snacking, ask:

LeaDeR LifeLine

On Day 4 children will hear the message of Jesus' death and resurrection. Since this may be a natural time for children to ask questions about salvation, you may want to photocopy and distribute the "Helping Children Follow Jesus" section (p. 181) to each staff member. Or refer leaders to page 14 of the Crew Leader's Pocket Guide.

✝ **The Point**

• **How is this food like God's love?** (It's good; it's healthy and nourishing; it's life-giving; it was a gift.)

• **How would you have felt if I'd left the delicious food up front, but never offered it to you?** (Hungry; annoyed; distracted; disappointed.)

Say: **Jesus commanded us to share something even better than food. Listen!** Read aloud today's Treasure Verse, "Go into all the world. Preach the good news to everyone" (Mark 16:15). Form three groups and ask each group to discuss one of the following questions:

• **Why does God want us to share the good news with the world?** (So everyone can live with God in heaven; so many people will love and follow God.)

• **What about this passage challenges you?** (The idea of going into the world; preaching; knowing enough about the good news.)

• **What about this passage excites you?** (The thought of everyone in the world knowing God; sharing God's love with so many people; the fact that God's love truly is good news!)

Allow groups to discuss their questions for three minutes, then blow your conch shell to call time. Let a member from each group report their responses.

✝ **The Point**

Say: **Today the kids at SCUBA will be challenged to** ✝ **share God's love. Although kids might be hesitant, encourage them and remind them that God's love is like this food—wonderful, life-giving, and good!**

Dismiss your staff with a huge word of thanks! Say: **You've made this week's Super Cool Undersea Bible Adventure a wonderful success. Thanks for sharing your gifts and talents with God's kids!**

LeaDeR LifeLine

This is a good time to distribute any thank you gifts or notes you've brought for your staff. For an easy, yet meaningful gift, check out the "Thank You" Shell (found in your catalog). Fill these shell-shaped containers with candy, confetti, or other "treasures!"

Leader Lifelines

HELPING CHILDREN FOLLOW JESUS

At **SCUBA** children don't just hear about God's love; they see it, touch it, sing it, taste it, and put it into action. As they travel from station to station, they go deeper into their understanding of God. Most importantly, children learn that God sent his Son, Jesus, to die for our sins because he loves us.

You'll notice that there's no "set" time for children to make a faith commitment. We feel that **SCUBA** helps children build relationships—with other children, with adults, and with Jesus. And since each child is at a different point in his or her relationship with Jesus, programming a time for commitment may be confusing to some children. However, if it's part of your church tradition to include a time for children to make a faith decision, feel free to add it in during the Sea Star Finale on Day 4.

Some children may want to know more about making Jesus part of their lives. If you sense that a child might like to know more about what it means to follow Jesus, give this simple explanation:

God loves us so much that he sent his Son, Jesus, to die on the cross for us. Jesus died and rose again so we could be forgiven for all the wrong things we do. Jesus wants to be our forever friend. If we ask him to, he'll take away the wrong things we've done and fill our lives with his love. As our forever friend, Jesus will always be with us and will help us make the right choices. And if we believe in Jesus, someday we'll live with him forever in heaven.

You may want to lead the child in a simple prayer inviting Jesus to be his or her forever friend. You may also want to share one or more of the following Scripture passages with the child. Encourage the child to read the Scripture passages with you from his or her own Bible.

- John 3:16
- Romans 5:8-11
- Romans 6:23
- Ephesians 2:4-8

Be sure to share the news of the child's spiritual development with his or her parent(s).

Oceans of extra Ideas!

You have all the basic **SCUBA** materials in your Starter Kit. If you want to add sparkle and pizazz to your program, check out some of the following items.

Station Leader Resources

• **Conch shells**—You and your station leaders will keep kids' attention the easy way with this spectacular sound from the sea! Children will easily hear the deep, echoing noise in a crowded room or on a playing field. As director, you'll use the conch shell to let Scuba Crews know when it's time to "swim" to their next stations. Encourage station leaders to use the conch shells any time they need to get kids' attention.

• **SCUBA staff T-shirts**—Outfit your station leaders and other helpers in style. These shirts are cool, eye-catching additions to your décor. Kids and adults will love them, and they'll wear them even after **SCUBA** is over.

• *Sing & Play Splash Music* **audiocassette or** *Sing & Play Splash Music* **CD**—Reinforce Bible learning by providing each station leader with his or her own *Sing & Play Splash Music* audiocassette or CD. Kids can hum along as they work in Undersea Crafts and Missions, play Splish Splash Games, and enjoy Dive-In Diner treats. You can also offer this audiocassette or CD to families to reinforce Bible learning at home.

• *Sing & Play Splash Music Video*—Let our Sing & Play kids teach your kids the words and actions to all twelve Sing & Play Splash songs. Kids will love watching, singing, and moving with this video—and the words are right on the screen, so it's even easier for readers to follow along!

Leader LifeLine

There's a little trick to blowing the conch shell. First, press your lips together. Now, keep your lips together, but blow out. (If you've ever played any kind of horn, you'll know what we're talking about!) It'll make a funny sound, but trust us. Finally, place the conch shell on your lips and try it. Wow! What a cool sound!

Leader LifeLines

• **SCUBA Clip Art, Song Lyrics, and Decorating CD**—This CD is jam-packed with oceans of cool clip art, Sing & Play Splash song lyrics, and dazzling decorating outlines. Use the clip art to create your own bulletin inserts, posters, or even jazz up your church Web page! Run off the song lyrics on transparency film, or (even better) use them to create your own PowerPoint presentation! And you'll love how easy it is to project the decorating designs onto an old bedsheet or a sheet of paper! What a simple way to transform a room into an undersea scene!

LeaDeR LifeLine

We've heard from many churches that they purchase cassettes about a month ahead of time and then use the songs in other children's ministry programs. This gives kids a chance to become familiar with the songs and motions long before your dive begins. (Remember, the more you order, the cheaper they are.)

DiVing Into tHe Home

WHy aRe Family ResouRces so ImpoRtant?

Your **SCUBA** will reach a variety of children from countless backgrounds. Each of these children (and their families) can benefit from having **SCUBA** resources at home. Not only do the following family resources remind kids of **SCUBA** fun, but they also provide excellent Bible reinforcement for months after your program has ended. A *Sing & Play Splash Music* audiocassette may be the only Christian music heard in some children's homes.

WHat aRe Family ResouRces?

On page 186 of this Director Manual, you'll find an order form that lists family resources that reinforce Bible learning. From our field tests, we know that kids love items such as the *Sing & Play Splash Music* audiocassette and CD and *Chadder's Undersea Bible Adventure* videotape. In fact, although we provide more cassettes each year, we keep selling out of them and have to order more!

Kids love to have mementos of their time at **SCUBA**. Items such as **SCUBA** T-shirts, caps, and iron-on transfers are great reminders of your program.

HoW can FamiLies Get THese ResOuRces?

We realize you're busy; after all, you've just directed a VBS program! So we've made it simple to get these important items into the hands of the kids in your program. On page 186 you'll find an order form for family resources. Now you have three options:

Option 1: Individual Orders

Distribute the order form at the end of Sing & Play Splash on Day 5. Let kids know that they can order the Sing & Play Splash music, Chadder video, and other fun stuff simply by taking the order form to their local Christian bookstore. Then send the forms home, and let kids and their families act from there.

Option 2: One Church Order

Distribute the order form at the end of Sing & Play Splash on Day 5. Let kids know that they can order the Sing & Play Splash music, Chadder video, and other fun stuff by having a parent help them fill out the order form. Tell kids they'll then need to bring their money and order form (in an envelope) to you by a specified date. You'll probably want to put the date in your church bulletin the following Sunday.

After the due date, tally the total number of each item, and fill it in on a blank order form or a photocopy of the form on page 186 of this manual. Be sure to keep the original order forms so you can distribute items accurately. Take the master order form to your local Christian bookstore and purchase the items, or order directly from Group (1-800-447-1070 or www.grouppublishing.com). The next Sunday, set up a table to distribute **SCUBA** materials.

Option 3: A Scuba Store

Make it extra easy for families to take home VBS fun by setting up a "scuba" store. Use the order form to order items a few weeks before your **SCUBA** begins. (Check out the box on page 185 to help determine quantities.) Then set a price for each item. Decide how much money you'll earn on each item you sell. Remember, any money you make can go to your church's missions or children's ministry program, or to local community outreach programs.

Then set up shop! Place the items on a table just outside the Sea Star Finale area. Staff your store with a few willing volunteers (or youth group members), and "open your doors" after Sea Star Finale ends. You'll be amazed at the overwhelming response!

Recommended advance Order Quantities

Item	Quantity
Chadder's Undersea Bible Adventure video	10 percent of VBS enrollment
Sing & Play Splash Music audiocassette	75 percent of VBS enrollment
Sing & Play Splash Music CD	75 percent of VBS enrollment
Sing & Play Splash Music Video	10 percent of VBS enrollment
SCUBA souvenir photo frame	75 percent of VBS enrollment

It's that easy!

Field Test Findings

In all of our field test experience, we've found that families really wanted to purchase mementos of a spectacular, meaningful week. You'll be amazed at the overwhelming response when you make these items available.

Family Resources Order Form

Name _____

Address _____

_____

City _____ State _____ ZIP _____

Phone _____

Complete this order form and return it to your **VBS director.** Or inquire at your local Christian bookstore for these great **SCUBA** items!

HOW MANY	TITLE	ITEM NO.	PRICE	TOTAL COST
_____	Sing & Play Splash Music audiocassette	#646847-13004-5	$11.99	_____
_____	Sing & Play Splash Music CD	#646847-13002-1	$16.99	_____
_____	Sing & Play Splash Music Video	#646847-13003-8	$24.99	_____
_____	Sing & Play Splash Music DVD	#646847-10543-2	$24.99	_____
_____	Chadder's Undersea Bible Adventure video	#646847-13013-7	$19.99	_____
_____	Chadder's Undersea Bible Adventure DVD	#646847-10533-3	$24.99	_____
_____	Chadder puppet	#9056	$35.99	_____

Subtotal $ _____

Shipping & Handling $ _____

Sales tax (AZ 5%, CA 7.25%, CO 3%, FL 6%, GA 4%, IA 5%, IN 5%, MI 6%, MN 6.5%, NC 6%, OH 5%, PA 6%, TX 6.25%, VA 4.5%) $ _____

TOTAL $ _____

You can also mail this completed order form and payment to:
Group Publishing, Inc., P.O. Box 485, Loveland, CO 80539

PLEASE ADD SHIPPING AND HANDLING FROM THE CHART BELOW.

SHIPPING & HANDLING ORDER SUBTOTAL	SHIPPING & HANDLING
Up to $12	$3.50
$12.01-$20.00	$4.90
$20.01-$50.00	$5.90
$50.01-$75.00	$7.90
$75.01-$100.00	$11.90
$100.01-$150.00	$15.90
$150.01-$200.00	$19.90
$200.01+	$24.90

Leader Lifelines

HeaLtH anD safety concerns

Each station leader manual gives safety tips for specific station activities. As director, however, you're responsible for larger health and safety concerns that may affect the entire VBS. The information below may alert you to health and safety concerns that require your attention.

HeaLtH Issues

You'll want to maintain a first-aid kit in a central station. Stock your first-aid kit with adhesive bandages of different sizes, first-aid cream, antibacterial ointment, sterile gauze pads, and insect repellent. You may also want to provide a place for children to lie down if they feel ill. Keep children's registration forms near your first-aid area so that you can call parents or caregivers in case of serious injury.

Your **SCUBA** registration form provides a place for parents or caregivers to identify food allergies. Dairy allergies are common, but you may also have children who are allergic to gluten (wheat, rye, barley, or oats), nuts, or other foods.

Most of the snacks suggested in the Dive-In Diner Leader Manual will require only slight modifications for children with food allergies. Consult with the Dive-In Diner Leader about modifying snacks or substituting flavored rice cakes, popcorn, fruits, or raw vegetables to accommodate children with food allergies.

Insurance: MaKe Sure you're covereD

Your church probably already has an insurance policy or policies that are intended to protect you from loss as a result of fire, theft, injury, or lawsuits. Your program is probably covered by your regular insurance, but you should double-check with your insurance agent to be sure. You're not likely to have serious injuries, but you'll want to be prepared just in case.

LeaDeR LifeLine

Some churches require volunteers to go through a short class, seminar, or workshop on appropriate actions when working with children. This is an excellent idea, especially if less-experienced teenagers and adults will be helping out. Check with your church leaders to see if they know of (or have led) a class that would be helpful to you. Or check out www.childrensministry.com. There you'll find back issues of Children's Ministry Magazine containing articles on making your church a safe place.

LeaDeR LifeLine

The Crew Leader's Pocket Guide (one for elementary leaders and one for preschool leaders) is filled with practical, easy tips on child-safety. Be sure to equip your staff with these handy guidebooks!

FaCiLities: Keeping your SCUBa Site Safe

Many accidents can be prevented by well-maintained facilities. After you've selected station meeting areas, check each area for potential hazards. Remove broken or dangerous items, and be sure to lock storage areas that contain chemicals, cleaning solutions, or other toxic materials.

Your church is about to become a high-traffic area! Keep in mind that you'll probably need to clean bathrooms and empty trash daily. You'll also want to spot-check hallways, lobbies, and meeting rooms for trash, stray Scuba Crew bags, and lost-and-found items.

CHiLD aBUSe: Keeping KiDS Safe

Child abuse can take many forms. While you may feel sure that no one in your church would physically or sexually abuse a child in your program, emotional abuse or neglect can be harder to detect. Prevent child abuse by enlisting only staff members that you know and trust and by discussing your concerns and expectations with them ahead of time.

SCUBA field test directors reported few or no discipline problems. But you'll want to talk with your staff about how you'll handle any that do arise. Discuss appropriate and inappropriate staff responses to situations that require discipline. Photocopy and distribute the "What's a Scuba Crew Leader?" handout from page 135 of this manual. This handout suggests positive-language responses for easy classroom management. Remind staff members that you expect them to model Jesus' love in all they say and do.

SCUBA activities are designed so that children are always supervised by a Scuba Station Leader and several Scuba Crew Leaders. You may want to point this out to parents who are concerned about adequate supervision. To avoid even the appearance of impropriety, encourage each staff member to avoid spending time alone with a child. Suggest that staff members escort children in pairs or small groups for bathroom and drinking fountain stops. A good rule for safe touching is to never touch a child where his or her bathing suit would cover.

Use these health and safety tips to set up a **SCUBA** program that ensures the physical, emotional, and spiritual well-being of everyone involved.

Kids With Special Needs

Physical Disabilities

If you know you'll have physically challenged children at your program, you'll need to make sure your station areas are wheelchair accessible. You may also want to recruit a staff member to look out for these children. This staff member can ask parents or caretakers about specific needs such as

- whether kids have special equipment such as wheelchairs,
- what kids can and cannot eat,
- what kids need help doing,
- what kids like to do for themselves, and
- what kids enjoy most.

Because children work together and help one another in Scuba Crews, most physically challenged children will get the help they need from their crew members and Scuba Crew Leaders. However, if a physically challenged child needs constant help to participate in station activities, consider assigning an additional Scuba Crew Leader to his or her crew. For this position, choose someone who will be sensitive and who is capable of responding to the child's needs.

Physically challenged children may be shy, but often they're very bright and innovative. Scuba Crew Leaders can encourage them to shine in stations that include group discussion, such as Chadder's Undersea Bible Adventure or Deep Bible Adventures. (Plus, as kids carry out their crew roles, they'll all discover how important each crew member is!)

LeaRNING DiSaBiLitieS

Educators estimate that up to 20 percent of today's children have some type of learning disability. That means that in a program of one hundred children, up to twenty kids could be battling with dyslexia, attention-deficit/hyperactivity disorder, or other learning disabilities. Kids with learning disabilities aren't lazy or dumb—they just learn differently from other children.

SCUBA works for children with learning disabilities! Here's why:

• **It doesn't rely heavily on reading skills.** Children who enjoy reading can volunteer to be Readers for their Scuba Crews. Children who have trouble reading can choose other, equally important jobs.

• **It allows kids processing time.** Because each Scuba Crew has a Scuba Crew Leader, station leaders don't have to single out kids who need special help. Crew leaders can help the kids in their Scuba Crews work at their own pace. And station leaders are free to go around and check in with children as they complete their activities.

• **It doesn't require children to think sequentially.** Fifty percent of all students are frustrated by sequential-type assignments. At **SCUBA**, children don't have to master a new set of information each day. Instead, they learn one basic Point that's reinforced in different ways for different kinds of learners.

If you know or suspect that kids with learning disabilities will be attending your program, let your teachers know. Encourage them to help these children by
• giving instructions one at a time,
• using the positive-language suggestions in the "What's a Scuba Crew Leader?" handout (p. 135) or the Crew Leader's Pocket Guide,
• ignoring harmless annoying behaviors, and
• praising children sincerely and often.

For more information on attention-deficit/hyperactivity disorder (ADHD), use the address below to contact Children and Adults With Attention-Deficit/Hyperactivity Disorders.

Children and Adults With Attention-Deficit/Hyperactivity Disorders
8181 Professional Pl., Ste. 201
Landover, MD 20785
www.chadd.org

FieLD Test FiNDiNGS

We've received many touching letters and e-mail messages from parents of special-needs children. These adults were surprised and delighted at how much their kids got out of Group's VBS. Parents of special-needs kids are used to classroom situations and children's ministry functions that are unwelcoming and difficult for their kids. It's a delight to hear that this VBS model is friendly and effective for all types of children!

LeaDeR LifeLiNes

Welcoming Newcomers

Summer is a busy time for families. Some kids may come to **SCUBA** all five days; some may come for two or three days and then drop out; others may join your **SCUBA** program midcourse. Use the following ideas to welcome newcomers to your adventure.

• **Start with small Scuba Crews.** When you assign kids to Scuba Crews, limit some crews to three or four kids instead of five. If new kids join your program, you can assign them to Scuba Crews in which you've left openings. Even if you don't have many visitors, kids in smaller crews will love the additional attention they'll get from their Scuba Crew Leaders. If you want to encourage visitors to attend, challenge kids to fill their crews by inviting their friends.

• **Have kids introduce new Scuba Crew members.** Instead of escorting a visitor to a Scuba Crew yourself, invite one of the crew members to do it. Recruit an outgoing member of the visitor's assigned crew (a Coach may be a good candidate for this job), and then introduce the visitor to the other child one-on-one. Help the child describe the Scuba Crew, including the crew name, the crew jobs, and the daily schedule. Then send the pair of children back to meet the rest of the crew.

• **Cheer for visitors each day during Sing & Play Splash.** Have the Sing & Play Splash Leader invite Scuba Crews to stand if they have new members. Have Coaches introduce their new crew members, and then have the Sing & Play Splash Leader lead everyone in shouting, "Welcome!"

• **Use the Bible Point Crafts.** Since these craft options can be completed in twenty minutes, it's OK if kids aren't able to come to all of **SCUBA**. These crafts are visitor-friendly because they aren't projects that span several days, and there's no messy paint or glue that must dry overnight. You won't find yourself with odds and ends of partially completed crafts, made by kids who miss part of your program. Nor will you face newcomers who didn't get to start the craft the day before.

RESPONSiBiLiTy: Let 'em Have It!

At **SCUBA**, Scuba Station Leaders provide fun, hands-on, Bible-learning activities. Scuba Crew Leaders shepherd and guide their Scuba Crews. But kids take responsibility for their own learning.

Even the most well-intentioned Scuba Station Leaders and Scuba Crew Leaders may be uncomfortable giving kids this much responsibility. After all, they're the leaders; they've prepared the material, and they know what kids should learn. Dive-In Diner Leaders may insist that it's easier to prepare snacks ahead of time instead of counting on kids to complete the work. Scuba Crew Leaders may be tempted to complete Bible Point Crafts for kids instead of helping them complete their own.

Every activity at your **SCUBA** program has been field-tested, revised, retested, and revised again. So you can have confidence that kids will be able to follow directions and complete the activities successfully within the allotted times. Instead of doing kids' work for them, leaders should encourage Scuba Crew members to help kids dive deeper into God's love by helping one another complete activities.

By the end of the week, you'll hear reports of kids leading their own discussions, helping one another complete projects, and cheering one another on. Trust the Lord, and trust your kids—and watch God's love surround your program!

FOLLOW-UP

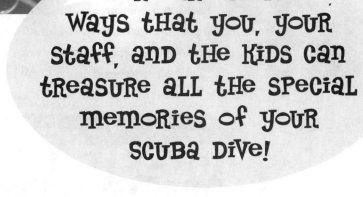

HERE ARE SOME WAYS THAT YOU, YOUR STAFF, AND THE KIDS CAN TREASURE ALL THE SPECIAL MEMORIES OF YOUR SCUBA DIVE!

Thanks for joining us at Group's Super Cool Undersea Bible Adventure!

Admit it—as much fun as it was to go **SCUBA** diving, it's a great feeling to have "surfaced." And why not? After all, you just succeeded in putting on a top-notch, high-quality, Bible-based, and downright fun program for a group of wiggly kids! Such effective ministry takes a lot of mental, emotional, and physical energy. So now you can sit back and thank God for his blessings on your program. Then congratulate yourself and your staff on an awesome adventure! In this section, you'll find ideas that will help you wrap up your program and follow up with children and their families. You'll also find helpful evaluation forms you can use to get specific feedback from Scuba Station Leaders and Scuba Crew Leaders.

CLoSiNG PROGRAM: a Sea of BiBLe FuN

Reach out to parents, grandparents, and friends every day at SCUBA's Sea Star Finale!

If you want an easy way to give parents and church members a glimpse of your **SCUBA** fun, invite them to attend Sea Star Finale. This fun-filled Bible-learning time is already built in to your **SCUBA** program each day. Explain that parents can join the fun by arriving just twenty minutes early when they come to pick up their children. They'll see children singing Sing & Play Splash songs, telling what they did in each station, and actively reviewing the daily Bible story. Parents will really catch the **SCUBA** spirit as children celebrate God's love with a grand celebration on Day 5.

If you want to have a separate closing program, follow the steps below to set up a station "open house." Set up your open house in the evening or even on Sunday morning. Parents and kids will love it!

1. Have station leaders set up the following activities in their respective station areas. If you purchased additional *Sing & Play Splash Music* audiocassettes, encourage station leaders to play the **SCUBA** songs while people are visiting their areas.

Sing & Play Splash—Have the Sing & Play Splash Leader teach words and motions to all 12 songs (or as many as time allows). Or let kids request their favorites!

Preschool Tide Pool—Have the Preschool Tide Pool Director set up five or six Scuba Discovery Stations that children can visit with their parents. Choose from the activities suggested below, or let the preschool director suggest kids' favorites.

- See the Sea
- Turtle Pals
- Hidden Shells
- Oceans of Love

Undersea Crafts and Missions—Have the Undersea Crafts and Missions Leader display his or her sample Bible Point Crafts (or have kids display the crafts they made—if they're willing to part with them for a little while). Ask the crafts leader to explain the stories of Cesar, Alexandra, and Ishmael on the Operation Kid-to-Kid posters. Have the crafts leader encourage kids to show their parents the catch of shoes and socks that will be sent to needy kids around the world!

Splish Splash Games—Have the Splish Splash Games Leader lead families in The Nineveh Assignment game kids played on Day 2 or the Treasure Hunt Mix-Up from Day 3. Families will also enjoy Give It All You've Got!

Dive-In Diner—Have the Dive-In Diner Leader set out supplies for making Elijah's Altar. Display a sample snack, and let children and parents make their own tasty treats.

Chadder's Undersea Bible Adventure—Have the Chadder's Undersea Bible Adventure Leader play the *Chadder* video. Set out paper, markers, and pencils; and let families design their own "Wanted" posters for the Coral Reef thief!

Deep Bible Adventures—Have the Deep Bible Adventures Leader set up the whale from Day 2, complete with smelly tuna and a helper making

LEADER LifeLine

If you really want to go the extra mile, check out *Scuba-Do's Dive: A Closing Production for Your Super Cool Undersea Bible Adventure*, in your **SCUBA** catalog for a closing production. This musical celebration includes Scuba-Do, the crazy canine kids will have grown to love during **SCUBA**. *Scuba-Do's Dive* provides an opportunity for friends and relatives to hear what kids have been learning, while enjoying the bubbly tunes of **SCUBA**. For more information, see page 14 of your catalog.

FOLLOW-UP

whale and ocean sound effects. Families can sit with "Jonah" for a few minutes, while he tells of his adventures and all he's learned about obeying God.

Sea Star Finale—Have the Sea Star Finale Leader lead people in the show from Day 2.

2. Begin by having everyone gather in the sanctuary or the fellowship hall for a brief introduction and a Sing & Play Splash time. Have your Sing & Play Splash Leader teach everyone the theme song, "Deeper With God." This is a great time to distribute **SCUBA** completion certificates. Simply photocopy the certificates on pages 199 and 200 (or purchase the leaders' and children's completion certificates); fill in children's, Scuba Crew Leaders', or Scuba Station Leaders' names; then sign and date each certificate.

3. Designate a thirty- to forty-five-minute time frame in which families can visit the stations. At the end of the designated time, use a conch shell to call everyone back to your original meeting area for Sea Star Finale.

4. Thank everyone for coming, and encourage them to join you in planning and preparing for next year's program.

Your **SCUBA** has ended, but helping kids know and love God never ends. You still have lots of time to share the good news about Jesus with the kids in your church and community. The outreach efforts you make will help you share God's love with your **SCUBA** participants and their families. Use the ideas below to design a follow-up plan that fits your church's needs.

• **Catch 'em with a party!** To get kids diving into God's love every week, you might want to host a Back to SCUBA Party, using our Back to SCUBA Follow-Up Kit! This "party-in-a-box" makes follow-up a breeze, allowing you to bring VBS kids back to church and introduce them to your regular children's ministry team! Plus, you'll have the chance to use your **SCUBA** decorations, hear Sing & Play Splash songs, review the Bible stories and Bible Points kids learned at **SCUBA**, and see those adorable Bible Memory Buddies once more! We've even created back-to-school items like pocket folders, pencils, bookmarks, and backpack pulls that will encourage "faith-sharing" at school. The "Back to SCUBA" Follow-Up Kit is available from Group Publishing or your local Christian bookstore.

• **Send SCUBA follow-up postcards.** Kids love getting mail, so here's a surefire way to get kids back for Sunday school—a personal invitation from **SCUBA**. These colorful postcards help you make a long-term impact on kids by involving them in your regular Sunday school program. (Order these postcards from Group Publishing or your local Christian bookstore.)

• **Give away SCUBA photos.** Deliver framed photos to families of children who don't regularly attend your church. Kids will treasure these colorful, fun mementos, and you'll have an opportunity to invite the family to visit your church. (Order **SCUBA** souvenir photo frames from Group Publishing or your local Christian bookstore.)

• **Invite Chadder Chipmunk to visit a children's ministry event.** Schedule a return engagement of *Chadder's Undersea Bible Adventure* during another children's ministry event. Children who visited your church during **SCUBA** will want to come back and revisit their furry friend. You might even have a volunteer dress in the Chadder costume. Kids will love a visit from a giant, huggable Chadder! (Order *Chadder's Undersea Bible Adventure* video and Chadder costume patterns from Group Publishing or your local Christian bookstore.)

• **Sponsor a parents' day.** Build relationships with children's parents by having a parents' day during **SCUBA**. Encourage children to invite their parents or older siblings to join them. Provide adult and youth Bible studies or have family members visit the stations with their children's Scuba Crews. Also require parents to come inside to pick up their children so you can make contact with them.

• **Hold a SCUBA memory night.** Invite all the **SCUBA** participants to a get-together every month or every quarter. Make each memory night a fun event that fits the **SCUBA** theme. Serve Dive-In Diner food, play Sing & Play Splash tunes, and play Splish Splash Games. Show slides or video footage of your dive. You may even interview divers about what they're doing now that the adventure has ended.

• **Thank your staff members for all their hard work.** Your praise and appreciation will speak volumes to your volunteers...and can be integral in their decision to volunteer next year. So go the extra mile to show them how much you appreciate all they've done. A card with a personal, heartfelt message is always a good idea. Balloons, flowers, or baked goodies are even better. You might consider filling our "Thank You" Shells with marshmallow "pearls" or bright jelly bean "treasures." Add a note, saying "You were a gem

of a station leader at **SCUBA**!" Volunteers will appreciate a blue bag filled with Goldfish crackers and a note that reads, "I'm glad we caught you! Thanks for helping at **SCUBA**!" Or present each helper with a bottle of water and a fish-shaped note that says, "Thanks for getting your feet wet at **SCUBA**!"

• **Sign up a team for next year's program.** It's never too early to start recruiting, and your staff will be excited about the week they've just finished at **SCUBA**. There's no better time to collect the names of volunteers who might be interested in volunteering for next year's VBS program. Photocopy the **"We hope you're hooked on VBS after our SCUBA!"** handout on page 202, and post it around your facility. You may be surprised at the jump-start you'll get on next year's recruitment!

GROUP'S 2004 VBS!

SCUBA was a blast...but 2004 will be even better!
Be among the first to find out what Group's 2004
VBS theme is on July 15, by visiting
www.groupvbs.com/vbs2004

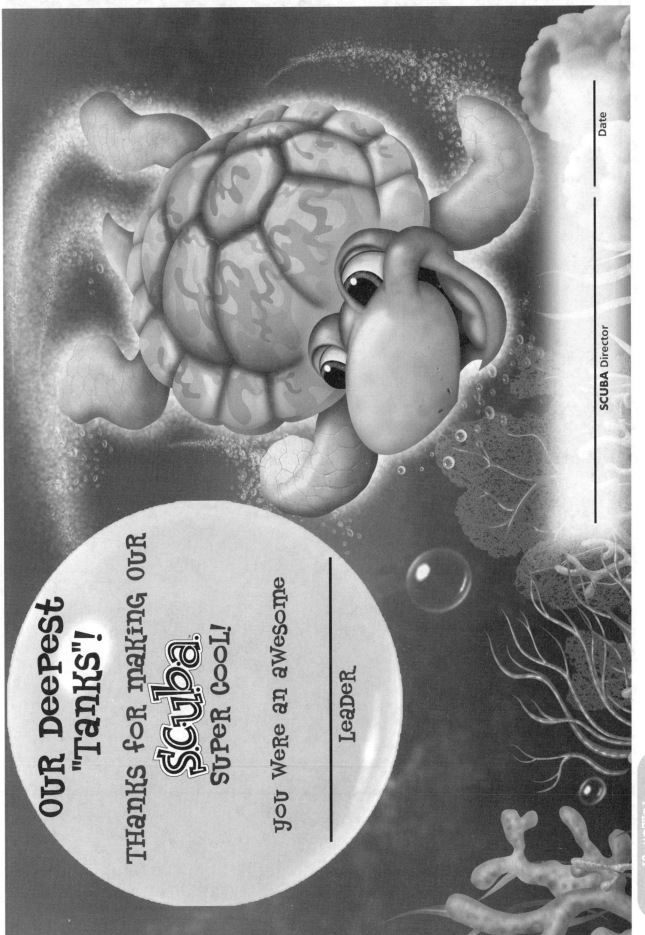

OuR DeePeSt "TanKS"!

THanKS foR maKing ouR **S.C.U.B.A.** SuPeR CooL!

you WeRe an aWeSome

LeaDeR

SCUBA Director

Date

FoLLoW-uP

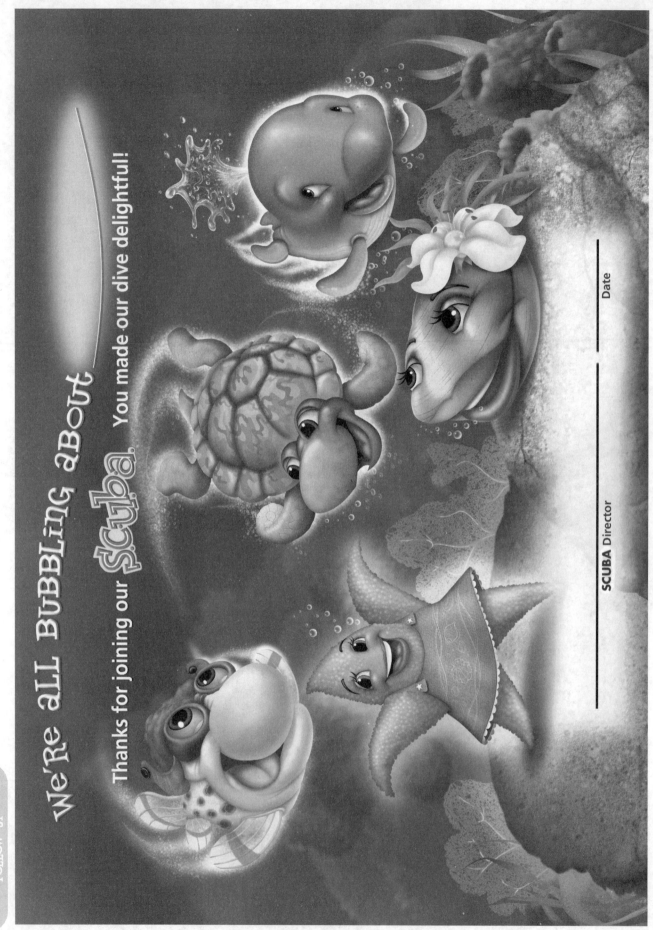

We're all Bubbling about Scuba.

You made our dive delightful!

Thanks for joining our

SCUBA Director _____

Date _____

oceans of thanks to
these "fin-tastic"
friends who made our
SCUBA super cool!

We Hope you're Hooked on VBS after our SCUBA!

You were a *fin*-tastic part of the 2003 **SCUBA** staff! We'd love to have you join our team for another adventure at next year's VBS. If you're interested, just sign below. We'll hang on to your name and information and let you know about opportunities for next year.

Name	PHone	at next year's VBS, I WOULD Be interested in...

FOLLOW-UP

evaluating your Scuba PROGRAM

After **SCUBA** you'll want to check in with your Scuba Station Leaders, Scuba Crew Leaders, and other staff members to see how things went.

Photocopy the "Scuba Station Leader VBS Evaluation" (p. 204) and the "Scuba Crew Leader VBS Evaluation" (p. 205), and distribute the photocopies to your staff. To help your evaluation process go smoothly, you may want to ask staff members to return their evaluations within two weeks of **SCUBA**. After two weeks, specific details will still be fresh in staff members' minds, and they'll have a good perspective on their overall experiences.

After you've collected Scuba Station Leader and Scuba Crew Leader evaluation forms, please take a few moments to fill out the "**SCUBA** Evaluation" on pages 207-208. Be sure to summarize the comments you received from Scuba Station Leaders and Scuba Crew Leaders. Keep a copy of your completed evaluation for your records; then return the original to Group's VBS Coordinator. Your detailed feedback will help us meet your needs as we plan an all-new program for next year.

LeaDeR LifeLine

You can customize the evaluation forms by adding additional questions in the "Other comments about our **SCUBA** program" section. For example, you may want to ask about facilities or about the dates and times of your VBS. This is also a good time to recruit volunteers for next year's VBS. Scuba Station Leaders and Scuba Crew Leaders will have had so much fun that they'll want to sign on again!

THANKS FoR ReaCHiNG So many KiDS WiTH GRoUP'S SCUBa!

SCUBA Station Leader VBS evaluation

Thanks for joining us at SCUBA! Please complete this evaluation form to help us plan for next year's VBS.

1. I led the _____Station.

2. Were the instructions in your station leader manual clear and easy to follow? Explain.

3. What did you like best about your station? What did kids like best?

4. What would you like to change about your station?

Other comments about our **SCUBA** program:

FOLLOW-UP

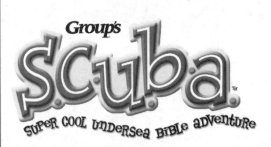

SCUBa CReW LeaDeR VBS evaLuation

Thanks for joining us at SCUBA! Please complete this evaluation form to help us plan for next year's VBS.

1. What was the best thing about working with your Scuba Crew?

2. What was the hardest thing?

3. Did the "For Scuba Crew Leaders Only" handouts or Crew Leader's Pocket Guide help you as you worked with kids? Explain.

4. What's one thing you'd like more help with in your role?

FoLLoW-UP

SCUBA VBS EVALUATION

THANKS FOR TAKING KIDS DEEPER AND DIVING WITH US!

We appreciate you joining us for unforgettable, fun Bible learning...and we look forward to introducing you to an all-new VBS next year!

Will you help us make next year's VBS even better? Take a few moments at the end of your program to fill out this survey. Drop it in the mail, and let us know what you think!

Check out www.groupvbs.com to see how you can fill out this evaluation electronically!

Thank You!

Jody Brolsma

Jody Brolsma
SCUBA Dive Master

Instruction: Use blue or black pen to completely fill in the response " ⭘ " when appropriate.

Incorrect Marks ✓ Ⓧ ◉ ⭘   Correct Mark ●

FOLD

1. As a director, what was the best part of SCUBA?

2. If you could change or improve anything about Group's VBS, what would it be?

3. Was there an aspect of SCUBA that you were dissatisfied with? If so, what?

4. Do you have any great SCUBA stories you'd like to share with us?   FOLD

5. What was the number one reason you chose Group's SCUBA?
- ⭘ Bible stories
- ⭘ strong life application
- ⭘ crafts
- ⭘ format
- ⭘ past success with Group's VBS
- ⭘ music
- ⭘ theme
- ⭘ other (please explain)

6. Tell us how you learned about Group's SCUBA.
- ⭘ bookstore
- ⭘ mailing
- ⭘ advertisement
- ⭘ word of mouth
- ⭘ SCUBA Splash Party
- ⭘ Children's Ministry Magazine
- ⭘ bookstore preview
- ⭘ Children's Ministry Magazine Live
- ⭘ other (please specify)

7665312246

Instruction: Use blue or black pen to completely fill in the response " ◯ " when appropriate.

Incorrect Marks ✓ Ⓧ ● ◯   Correct Mark ●

7. Where did you purchase your VBS items?

◯ bookstore   ◯ I called Group

◯ I went to www.groupvbs.com

◯ I went to www.groupoutlet.com

Why?

Tell us about your purchasing experience.

8. Did you attend a Scuba Splash (Director) Party?

◯ yes   ◯ hosted   ◯ no

Would you like to attend a Group VBS directors party in the future?

◯ yes   ◯ no

FOLD   **Would you like to host a Group's VBS directors party in the future?**   FOLD

◯ yes   ◯ no

9. How many years have you used Group's VBS?

◯ 1   ◯ 2   ◯ 3   ◯ 4   ◯ 5   ◯ 6   ◯ 7   ◯ 8

If you said something nice about Group's VBS, may we quote you?

◯ Yes

10. How easy was it to recruit your volunteers?

◯ Very easy! I hardly had to do a thing!

◯ Easy, but I did have to work at finding enough helpers.

◯ Somewhat difficult. I really had to be creative and get folks "on board."

◯ Difficult - it was like pulling teeth!

11. What recruiting helps did you use?

◯ Ideas in the SCUBA Director Manual

◯ Recruiting Commercials from the Pass-Along Recruitment Video

◯ E-cruiting Service

12. What would you need to continue using Group's VBS each year?

Permission to photocopy this evaluation form from Group's SCUBA Director Manual granted for local church use. Copyright © Group Publishing, Inc., P.O. Box 481, Loveland, CO 80539. **www.groupvbs.com**

FOLD   FOLD

Name

Address

City   **State**   **Zip**

E-mail

NO POSTAGE NECESSARY IF MAILED IN THE UNITED STATES

BUSINESS REPLY MAIL

FIRST-CLASS MAIL   PERMIT NO 16   LOVELAND CO

POSTAGE WILL BE PAID BY ADDRESSEE

VBS COORDINATOR
P.O. BOX 481
LOVELAND, CO 80539-9985

InDeX

Weaving Faith Into Life

Keep them plugged in all week long!

FaithWeaver™ Sunday school curriculum offers memorable Bible lessons that help learners –*of all ages*–apply God's Word to their lives. They get opportunities every week to put their faith into action.

And FaithWeaver is easy to use for teachers and flexible to fit just about any church size.

FaithWeaver Bible Curriculum helps you cover the significant Bible stories you want learners to know and trust (you get an overview of the Bible every three years, with an overview of the New Testament *every* year.) And you'll find most of the preparation already done for you, so you can spend time building relationships with your learners!

Download a **FREE** sample lesson at www.faithweaver.com today to check out how FaithWeaver works across all age levels. Or visit your Christian curriculum supplier. And let FaithWeaver help you keep learners of all ages plugged into the Bible all week long!

Welcome to FW Friends™!
See kids grow in faith, in
actions and in outreach!

FW Friends is a revolutionary midweek program that helps you see kids' real spiritual growth! Every week kids have a blast exploring God's Word and learning how to apply it to their lives. So you can watch them grow in Christ! You can use FW Friends as a midweek program or for Sunday school, an after-school program or anywhere you want kids to grow in faith, in actions and in outreach.

Everything about FW Friends emphasizes lasting spiritual growth. Kids begin at the Opening Celebration, separate to join their Circle of Friends as they rotate through Discovery Centers, take time for quiet reflection with their journals, then rejoin the other groups for the Closing Celebration.

FW Friends is easy and flexible. Every lesson and activity is clearly and visually laid out in several handy See-It Do-It™ leader guides. Any leader can actually sit down with a group of kids—See-It Do-It guide in hand—and lead them through any activity…with very little preparation needed!

FW stands for FaithWeaver™ and FW Friends is part of the FaithWeaver family of Christian growth resources. Contact us for more information about this family of resources that ties together Bible curriculum, children's church, midweek programming, and the home. FaithWeaver builds on the power of the family to encourage Christian growth.

2003 Vacation Bible School Catalog

Group's

S.C.U.B.A.™

SUPER COOL UNDERSEA BIBLE ADVENTURE

WHERE KIDS DIVE DEEPER INTO THEIR FAITH

		Bible Story	**Treasure Verse**	**Games—featu Bible Memory B**

Day 1

I'm ace!

Believe it or not, I'm a flying fish! There's only one true God who can *really* make a fish that can fly. I'll remind kids to believe in God. Wahoo!

BiBLe PoiNT: Believe in God.

Elijah confronts the Prophets of Baal (1 Kings 18:16-39)

"But you are the only true God" (Jeremiah 10:10a)

Day 2

It's me...SQUiRt!

It's super important for whales to listen and obey other whales. I want kids to learn to obey God.

BiBLe PoiNT: Obey God.

Jonah disobeys God (Jonah 1–3)

"Here is what it means to love God. It means that we obey his commands" (1 John 5:3)

Day 3

TaNK HeRe

Sea turtles have a built-in protection system. Kids don't have a shell...but they do have God. I'll help kids discover that they can trust God.

BiBLe PoiNT: Trust God.

Jesus calms a storm (Matthew 8:23-27)

"Trust in the Lord with all your heart. Do not depend on your own understanding" (Proverbs 3:5)

Day 4

I'm PeaRL

I want kids to know Jesus is God's Son— God's precious treasure! I'll remind kids to love God!

BiBLe PoiNT: Love God.

Jesus dies on the cross and rises again (Luke 23–24)

"Love the Lord your God with all your heart and with all your soul. Love him with all your strength" (Deuteronomy 6:5)

Day 5

I'm StaRLa!

When kids see my arms stretched out, they'll want to share God's love too!

BiBLe PoiNT: Share God's love.

Jesus appears to his followers as they fish (Matthew 28:18-20; John 21:1-17)

"Go into all the world. Preach the good news to everyone" (Mark 16:15)

NeW BaCK To SCuBa! Follow-Up Kit

I'm GiLL!

Invite your SCUBA kids back to my 2 hour party to relive and review what they learned at VBS.

BiBLe PoiNT: Follow God.

Jesus calls the disciples (Matthew 4:18-22)

"Follow me... and I will make you fishers of people" (Matthew 4:19)

SCUBA Bookmark

See WHat KiDs Do each DaY

Crafts	Snacks	Life Application Video

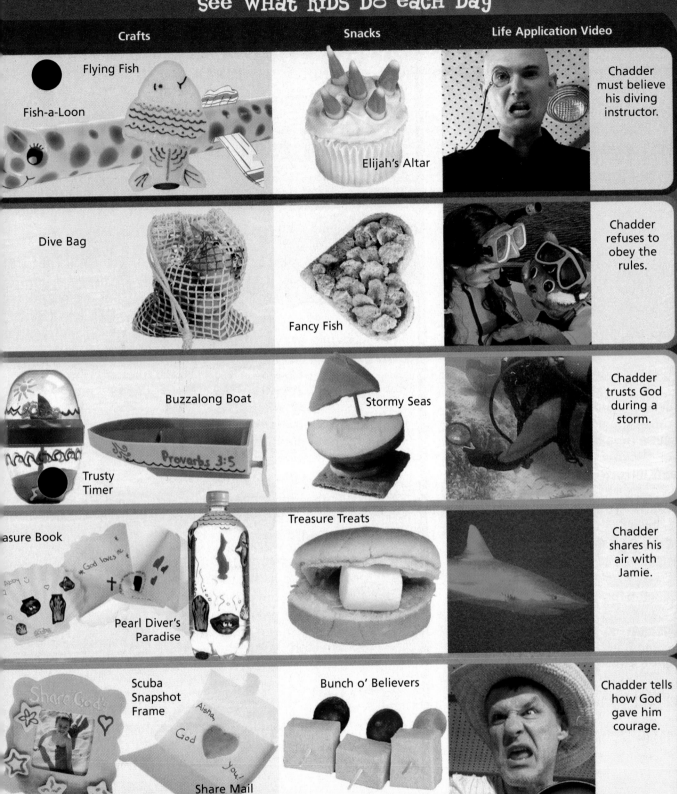

Flying Fish

Fish-a-Loon

Elijah's Altar

Chadder must believe his diving instructor.

Dive Bag

Fancy Fish

Chadder refuses to obey the rules.

Buzzalong Boat

Provorbs 3:5

Trusty Timer

Stormy Seas

Chadder trusts God during a storm.

asure Book

God loves me

Pearl Diver's Paradise

Treasure Treats

Chadder shares his air with Jamie.

Scuba Snapshot Frame

Aisha, God You!

Share Mail

Bunch o' Believers

Chadder tells how God gave him courage.

SCUBA Pocket Folder

SCUBA Pencils

SCUBA Zipper Pull

Re-capture the excitement of SCUBA after your official VBS with this new Back to SCUBA! Follow-Up Kit. The kit contains 2 hours of fun that will keep kids hooked on your children's ministry year-round. After the party, send your kids back to school with supplies that will help them share their faith...pocket folders, pencils, and more!

table of contents

www.groupvbs.com

4

With Scuba VBS it's easy to Sea the Difference

"Don't miss our Bible Memory Buddies™! J
one way we bring the Bible to life. See pag

- **Easy Bible Memory!** The Bi
  sinks into kids' hearts as life-
  changing lessons are reinforced
  every activity. Kids learn Bible
  verses, then learn to apply them
  to life every day.

- **Practical Life Application
  Activities and Questions
  in each Lesson!**
  To help you spot these
  important activities, just
  look for this logo throughout
  your leader manual.

  LIFE APPLICAT
  GO

- **Powerful music, worship and drama**
  will get your kids excited
  about God!

- **Oceans of Decorating Ideas**
  for turning your church into an
  unforgettable underwater world!
  Dive online at www.groupvbs.com
  to exchange more ideas with
  VBS Directors.

SING & PLAY SPLASH CD

- **Easy to Get Results!**
  Watch your children's ministry grow as kids bring their
  friends and build lasting relationships at VBS. It's so mu
  fun they'll keep coming to your church long after the
  program ends.

*"We had older boys
missing sports events
because they didn't
want to skip VBS—
that says a lot!"*
SANDY KEMNER
BROOKINGS, SD

ReCRUitinG YOUR VoLUnteeRS iS aS easy aS 1...2...3!

Our exclusive SCUBA Recruiting Campaign comes FREE in every Starter Kit. We've included everything you need to reel 'em in! Here's what you'll get:

1. THRee Ready-to-SHOW ViDeO ReCRUitinG CommeRCiaLS

Show them at church or whenever people are gathered.

2. COmPLete SteP-By-SteP ReCRUitinG CampaiGn

See pages 99-122 in the SCUBA Director Manual.

3. GROUP'S eXCLUSive e-CRUitinG SeRViCe

It's easy…customizable…and flexible. Pre-written e-mail messages are automatically delivered to you based on your VBS dates. Use them any way you want—customize them, personalize them, and then send them to potential volunteers.

> *"It was easy to put together! The jobs were so well laid out that I had volunteers coming out of the woodwork!"*
> SUSAN HEIDER
> MARINETTE, WI

HeRe'S HOW e-CRUitinG WORKS:

1. **SiGn UP!** Visit www.groupvbs.com and click on Group's E-Cruiting service to register. Be sure to tell us the starting date of your VBS.

2. **CHeCK YOUR inBOX!** We'll e-mail you a recruiting letter about three months before your SCUBA is set to begin. Simply customize and re-send this letter to as many people as you want.

3. **YOU'Ve GOt mORe maiL!** In the weeks that follow, you'll receive even more specialized e-mail recruiting pieces that you can personalize and send to potential volunteers, including 7 Station Leader job descriptions, a letter to SCUBA Crew Leaders, and more.

● **YOU'Re in COntROL!** You decide which messages to send and when. Pre-written messages can be sent as is or fully customized to add your personal touch. Recruiting made easy!

Group ➡ YOU

www.groupvbs.com

HeRe'S HoW SCUBa WoRKS...
WiTH eLeMeNTaRY-AGeD
STuDeNTS.

1. SCUBA CReWS

Elementary-age children form small groups of 5 called "Scuba Crews." Each Scuba Crew has an adult or teenage guide.

**We'Re not a CLaSS,
We'Re a CReW!**

2. SCUBa STaTions

Every day SCUBA crews rotate through 7 different stations—exploring the same simple Bible point at each one.

Sing&play Splash
large group opening—25 minutes

Chadder's undersea Bible adventure
life application video—20 minutes

dive-in diner
snacks—20 minutes

Splish Splash games
games—20 minutes

Undersea Crafts & missions
crafts—20 minutes

deep Bible adventures
Bible story time—20 minutes

Sea Star finale
large group closing—20 minutes

3. SCUBa WOW!

It's easy and fun for everyone because:
- SCUBA requires fewer trained teachers. Only 8 teachers are needed for a VBS of up to 150 kids...for small programs you may only need 2 or 3 teachers total.
- Teachers prepare only the material for their station.

- SCUBA is flexible. Its unique format allows you to condense the program for smaller churches and expand it for larger churches.
- Some leaders don't have to prepare anything, and those who do only prepare 20-25 minutes of material a day.

PRESCHOOLERS HAVE THEIR OWN AGE-APPROPRIATE PROGRAM DESIGNED JUST FOR THEM!

Just like elementary kids, preschoolers form crews, too! Then they rotate through age-appropriate stations within Preschool Tide Pool: Sing & Play Splash, Bible Story Adventures, Scuba Discovery Stations, Dive-In Diner, Chadder's Undersea Bible Adventure, Splash and Dash Playtime, and Sea Star Finale.

Preschoolers even join the big kids for opening and closing programs.

PRESCHOOLERS HAVE A WHALE OF a time!

See pages 10 and 28 for more splashy details.

Tide Pool Bible Book

Preschool Tide Pool Director Manual

WORKS!

FOR LEADERS:

● Our station-based format allows volunteers to use their natural gifts and teach only the things that they do best.

● Everyone knows...you never scuba dive alone! Group offers a virtual community of dive buddies at www.groupvbs.com. Ask questions, exchange ideas, offer prayer requests, and share your success stories with other SCUBA Directors. Help is just a click away!

● SCUBA Splash Parties allow you to network with other VBS Directors in your area. Share ideas on everything from decorating to raising money while having a whale of a time.

NEW!
CREW LEADER POCKET GUIDES

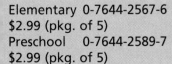

These guides provide your volunteers fun ideas to help build meaningful crew relationships, guidelines for what to do at each SCUBA station, plus practical tips for discipline, safety, and helping kids go deeper in their relationship with God. A must-have for each crew leader!

Elementary 0-7644-2567-6
$2.99 (pkg. of 5)
Preschool 0-7644-2589-7
$2.99 (pkg. of 5)

www.groupvbs.com

DiVE iNto tHese PROGRam essentials!

NOW available on DVD!

CHADDER'S UNDERSEA BIBLE ADVENTURE VIDEO

Check in with Chadder Chipmunk and his zany friends every day for aquatic adventures and a cliff-hanger mystery that doesn't get solved until week's end. Video clips are used every day in Chadder's theater.

VHS 646847-13013-7
Quantity Discounts:
1-9 copies	$19.99
10-29 copies	$9.99
30+ copies	$6.99

DVD 646847-10533-3
Quantity Discounts:
1-9 copies	$19.99
10+ copies	$9.99

SKITS & DRAMA CD

With music, drama, sound effects, and 5 wacky skits, you'll use this convenient CD every day of your undersea adventure. Shared among 3 stations.

646847-13032-8 $14.99

SING & PLAY SPLASH MUSIC VIDEO

On-screen lyrics help your kids bubble over with excitement as they follow along. This kid-friendly video teaches super-cool songs and actions that children, teenagers and adults will love.

NOW available on DVD!

VHS 646847-13003-8
Quantity Discounts:
1-9 copies	$24.99
10-29 copies	$12.99
30+ copies	$7.99

DVD 646847-10543-2
Quantity Discounts:
1-9 copies	$24.99
10+ copies	$12.99

SCUBA CLIP ART, SONG LYRICS, AND DECORATING CD

NOW a 2-CD set!

Features higher-quality, scalable images!

Something for everyone...clip art, customizable forms, song lyrics transparencies, and decorating patterns. A treasure chest of resources!

646847-13462-3 $19.99

BiBLe BooKS taKe KiDS DeePeR into GoD'S WoRD!

TiDe PooL BiBLe BooK
(PRESCHOOL)

0-7644-2508-0 $2.99

- 5 Bible stories with "read-along" pictures
- Daily activity pages
- Family-friendly take-home activities

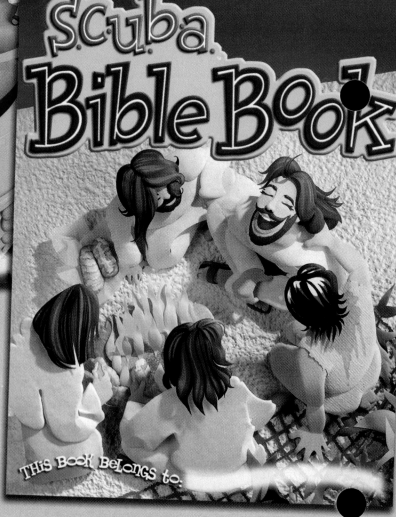

SCUBa BiBLe BooK
(ELEMENTARY)

0-7644-2509-9 $2.99

- Bright, colorful pages are easy to write on and easy to understand
- Five exciting Bible stories taken straight from the Bible
- Kid-friendly take-home pages

www.groupvbs.com

SURPRISE STICKERS

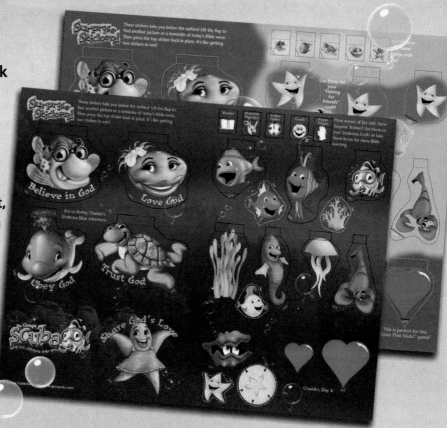

● in each student book

Both student books feature a jam-packed sheet of Surprise Stickers—the coolest thing you've never seen!

Each 2-part sticker delights kids with Bible points, fun art, affirmations, and jokes—such as, "Why are fish so smart? Because they swim in schools!"

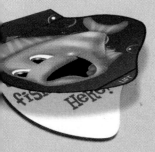

●ake a SPLaSH With BiBLe MeMoRY BuDDieS™!

STaRLa

Wondering how to get older boys into VBS? Kids at our field test went wild for these squirters!

BiBLe MeMoRY BuDDieS™

Adorable aquatic friends make the Bible leap to life! Ace, Squirt, Tank, Pearl, and Starla each have the daily treasure verse on them. Bible memory has never been this fun!

646847-10496-1 $3.99/set of 5

SQUIRT

aCe

PeaRL

QUANTITY DISCOUNTS

1-19 sets	$3.99
20-39 sets	$3.49
40+ sets	$2.99

DiVe BaG

Don't forget our Scuba Dive Bags! An essential piece of SCUBA gear, these ba●●ill hold 5 Bible Memory Buddies.

646847-10467-1
$15.99/pkg. of 10

TaNK
(SHOWN ACTUAL SIZE)

11

BiBLe Point CRafts

- Lasting mementos of BiBLe tRUTHs!
- InteRactive toys that swim, fLy, and stRetcH!
- KiD-testeD, KiD-fRienDLy!
- exclusive foR scuBa!

- **a VaLue!** Why spend money on things your kids will throw away? Since kids treasure keepsake reminders of the Bible truths they've learned, your dollars are being used wisely.

Day 1

FiSH-a-Loon ▼
A 3-foot inflatable flying fish delights kids as they learn that there's only one true God. Great for preschoolers, too!
INCLUDES: FISH-A-LOONS, DECORATABLE FISH FINS, AND RUBBER BANDS.

646847-10466-4 $6.99/pkg of 10
APPROXIMATELY 6" WIDE X 4 FT LONG

FLying FiSH ▼
What's more fun than foam fish that fly? Fill the tank with Alka-Seltzer and water and get ready for high-flying fun! After all, who could believe a fish could fly?
INCLUDES: FOAM FISH, SCUBA TANKS. ALKA-SELTZER NOT INCLUDED.

646847-10465-7
$8.99/pkg of 10
6" X 4"

Day 2

Dive Bag ▼
Kids love to personalize Dive Bag that hold their Bible Memory Buddies™. These see-through Di Bags remind them that they can hide from God (like Jonah tried so they learn they need to obey Great for preschoolers, too!
INCLUDES: COTTON NET D AGS.

646847-10467-1
$15.99/pkg of 10
5" X 7"

Day 3

◄ **Trusty Timer**
Kids assemble and decorate these clear egg-shaped sand-timers. Teach kids to trust God all the time...any time. INCLUDES: PACKETS OF COLORFUL SAND, 2-PIECE TIMER SETS.

646847-10468-8
$18.99/pkg of 10
4" HIGH X 2-1/2" DIAMETER

Buzzalong Boat ▼
After painting their boats kids wind them up, set them in water, and away they go! Bring back the excitement—and action—of today's Bible story. Great for preschoolers, too! INCLUDES: BOATS WITH WIND-UP MOTORS.

646847-10469-5 $11.99/pkg of 10
5" LONG X 2" WIDE X 1" HIGH

Day 4

◄ **Pearl Diver's Paradise**
Add this exclusive pearl diver and shell to the "aquarium" water bottle kids decorate. Squeeze the bottle and watch in amazement as the figure dives to the bottom. It's a hands-on reminder that Jesus is a priceless treasure. INCLUDES: DIVERS AND SHELLS. BOTTLES NOT INCLUDED.

646847-10471-8
$6.99/pkg of 10
2-3/4" LONG DIVER
6MM SHELL BEAD

Day 5

Scuba Snapshot Frame ▼
Sturdy wooden photo frames and wooden stars beg for decoration as children learn to reach out to others—like a sea star—with the love of God! INCLUDES: FRAMES AND PUNCH-OUT STARS.

646847-10475-6
$11.99/pkg of 10
4-1/2" X 4-3/4"

Treasure Book ▼
You'll be touched when kids draw pictures of their love for God in this expandable shell-shaped journal. An ongoing reminder of how God gave Jesus—his treasure—for us. Great for preschoolers, too! INCLUDES: BOOK COVERS AND EXPANDABLE JOURNAL PAGES.

646847-10470-1
$9.99/pkg of 10
6" X 8"

Share Mail Postcard ►
Kids use squishy colorful "Paint Dough" to make 3-D designs on fold-up postcards, expressing God's love...then mail the card to someone else. It's an indescribable way for kids to share God's love. INCLUDES: FOLD-UP POSTCARDS, 4 ASSORTED TUBS OF PAINT DOUGH FOR EVERY 10 KIDS.

646847-10476-3
$7.99/pkg of 10
3-1/2" X 5"
FOLDED

Make a SPLASH With Great Music!

Sing & Play Splash Music Video

On-screen lyrics help your kids follow along. This music video teaches kid-pleasing songs and actions that children, teenagers and adults will love.

646847-13003-8
Quantity Discounts:

1-9 copies	$24.99
10-29 copies	$12.99
30+ copies	$7.99

◀ Sing & Play Splash Audiocassette

Includes all 12 SCUBA songs. Play as background music during snacks, crafts, and game time...or before and after your program. Recorded in split-track format.

646847-13004-5
Quantity Discounts:

1-19 copies	$11.99
20-39 copies	$5.99
40-59 copies	$4.99
60+ copies	$3.99

ALL NEW! Now on DVD!

◀ Sing & Play Splash Music DVD

Take advantage of the quality and convenience that DVD offers.

646847-10543-2
Quantity Discounts:

1-9 copies	$24.99
10+ copies	$12.99

Sing & Play Splash Music CD ▶

Worship to change kids' hearts. Includes all 12 SCUBA songs. Recorded in split-track format.

646847-13002-1
Quantity Discounts:

1-9 copies	$16.99
10-29 copies	$10.99
30+ copies	$7.99

Scuba-Do's Dive Closing Production ▶

Scuba-Do's Dive is this year's all-new closing drama. It's interactive. Memorable. Great for outreach. Invite parents, grandparents, and neighbors to share in moving worship and humor as they dive deeper into God's love. CD included with pre-recorded soundtrack, including every line, every song, and every sound, plus easy-to-use clip art.

0-7644-2507-2 $19.99

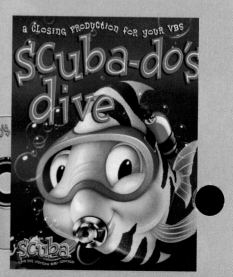

a closing production for your VBS

Scuba-do's dive

GRAB YOUR SCUBA GEAR!

◀ Front

Staff T-Shirt ▶
Spot SCUBA Leaders at a glance. Staff T-Shirt features the SCUBA logo. 100% cotton. Adult medium or XL.

Med   646847-10489-3
XL   646847-10445-9
Quantity Discounts:
1-9 shirts $15.99
10+ shirts $10.99

▲ Back

▲ CREW LEADER CAPS
Functional and fashionable, these comfy caps help your leaders stand out.

646847-10450-3
Quantity Discounts:
1-9 hats $9.99
10+ hats $6.99

Dive into God's Love!

▲ Buttons
Put a smile on every child's face with SCUBA Buttons. Make great prizes or gifts! 1 3/8" diameter with safety pin.

646847-10480-0 $9.99/pkg. of 30

CREW#

NAME:

◀ CHADDER Costume Pattern
Bring Chadder to life at your VBS every year. This pattern allows plenty of room and requires only moderate sewing skills.

646847-09055-4 $9.99

▲ Name Badges
You'll help your children feel cherished when you call them by name. Sturdy name badges last all week.

646847-10479-4 $3.99/pkg. of 10

◀ Iron-on Transfers
Craft your own T-shirts or tote bags as gifts for kids or leaders. Get creative... there's a sea of possibilities! 8 1/2" x 5 1/2"
646847-10451-0 $12.99/pkg. of 10

Don't Dive Alone!
Share your Super Cool Undersea Bible Adventure with everyone!

FOR oceans of fun Join us at Vacation Bible School

Group's S.C.U.B.A. Super Cool Undersea Bible Adventure!

Dive into God's Love!

Join us at Vacation Bible School!

Group's S.C.U.B.A. Super Cool Undersea Bible Adventure

2003 Vacation Bible School

Group's S.C.U.B.A. Super Cool Undersea Bible Adventure

www.groupvbs.com

DOORKNOB DANGLERS ▶

Boost attendance with these sturdy invitations. Flood your community with them for a tidal wave of visitors! Pairs of perforated danglers are included on 8 1/2" x 11" sheets. Easy to photocopy.

0-7644-2578-1
$7.99/pkg. of 50

FOR Oceans of fun...

Group's

Dive into

S.cuba.

SUPER COOL UNDERSEA BIBLE ADVENTURE

Come "sea" us at Group's
S.cuba.
SUPER COOL UNDERSEA BIBLE ADVENTURE

◀ INVITATION POSTCARDS

Kids love to get mail! Send these convenient postcards and watch them pour in. Four perforated postcards per 8 1/2" x 11" sheet for easy backside copying.

0-7644-2580-3
$8.99/pkg. of 52

PUBLICITY VALUE PACK!

SAVE MORE THAN 20%

FOR Oceans of fun Join US at Vacation Bible School

DIVE into GOD'S LOVE!
Join us at Vacation Bible School!

Group's
S.cuba.

Save some sand dollars with this assortment of publicity items!

Package includes:
1 Doorknob Danglers (pkg. of 50)
1 Invitation Postcards (pkg. of 52)
1 Heavy-Duty Outdoor Theme Banner
1 Publicity Posters (pkg. of 5)

Publicity Value Pack
646847-10464-0
A $46.96 value for only $36.99!

take KiDS eVen DeePeR in tHeiR faitH!

BacK to SCUBa!
FOLLOW-UP KIT

After your official VBS, invite kids back to your church for a fun 2-hour party that relives and reviews what they learned at SCUBA VBS. Kids will enjoy a Bible story, games, snack, craft, and music. The Bible focus is "Follow God," using the story from Matthew 4:19 of Jesus calling the disciples.

Your Back to SCUBA Party will:

- welcome VBS kids back into your church,
- provide you an opportunity to highlight all of your church's children's ministry programs,
- solidify VBS Bible learning through review, and
- plug families into your church right away!

The Back to SCUBA kit includes:

- a 40-page Party Planner,
- a package of 52 Follow-Up Postcards, and
- samples of SCUBA back to school supplies: 1 SCUBA bookmark, 1 SCUBA zipper pull, 1 SCUBA pencil, and 1 SCUBA pocket folder. See items below.

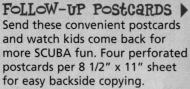

afteR tHe PaRty, SenD yOUR KiDS BacK to SCHooL WitH fUn, faitH-SHaRinG SUPPLies!

FOLLOW-UP POStCaRDS ▶

Send these convenient postcards and watch kids come back for more SCUBA fun. Four perforated postcards per 8 1/2" x 11" sheet for easy backside copying.

0-7644-2579-X
$8.99 (pkg. of 52)

▼ SCUBa BooKmaRKS

Colorful plastic clip-on bookmarks have Matthew 4:19 on the back. 2 1/2" x 2 1/2"

646847-10494-7
$11.99 (pkg. of 10)

SCUBa PocKet FoLDeRS ▶

Eye-catching sturdy folders make it easy to share God's Word. Matthew 4:19 printed inside. 9" x 12"

646847-10491-6
$9.99 (pkg. of 10)

◀ SCUBa ZiPPeR PULLS

Kids will love clipping this 2" Gill to backpacks, lunchboxes, keychains and more! Features Matthew 4:19.

646847-10495-4
$11.99 (pkg. of 10)

▼ SCUBa PenCiLS

These fun pencils can be shared with friends at school. Standard size pencil.

"FoLLoW me..." (Matthew 4:19)

646847-10490-9 $5.99 (pkg. of 10)

ORDER FORM FOR GROUP'S SCUBA VBS

CHURCH NAME

DENOMINATION | CHURCH SIZE

ADDRESS (street address necessary for UPS shipments)

CITY | STATE | ZIP

CHURCH PHONE | CHURCH FAX

PERSON PLACING ORDER | TITLE

E-MAIL

SHIP TO (if different)

NAME

ADDRESS

CITY | STATE | ZIP

DAYTIME PHONE

DATE OF YOUR VBS

Group's
S.C.U.B.A
SUPER COOL UNDERSEA BIBLE ADVENTURE

www.groupvbs.com

Check out our
OUTLET STORE
for bargains on decorating
resources, craft supplies,
and more!
www.groupoutlet.com

SCUBA STARTER KIT
(SEE PGS. 8-9 IN CATALOG)

1 Dive Deep! Recruitment, Overview &
  Pass-Along Training Video
1 SCUBA Director Manual
1 Preschool Tide Pool Director Manual
1 [Tide] Bible Adventures Leader Manual
1 [Chadd]er's Undersea Adventure
  Leader Manual
1 Undersea Crafts & Missions
  Leader Manual
1 Splish Splash Games Leader Manual
1 Sea Star Finale Leader Manual
1 Dive-in Diner Leader Manual
1 Sing & Play Splash Leader Manual
1 Elementary Crew Leader Pocket guide
1 Tide Pool Bible Book (Preschool)
1 SCUBA Bible Book (Elementary)
1 Sing & Play Splash Music CD
1 Set of Bible Memory Buddies™
1 Bible Memory Buddies™ Sticker Sheet

To preview Group's SCUBA, order a Starter Kit. Here's what you'll receive:

1 Craft Sample Pack containing:
  1 Dive Bag
  1 Treasure Book
  1 Fish-a-loon
  1 Buzzalong Boat
  1 Trusty Timer
  1 SCUBA Snapshot Frame
  1 Flying Fish
  1 Pearl Diver's Paradise
  1 Share Mail Postcard
1 Publicity Pack containing:
  1 Bulletin Insert
  1 Doorknob Dangler
  1 Invitation Postcard
  1 Name Badge
  1 Publicity Poster
  1 Certificate of Completion
  1 Iron-On Transfer
  1 Thank You Shell

Send me _____ STARTER KITS   0-7644-2562-5 $59.99 _____

PROGRAM ESSENTIALS (SEE PGS. 8-9, 19 IN CATALOG)

	Chadder's Undersea Bible Adventure Video	646847-13013-7		
_____		Quantity Discounts 1-9 copies	$19.99	_____
_____		10-29 copies	$9.99	_____
_____		30+ copies	$6.99	_____
	Chadder's Undersea Bible Adventure DVD	646847-10533-3		
_____		Quantity Discounts 1-9 copies	$19.99	_____
_____		10+ copies	$9.99	_____
_____	SCUBA Skits & Drama CD	646847-13032-8	$14.99	_____
_____	SCUBA Clip Art, Song Lyrics, and Decorating CD	646847-13462-3	$19.99	_____
_____	Preschool Crew Leader's Pocketguide (5)	0-7644-2589-7	$2.99	_____
_____	Elementary Crew Leader's Pocketguide (5)	0-7644-2567-6	$2.99	_____
_____	Operation Kid-to-Kid Missions Kit (page 19)	646847-10460-2	$9.99	_____

STUDENT ESSENTIALS (SEE PGS. 10-11 IN CATALOG)

_____	Tide Pool Bible Book (Preschool)	0-7644-2508-0	$2.99	
_____	SCUBA Bible Book (Elementary)	0-7644-2509-9	$2.99	●
_____	Bible Memory Buddies™ (set of 5)	646847-10496-1		
_____	Quantity Discounts	1-19 sets	$3.99	_____
_____		20-39 sets	$3.49	_____
_____		40+ sets	$2.99	_____

BIBLE POINT CRAFTS (SEE PGS. 12-13 IN CATALOG)

_____	Fish-a-loon (pkg. of 10)	646847-10466-4	$6.99	_____
_____	Flying Fish (pkg. of 10)	646847-10465-7	$8.99	_____
_____	Dive Bag (pkg. of 10)	646847-10467-1	$15.99	_____
_____	Trusty Timer (pkg. of 10)	646847-10468-8	$18.99	_____
_____	Buzzalong Boat (pkg. of 10)	646847-10469-5	$11.99	_____
_____	Pearl Diver's Paradise (pkg. of 10)	646847-10471-8	$6.99	_____
_____	Treasure Book (pkg. of 10)	646847-10470-1	$9.99	_____
_____	SCUBA Snapshot Frame (pkg. of 10)	646847-10475-6	$11.99	_____
_____	Share Mail Postcard (pkg. of 10)	646847-10476-3	$7.99	_____

PUBLICITY ITEMS (SEE PGS. 16-17 IN CATALOG)

_____	Bulletin Inserts (pkg. of 100)	0-7644-2575-7	$9.99	●
_____	Doorknob Danglers (pkg. of 50)	0-7644-2578-1	$7.99	_____
_____	Outdoor Banner	0-7644-2574-9	$19.99	_____
_____	Invitation Postcards (pkg. of 52)	0-7644-2580-3	$8.99	_____
_____	Publicity Poster (pkg. of 5)	0-7644-2577-3	$9.99	_____
_____	Publicity Value Pack	646847-10464-0	$36.99	_____

GREAT MUSIC (SEE PG. 14 IN CATALOG)

	Sing & Play Splash Music Audiocassette	646847-13004-5		
_____	Quantity Discounts	1-9 copies	$11.99	_____
_____		20-39 copies	$5.99	_____
_____		40-59 copies	$4.99	_____
_____		60+ copies	$3.99	_____
	Sing & Play Splash Music CD	646847-13002-1		
_____	Quantity Discounts	1-9 copies	$16.99	_____
_____		10-29 copies	$10.99	_____
_____		30+ copies	$7.99	_____
	Sing & Play Splash Music Video	646847-13003-8		
_____	Quantity Discounts	1-9 copies	$24.99	_____
_____		10-29 copies	$12.99	●
_____		30+ copies	$7.99	

GREAT MUSIC CONTINUED (SEE PG. 14 IN CATALOG)

	Sing & Play Splash Music DVD	646847-10543-2		
		Quantity Discounts 1-9 copies	$24.99	_____
_____		10+ copies	$12.99	_____
_____	SCUBA-DO's Dive Closing Production	0-7644-2507-2	$19.99	

SCUBA WEARABLES (SEE PG. 15 IN CATALOG)

	Buttons (pkg. of 30)	646847-10480-0	$9.99	_____
_____	Chadder Costume Pattern	646847-09055-4	$9.99	_____
_____	Crew Leader Cap	646847-10450-3		
_____		Quantity Discounts 1-9 caps	$9.99	_____
_____		10+ caps	$6.99	_____
_____	Iron-On Transfers (pkg. of 10)	646847-10451-0	$12.99	_____
_____	Name Badges (pkg. of 10)	646847-10479-4	$3.99	_____
	Staff T-Shirt, X-Large	646847-10445-9		
_____		Quantity Discounts 1-9 shirts	$15.99	_____
_____		10+ shirts	$10.99	_____
	Staff T-Shirt, Medium	646847-10489-3		
_____		Quantity Discounts 1-9 shirts	$15.99	_____
_____		10+ shirts	$10.99	_____

BACK TO SCUBA FOLLOW-UP ITEMS (SEE PG. 18 IN CATALOG)

	Back to SCUBA Follow-Up Kit	646847-10461-9	$14.99	_____
_____	Back to SCUBA Postcards (pkg. of 52)	0-7644-2579-X	$8.99	_____
_____	Pencils (pkg. of 10)	646847-10490-9	$5.99	_____
_____	Gill Zipper Pulls (pkg. of 10)	646847-10495-4	$11.99	_____
_____	Bookmarks (pkg. of 10)	646847-10494-7	$11.99	_____
_____	Pocket Folders (pkg. of 10)	646847-10491-6	$9.99	_____

DECORATING RESOURCES (SEE PGS. 20-25 IN CATALOG)

	Bible Point Posters (set of 5)	646847-10458-9	$9.99	_____
_____	Bible Story Posters (set of 5)	646847-10446-6	$9.99	_____
_____	Treasure Verse Posters (set of 5)	646847-10459-6	$9.99	_____
_____	Mural Decorating Kit	646847-10477-0	$14.99	_____
_____	Gill Inflatable	646847-10488-6	$11.99	_____
_____	Theme Balloons (pkg. of 30)	646847-10456-5	$8.99	_____
_____	Church Display	646847-10481-7	$19.99	_____

SCUBA SURPRISES (SEE PGS. 26-27 IN CATALOG)

_____	Bible Memory Buddies™ Sticker Sheets (pkg. of 10)	646847-10485-5	$6.99	_____
_____	Certificate of Completion (pkg. of 10)	646847-10454-1	$2.99	_____
_____	Chadder Plush Puppet	646847-09056-1	$35.99	_____
_____	Conch Shell Noisemaker	646847-10487-9	$16.99	_____
_____	Crew Bags (pkg. of 10)	646847-10455-8	$5.99	_____
_____	Souvenir Photo Frame (pkg. of 10)	646847-10449-7	$6.99	_____
_____	Thank You Shell (pkg. of 10)	646847-10457-2	$9.99	_____
_____	Water Bottle	646847-10484-8	$2.99	_____

LEADER MANUALS (SEE PGS. 28-29 IN CATALOG)

_____	SCUBA Director Manual	0-7644-2500-5	$14.99	_____
_____	Preschool Tide Pool Director Manual	0-7644-2510-2	$12.99	_____
_____	Deep Bible Adventures Leader Manual	0-7644-2505-6	$9.99	_____
_____	Chadder's Undersea Bible Adventure Leader Manual	0-7644-2503-X	$9.99	_____
_____	Undersea Crafts and Missions Leader Manual	0-7644-2504-8	$9.99	_____
_____	Splish Splash Games Leader Manual	0-7644-2502-1	$9.99	_____
_____	Sea Star Finale Leader Manual	0-7644-2517-X	$9.99	_____
_____	Sing & Play Splash Leader Manual	0-7644-2501-3	$9.99	_____
_____	Dive-In Diner Leader Manual	0-7644-2506-4	$9.99	_____
_____	Dive Deep! Recruitment, Overview, and Pass-Along Training Video	646847-13033-5	$14.99	_____

Total $ _____

ORDER TODAY!

TOUCH CHILDREN aROUND tHe WORLD.

...your kids will not only dive
...o their faith...they'll send the news
...ve across the globe! This hands-on mission
...lled Operation Kid-to-Kid™, allows kids in
...erica to send desperately needed socks and
...rphan children around the world.

ReaL KiDS, ReaL neeDS, ReaL SeRViCe.

◀ **OPeRation KiD-to-KiD Kit**
Bring missions to life with a video that shows
Operation Kid-to-Kid in action. Plus, 3 touching
posters to help your kids connect with needy
children.

646847-10460-2 $9.99

Dive into Decorating!

Atmosphere and environment enhance learning, so decorations are an integral part of SCUBA. They can set the mood for the week and get children excited about God's love.

Think about all the things you might find at the bottom of the ocean. A sunken ship? Ask your congregation members for an old rowboat that you can lay in a corner. A treasure chest? Cover an old toy chest with brown paper, dangle some toy jewelry from the opening, and set it near a doorway.

FiSHiNG foR DeCoRatiNG iDeas?

By letting your imagination and creativity go wild, you can create a setting that's swimming with personality. Go for it!

COLORFUL CORAL! Make colorful coral by using long balloons (the kind you make balloon animals with). Use an air pump to blow up about ten balloons. Twist and bend them so they're not straight, then bundle them together with masking tape at one end. Slip a piece of heavy-gauge wire into the middle of the bundle. Poke the wire into a Styrofoam cooler lid you've set on the floor. Cover the lid with blue, green, or tan material. Finally, tape a paper fish to the end of the wire so kids won't get poked!

DiVe BUDDY WeLCome! Add warmth and friendliness to your SCUBA by making door-size pictures of the Bible Memory Buddies™ to place on each station door. Use the clip art on the *SCUBA Clip Art, Song Lyrics, and Decorating* CD to make these dive buddies!

HaVe CoStuMeD StaFF oN HanD. Have volunteers dressed in SCUBA gear—flippers, masks, snorkels, or even wet suits—to greet and welcome children each day.

GoiNG DeePeR!

Use the clip art on the *SCUBA Clip Art, Song Lyrics, and Decorating* CD to make your decorations sparkle. Simply print out the clip art onto transparency paper, then use an overhead projector to make these dazzling designs larger than life. Project the designs onto bed sheets or butcher paper, trace them, and then color them in.

SCHoOLS of fiSH! Blow up brightly colored balloons, then tape streamers or tissue paper to them to create puffer fish. Use fishing line (what else?) to hang the fish from your ceiling.

...NG POSTERS OF REAL SEA CRITTERS. Find ...ters of fish, octopuses, shells, or crabs. Look through ...ure magazines for the pictures, and then post them ...rywhere. You can even purchase Treasure Verse ...ters, which feature vibrant undersea photos along ...n each day's Treasure Verse.

WATERY ENTRY! Dangle blue crepe paper streamers or strips of shiny blue metallic paper in your doorway so kids feel like they're entering a deep, blue, watery world.

GET CRABBY! Cover round tables with red paper, and tape red poster board "claws" to one side to create enormous crabs! Rectangular tables can be made into aquariums. Just drape blue paper over the tables, and attach fish stickers that "swim" over the blue background.

THIS ROCKS! Cover unused bookshelves or ...s with ... material to create rocks. Drape plastic "seaweed" on your rocks.

FISHING FOR FUN? Bright, colorful fish will be a welcome sight as kids enter your SCUBA site. Cut simple fish shapes from neon poster board, then use black paint to add eyes, fins, and scales to each fish. Dangle the fish from clear fishing line, and shine a black light on them for an eye-catching effect!

CREATE A MARINE SCENE IN EACH WINDOW. Use blue tempera paint (tempera paint with a few drops of liquid soap added will wash right off) to make waves in the windows. This is a fun and easy way to communicate your theme to those inside and out.

WHO'S UP THERE? Stuff the legs of a wet suit with fiberfill or newspaper. Use electrical tape to attach flippers, then hang the legs from your ceiling. Wrap poster board into tubes to create simple scuba tanks. Kids will look up to see a diver swimming above their heads!

A WATERY WORLD. To create the illusion of being under the sea, spray old sheets with varying shades of blue and green dye. When the sheets have dried, hang them on the walls, drape them on your table, or place them over any church furniture that's lying around! Or go the extra mile and rent a bubble machine from a party supply store. Have bubbles floating around your registration table to make kids feel like they're really diving underwater!

SPLASHY STAGE! Trim your stage with giant cardboard coral shapes. Spray paint them in a variety of bright, undersea colors! Hang blue material from the ceiling. If you have a high ceiling, string a length of fishing line across your stage, as high as you possibly can. Then drape the blue material from the fishing line. String clear balloon "bubbles" on fishing line, and hang these from the ceiling or doorways. Turn an old refrigerator box into an enormous treasure chest. (You'll put each day's Treasure Verse treasure inside!) Dangle plastic ivy "seaweed" from the ceiling, or drape it over papier-mâché rocks. For more decorating supplies and ideas, go to www.groupoutlet.com.

make a SPLASH With these items!

Jesus appears to His Followers as They Fish (Matthew 28:18-20, John 21:1-17).

Elijah confronts the Prophets of Baal (1 Kings 18:16-39).

Jonah Disobeys God (Jonah 1-3).

Jesus Dies on the Cross and Rises Again (Luke 23-24).

Jesus Calms a Storm (Matthew 8:23-27).

BIBLE STORY POSTERS ▲
Bright Bible art helps kids remember each day's Bible story with ease. 22" x 34".

646847-10446-6
$9.99/set of 5

◀ Giant Gill inflatable
You'll want a school SCUBA's favorite ma swimming all over y church. Inflate with hand pump. 2 FT x 3 FT.

646847-█████-6
$11.99

Theme Balloons ▼
Here's a super-easy way to jump in with both feet! Scatter oceans of balloons around the floor or fill them with helium and let them float like bubbles. Assorted colors.

646847-10456-5
$8.99/pkg. of 30

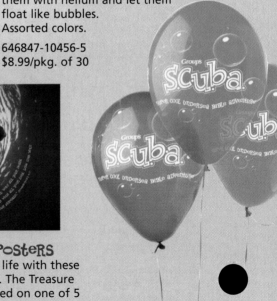

◀ Treasure Verse Posters
Make Bible memory come to life with these bright Treasure Verse Posters. The Treasure Verse for each day is reinforced on one of 5 beautiful underwater photos. 22" x 34".

646847-10459-6
$9.99/set of 5

24

BIBLE POINT POSTERS ▶

Our popular Bible Memory Buddies™ remind kids of each day's Bible Point. These colorful posters are the perfect touch for your decorating. 22" x 34".

6847-10458-9 $9.99/set of 5

GIANT DISPLAY ▼

Durable sign features SCUBA's favorite mascot with room to write your church's information. A sure-fire way to draw attention to your VBS. APPROXIMATELY 5 FT TALL.

646847-10481-7 $19.99

MURAL DECORATING KIT ▼

Dive into adventure with these beautiful illustrations. Advertise your SCUBA VBS on walls and other blank surfaces with easy-to-use murals! 68" x 66" (separate posters each 34"x 33")

6847-10 7-0 $14.99

68"

66"

a treasure trove of gifts for kids and volunteers!

Certificate of Completion
These colorful certificates reward a job well done. 10 3/8" x 8 3/8" sheets.

646847-10454-1
$2.99/pkg. of 10

Souvenir Photo Frame ▶
Capture special moments with your cutest sea creatures. These colorful frames hold pictures and drawings as mementos of your voyage. Great gifts for parents and volunteers! Souvenir frames are 5" x 7".

646847-10449-7
$6.99/pkg. of 10

◀ Chadder Puppet
Kids of all ages love Chadder. This 17" fuzzy friend has a moveable mouth. Use him in all your children's ministry programs!

646847-09056-1 $35.99

www.groupvbs.com

26

ater ottLe ▶
ieve us, e know the importance of
O. These snappy water bottles make
gifts and prizes. Water bottle is
high.

6847-10484-8 $2.99

ew Bags ▼
ong 16" x 18" plastic bags
d Student Books, crafts, treats
d treasures.

6847-10455-8 $5.99/pkg. of 10

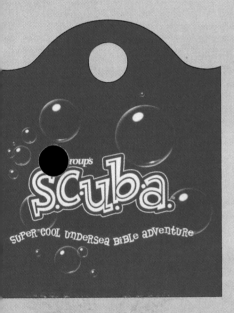

THaNK you SHeLL ▼
Your SCUBA VBS would be sunk
without the efforts of your
busy volunteers. Delight
them with this special
SCUBA "Thank you."

646847-10457-2
$9.99/pkg. of 10

FRONT

BACK

"FOR WHeRe
youR TReasuRe is,
tHeRe youR HeaRt
WiLL Be aLso".

Matthew 6:21

THaNKS
FoR SHaRiNG
GOD'S Love at
Scuba

BiBLe MeMoRy BuDDies™
STiCKeR SHeets ▶
Stick these stylin' sea friends on
Dive Bags, coloring books, Bible
books...even kids!

646847-10485-5
$6.99/pkg. of 10

Get Hooked on teaching and Sea the Difference you make!

Scuba Director Manual ▼
Here's everything you need to know. Day-by-day instructions, a planning calendar, an overview of the entire VBS, and more helpful tools.

0-7644-2500-5 $14.99

Preschool Tide Pool Director Manual ▼
Everything you'll need to help your little minnows learn and grow.

0-7644-2510-2 $12.99

Buy two sets of manuals—one for your Leaders and one to keep for yourself!

◀ Sing & Play Splash Leader Manual
Openings, words, skits, music, actions, and accompaniment...it's all right here. New! The mu score is now included.

0-7644-2501-3
$9.99

> "The kids love it...the staff loves it... the parents love it...and I love it! As long as I'm the VBS director, I can't imagine using anything else."
> ANONYMOUS FROM MESSAGE BOARD

SPLISH SPLASH Games Leader Manual ▶

Buckets of games and SCUBA starters.

0-7644-2502-1
$9.99

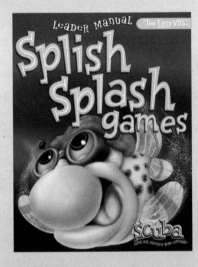

◀ Dive-In Diner Leader Manual

Creative, easy instructions for crafts that reinforce each day's Bible point.

0-7644-2506-4
$9.99

Sea Star ▶ Finale Leader Manual

Larger-than-life adventures to wrap up each day.

0-7644-2517-X
$9.99

◀ Undersea Crafts and Missions Leader Manual

Step-by-step instructions for crafts, plus fun bonus ideas.

0-7644-2504-8
$9.99

Chadder's ▶ Undersea Bible Adventure Leader Manual

Action-packed video leader's guide, plus ways to use the Student Books.

0-7644-2503-X
$9.99

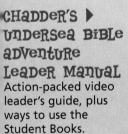

◀ Deep Bible Adventures Leader Manual

Multi-sensory Bible experiences that engage kids in the Bible story.

0-7644-2505-6
$9.99

Order Chadder's Undersea Bible Adventure video, see page 9.

SCUBA BUDDiES unite!

Here's your chance to network with other SCUBA VBS Directors from your community!

On a Saturday morning in March or April, you'll get together and
- share ideas for everything from decorating to fundraising,
- get a hands-on sneak-peek of SCUBA Bible adventure, snacks, crafts, and music, and
- each church will receive fun SCUBA products and surprises!

So strap on your flippers and get to a SCUBA Party near you!

Registration is $20.00 for the first person from each church and only $10.00 for each additional attendee.

See registration details on page 35.

abama

baster First United
thodist Church
urday, ...ch 01, 2003
Mon...o Rd.
baster, AL 35007

nryville United
thodist Church
urday, April 05, 2003
...20 US Hwy 431 N
ntersville, AL 35976

n City Baptist Church
urday, March 08, 2003
Mandy Lane
niston, AL 36207

ler Court Ministries
urday, March 01, 2003
Keller Ln. #I-7
cumbia, AL 35674

d of the Harvest
tist Church
urday, March 15, 2003
. Box 899
rthport, AL 35473

cedonia Baptist Church
urday, March 15, 2003
21 S. Chapel Hill Rd.
catur, AL 35603

lbrook First United
thodist Church
urday, March 08, 2003
. Box 609
lbrook, AL 36054

aska

rbanks Lutheran Church
urday, March 29, 2003
2 Cowles St.
rbanks, AK 99701

IZONA

phany Lutheran Church
urday, March 15, 2003
West Ray Road
andler, AZ 85225

surrection Lutheran
urch
urday, March 08, 2003
75 N. 1st St.
Valley, AZ 85737

kansas

urch of the Nazarene
urday, April 05, 2003
NW 3rd St.
ntonville, AR 72712

st Landmark
otist Church
urday, April 05, 2003
West Center
eridan, AR 72150

st United
thodis...rch
urday, ...ch 01, 2003
N. Main
ebe, AR 72012

CALIFORNIA

Calvary Church
Saturday, March 29, 2003
1010 N. Tustin Ave.
Santa Ana, CA 92705

Evangel Assembly of God
Saturday, March 01, 2003
265 W. Hwy 246
Buellton, CA 93427

**First Baptist Church
of Torrance**
Saturday, March 29, 2003
2118 W. Carson St.
Torrance, CA 90501

First Family Church
Saturday, March 15, 2003
8434 S. Greenleaf Ave.
Whittier, CA 90602

First Lutheran Church
Saturday, March 15, 2003
1200 Pinecrest St.
Placerville, CA 95667

First Presbyterian Church
Saturday, March 08, 2003
1705 17th St.
Bakersfield, CA 93301

Heart of the Valley Church
Saturday, March 15, 2003
18644 Sherman Way
Reseda, CA 91335

Hillside Church of Marin
Saturday, March 08, 2003
5461 Paradise Dr.
Corte Madera, CA 94925

**Placentia Presbyterian
Church**
Saturday, March 08, 2003
849 N. Bradford Ave.
Placentia, CA 92870

ShadowRidge Church
Saturday, March 22, 2003
5635 Douglas Blvd.
Granite Bay, CA 95746

Susanville Assembly of God
Saturday, March 22, 2003
473-465 Richmond Road
Susanville, CA 96130

**The Church of the
Incarnation**
Saturday, April 05, 2003
550 Mendocino Ave.
Santa Rosa, CA 95401

The Salvation Army
Saturday, March 29, 2003
351 Mission Ave.
San Rafael, CA 94901

Tulare First Church of God
Saturday, April 05, 2003
833 N. Blackstone
Tulare, CA 93274

COLORADO

Calvary Temple
Saturday, March 01, 2003
200 S. University Blvd.
Denver, CO 80209

Christ Christian Church
Saturday, March 08, 2003
675 E. 20th St.
Greeley, CO 80631

Christ's Church
Saturday, March 15, 2003
9675 S. Timberhawk C #11
Highlands Ranch, CO 80126

First Baptist Church
Saturday, March 08, 2003
720 Grand Ave.
Grand Junction, CO 81501

Grace Church of Arvada
Saturday, March 22, 2003
6969 Sheridan Blvd.
Arvada, CO 80003

Grace Place Church
Saturday, March 01, 2003
250 Mountain Ave.
Berthoud, CO 80513

Mountain Springs Vineyard
Saturday, March 08, 2003
7345 E. Woodman Rd.
Colorado Springs, CO 80908

Peace With Christ
Saturday, March 08, 2003
3290 South Tower Rd.
Aurora, CO 80013

Zion Lutheran Church
Saturday, April 05, 2003
1400 Skeel St.
Brighton, CO 80601

CONNECTICUT

**Kensington Congregational
Church**
Saturday, March 08, 2003
312 Percival
Kensington, CT 06037

**St. Stephen's Episcopal
Church**
Saturday, March 22, 2003
351 Main Street
Ridgefield, CT 06877

DELAWARE

Praise Assembly of God
Saturday, March 22, 2003
1421 Old Baltimore Pike
Newark, DE 19702

FLORIDA

Chapel by the Sea
Saturday, March 01, 2003
8240 S. A1A
Melbourne Beach, FL 32951

Community Baptist Church
Saturday, March 08, 2003
12534 Roseland Rd.
Sebastian, FL 32958

Epiphany Lutheran Church
Saturday, April 05, 2003
1498 Tuskawilla Rd.
Oviedo, FL 32765

**First United
Methodist Church**
Saturday, March 29, 2003
103 1st St. SE
Ft. Walton Beach, FL 32548

**First United
Methodist Church**
Saturday, March 15, 2003
973 S. Marion Ave.
Lake City, FL 32025

**First United Methodist
Church of Coral Gables**
Saturday, March 01, 2003
536 Coral Way
Coral Gables, FL 33134

Holy Cross Lutheran Church
Saturday, March 01, 2003
760 N. Sun Dr.
Lake Mary, FL 32746

**Hyde Park
United Methodist Church**
Saturday, March 08, 2003
500 W. Platte St.
Tampa, FL 33606

Immanuel Lutheran Church
Saturday, March 01, 2003
2655 SW Immanuel Dr.
Palm City, FL 34990

**Indian River
Presbyterian Church**
Saturday, April 05, 2003
2499 Virginia Ave.
Fort Pierce, FL 34982

The Salvation Army
Saturday, April 05, 2003
1100 W. Sligh Ave.
Tampa, FL 33604

Sarasota Baptist Church
Saturday, March 15, 2003
7091 Proctor Road
Sarasota, FL 34241

**South Lake Wales
Church of God**
Saturday, March 15, 2003
210 Presidents Dr.
Lake Wales, FL 33859

**St Luke's United
Methodist Church**
Friday, March 28, 2003
(9:30-12:30)
4851 Apopka Vineland Rd.
Orlando, FL 32819

St. Bernard's Church
Saturday, March 01, 2003
248 S. Harbor Dr.
Holmes Beach, FL 34217

**St. Paul United
Methodist Church**
Saturday, April 05, 2003
8264 Lone Star Rd.
Jacksonville, FL 32211

Wahoo First Baptist Church
Saturday, March 01, 2003
4517 CR 319
Bushnell, FL 33513

Check www.groupvbs.com
for additional locations!

Wakulla Presbyterian Church
Saturday, March 15, 2003
3383 Coastal Hwy.
Crawfordville, FL 32327

GEORGIA

Cannon United Methodist Church
Saturday, March 22, 2003
2424 Web Gin House Rd.
Snellville, GA 30078

Chattanooga Valley Church of the Nazarene
Saturday, March 01, 2003
2853 Chattanooga Valley Rd.
Flintstone, GA 30725

Church of St. Andrew
Saturday, March 22, 2003
5855 Riverside Dr.
Atlanta, GA 30327

Crossroads United Methodist Church
Saturday, April 05, 2003
2460 Hwy 138 NE
Conyers, GA 30013

Due West United Methodist Church
Saturday, March 29, 2003
3956 Due West Rd.
Marietta, GA 30064

First Baptist Church
Saturday, March 15, 2003
95 W. Morse St.
Forsyth, GA 31029

First Presbyterian Church
Saturday, March 29, 2003
1100 1st Ave.
Columbus, GA 31902

First United Methodist Church
Saturday, March 08, 2003
100 Memorial Drive
Hinesville, GA 31313

Mt. Zion Baptist Church
Saturday, March 15, 2003
4141 Highway 358
Danville, GA 31017

Pierce Chapel
Saturday, March 08, 2003
5122 Pierce Chapel Rd.
Midland, GA 31820

Reid Memorial Presbyterian Church
Saturday, March 22, 2003
2261 Walton Way
Augusta, GA 30904-4301

Sugarloaf United Methodist Church
Saturday, March 01, 2003
1795 Old Peachtree Rd.
Duluth, GA 30097

The Church at Northside
Saturday, March 08, 2003
3006 Martha Berry Hwy
Rome, GA 30165

ILLINOIS

Fair Oaks Presbyterian Church
Saturday, March 15, 2003
744 Fair Oaks
Oak Park, IL 60302

Fairfield Cumberland Presbyterian Church
Saturday, March 15, 2003
RR 4 Outer West Delaware
Fairfield, IL 62837

Family of God Baptist Church
Saturday, April 05, 2003
5313 Rt. 34
Oswego, IL 60543

First Baptist of Joy
Saturday, March 15, 2003
200 E. Edwards St.
Joy, IL 61260

First Church of Christ
Saturday, March 01, 2003
405 N. Maple
Mulberry Grove, IL 62262

Grayville United Methodist Church
Saturday, March 29, 2003
115 W. North St.
Grayville, IL 62844

Immanuel Lutheran Church
Saturday, March 15, 2003
178 McHenry Ave.
Crystal Lake, IL 60014-6099

McHenry Evangelical Free Church
Saturday, March 01, 2003
2614 Ringwood Rd.
McHenry, IL 60050

Meadows Baptist Church
Saturday, March 22, 2003
2401 Kirchoff Rd.
Rolling Meadows, IL 60008

Mount Olive
Saturday, March 01, 2003
3850 N. Tripp
Chicago, IL 60641

SonLife Church
Saturday, March 08, 2003
1203 Vandalia
Collinsville, IL 62234

State Road Community Church
Saturday, March 29, 2003
RR 2
Cambridge, IL 61238

INDIANA

Faith Community Church
Saturday, March 22, 2003
Promise Rd.
Noblesville, IN 46060

First United Methodist Church
Saturday, March 15, 2003
352 South Main
Crown Point, IN 46307

Free Methodist Church
Saturday, March 01, 2003
1603 Troy Road
Washington, IN 47501

Mt. Calvary Evangelical Lutheran Church
Saturday, March 01, 2003
1819 Reservation Dr.
Fort Wayne, IN 46819-2000

Portage Grace Church of the Nazarene
Saturday, March 29, 2003
5360 Clem Rd.
Portage, IN 46368

Spiceland Friends Church
Saturday, March 01, 2003
401 W. Main, P.O. Box 27
Spiceland, IN 47385

St. Lawrence Catholic Church
Saturday, April 05, 2003
6944 E. 46th Street
Indianapolis, IN 46226

Vineyard Community Church
Saturday, March 15, 2003
1265 N. Madison Ave.
Greenwood, IN 46142

Wakarusa Missionary Church
Saturday, March 08, 2003
202 W. Waterford
Wakarusa, IN 46573

Wesley Chapel United Methodist Church
Saturday, March 29, 2003
13733 Wesley Chapel Rd.
Churubusco, IN 46723

IOWA

Central Community Free Methodist Church
Saturday, March 22, 2003
8105 Douglas Ave.
Urbandale, IA 50322

Eldora United Methodist Church
Saturday, April 05, 2003
1415 12th St.
Eldora, IA 50627

First Baptist Church
Saturday, March 01, 2003
543 Division St.
Webster City, IA 50595

Hammond Avenue Brethren Church
Saturday, March 29, 2003
1604 Hammond Ave.
Waterloo, IA 50702

Living Word Christian Fellowship
Saturday, March 08, 2003
4187 Landon Ave. SW
Iowa City, IA 52240

Ottumwa Community Church
Saturday, March 29, 2003
305 S. Walnut
Ottumwa, IA

Solid Rock Church of God
Saturday, March 08, 2003
Rock Valley Road
Centerville, IA 52544

St. Matthew Lutheran Church
Saturday, March 01, 2003
1915 W. Kimberly Road
Davenport, IA 52806

KANSAS

Bethany Lutheran
Saturday, April 05, 2003
1000 W. 26th St. South
Wichita, KS 67217

First Christian Church
Saturday, March 08, 2003
128 W. Elm
Columbus, KS 66725

KENTUCKY

Crofton Christian Church
Saturday, April 05, 2003
175 E. Mill St.
Crofton, KY 42217

Drakesboro United Methodist Church
Saturday, March 08, 2003
201 Mose Rag___ ___d.
Drakesboro, K___ ___337

Gardenside Baptist Church
Saturday, March 22, 2003
1667 Alexandria Dr.
Lexington, KY 40504

Madison Hills Christian Church
Saturday, March 29, 2003
960 Red House Rd.
Richmond, KY 40475

Parkwood Baptist Church
Saturday, March 29, 2003
7009 Manslick Rd.
Louisville, KY 40214

St. Margaret Mary Church
Saturday, March 08, 2003
7813 Shelbyville Rd.
Louisville, KY 40222

LOUISIANA

First United Methodist Church
Saturday, April 05, 2003
200 East Pine St.
Ponchatoula, LA 70454

Gilliam United Methodist Church
Saturday, March 01, 2003
Adgers Rd.
Gilliam, LA 7___

Journey Christian Church
Saturday, March 22, 2003
2616 Sharon St.
Kenner, LA 70062

Check www.groupvbs.com for additional locations!

rd of Life
urday, March 08, 2003
. Box 1006
naldsonille, LA 70346

INE

xton United
thodist Church
urday, March 22, 2003
5 Chicopee Rd.
xton, ME 04093

st Congregational Church
Pittston
turday, March 08, 2003
4 Box 6720
rdiner, ME 04345

ckland
ngregational Church
turday, March 15, 2003
0 Limerock St.
ckland, ME 04841

ARYLAND

undel Christian Church
turday, March 08, 2003
20 Connelley Dr.
nover, MD 21076

rnerstone
sembly of God
turday, March 01, 2003
010 Annapolis Rd.
wie, MD 20715

nsdowne Worship Center
turday, th 15, 2003
30 Smi e.
nsdowne, MD 21227

. Andrew Lutheran Church
turday, March 29, 2003
01 Taylor Ave.
ltimore, MD 21234

assachusetts

st Baptist Church
turday, March 08, 2003
4 Washington St.
aintree, MA 02184

ICHIGAN

ngregational Church of
rmingham, United Church
Christ
turday, March 15, 2003
00 Cranbrook Rd.
oomfield Hills, MI 48304

st United
thodist Church
turday, March 22, 2003
89 W. Maple Rd.
rmingham, MI 48009

apleview Free
thodist Church
turday, March 29, 2003
31 Niles chanan Rd.
les, MI 0

artin United Methodist
turday, April 05, 2003
59 E. Allegan
artin, MI 49070

**North Park
Presbyterian Church**
Saturday, March 08, 2003
500 N. Park St.
Grand Rapids, MI 49525

**River Terrace Christian
Reformed Church**
Saturday, March 22, 2003
1509 River Terrace Drive
East Lansing, MI 48842

**South Lansing
Christian Church**
Saturday, March 29, 2003
6300 Aurelius Road
Lansing, MI 48910

Sparta Baptist Church
Saturday, March 22, 2003
38 S. State St.
Sparta, MI 49345

**West Goodland United
Methodist Church**
Saturday, March 15, 2003
2008 N. Van Dyke Rd.
Imlay City, MI 48444

MINNESOTA

Christ Community Church
Saturday, March 08, 2003
4570 Churchill St.
Shoreview, MN 55126

Grace Fellowship
Saturday, March 29, 2003
8601 101th Ave N.
Brooklyn Park, MN 55445

**Grace Lutheran Church of
Apple Valley**
Saturday, March 01, 2003
7800 West County Rd. 42
Apple Valley, MN 55124

Prairie Lutheran Church
Saturday, March 22, 2003
11000 Blossom Rd.
Eden Prairie, MN 55347

MISSISSIPPI

Oakland Baptist Church
Saturday, March 01, 2003
2959 Oak Ridge Rd.
Vicksburg, MS 39183

Russell Baptist Church
Saturday, March 01, 2003
1844 Hwy. 11-80
Meridian, MS 39301

MISSOURI

First Church of the Nazarene
Saturday, March 22, 2003
603 E. Hale Lake Rd.
Warrensburg, MO 64093

**Marshfield United
Methodist Church**
Saturday, March 08, 2003
220 S. Elm
Marshfield, MO 65706

**Representatives of Christ
Fellowship**
Saturday, March 15, 2003
1125 N. 10th, P.O. Box 696
St. Joseph, MO 64502

Trinity Lutheran Church
Saturday, March 08, 2003
14088 Clayton Rd.
Chesterfield, MO 63017

Zion Lutheran Church
Saturday, March 29, 2003
123 Carson Rd.
Ferguson, MO 63135

Zion United Church of Christ
Saturday, March 01, 2003
5710N Hwy 67
Florissant, MO 63034

NEBRASKA

**Grace United
Methodist Church**
Saturday, March 15, 2003
1832 W. 9th Street
Hastings, NE 68901

Shepherd of the Hills ELCA
Saturday, March 01, 2003
6901 Panama Rd.
Hickman, NE 68372

NEVADA

Faith Bible Church
Saturday, March 08, 2003
875 Fremont Lane
Fernley, NV 89408

NEW HAMPSHIRE

**Londonderry Presbyterian
Church**
Saturday, March 15, 2003
126 Phillsbury Rd.
Londonderry, NH 03053

St. John's Episcopal Church
Saturday, April 05, 2003
101 Chapel St.
Portsmouth, NH 03801

NEW JERSEY

**Bound Brook
Presbyterian Church**
Saturday, March 01, 2003
409 Mountain Ave.
Bound Brook, NJ 08805

Holy Family Parish
Saturday, March 22, 2003
213 Pershing Ave.
Carteret, NJ 07008

**Knowlton United
Methodist Church**
Saturday, March 01, 2003
509 Route 94
Columbia, NJ 07832

Margate Community Church
Saturday, March 01, 2003
8900 Ventnor Ave.
Margate, NJ 08402

**North Hunterdon United
Methodist Church**
Saturday, March 08, 2003
51 County Road 635
Hampton, NJ 08827

Pilgrim Church
Saturday, March 15, 2003
18 Essex Street
Paramus, NJ 07652

NEW MEXICO

**Aztec First United
Methodist Church**
Saturday, March 15, 2003
123 E. Chaco
Aztec, NM 87410

Los Altos Christian Church
Saturday, March 01, 2003
11900 Haines, N.E.
Albuquerque, NM 87112

NEW YORK

**First United
Methodist Church**
Saturday, March 29, 2003
3890 Main St.
Warrensburg, NY 12885

**Lyall Memorial
Federated Church**
Saturday, March 29, 2003
30 Maple Ave.
Millbrook, NY 12545

Sacred Heart Church
Saturday, March 22, 2003
380 E. Fairmount Ave.
Lakewood, NY 14750

St. Andrew's
Saturday, March 15, 2003
30 Brooksite Dr.
Smithtown, NY 11787

**The Church of Christ at
Greenpoint**
Saturday, April 05, 2003
199 North Henry Street
Brooklyn, NY 11222

NORTH CAROLINA

**Grace United
Methodist Church**
Saturday, March 08, 2003
401 Grace St.
Wilmington, NC 28401

**Hendersonville Pentecostal
Holiness Church**
Saturday, March 22, 2003
2295 Washington St.
Hendersonville, NC 28793

**Immanuel Temple
SDA Church**
Sunday, Mar. 9, 2003 (3-6 pm)
2102 S. Alston Ave.
Durham, NC 27703

**Oak Ridge United
Methodist Church**
Saturday, March 15, 2003
2424 Oak Ridge Rd.
Oak Ridge, NC 27358

White Plains United Methodist Church
Saturday, March 01, 2003
313 SE Maynard Rd.
Cary, NC 27512

OHIO

Beverly United Methodist Church
Saturday, April 05, 2003
700 Park St.
Beverly, OH 45715

Burton Congregational Church
Saturday, March 08, 2003
14558 W. Park St.
Burton, OH 44021

Christ United Methodist Church
Saturday, March 08, 2003
600 E. Gorgas St.
Louisville, OH 44641

First Church of God
Saturday, March 15, 2003
561 Carter Rd.
Defiance, OH 43512

First Presbyterian Church
Saturday, March 22, 2003
143 S. Prospect St.
Marion, OH 43302

First United Methodist Church
Saturday, March 01, 2003
225 Ludlow St.
Hamilton, OH 45011

Grace Baptist Church
Saturday, March 22, 2003
3475 Paris Blvd.
Westerville, OH 43081

Johnsville Grace United Methodist Church
Saturday, March 15, 2003
7459 County Rd. 242
Shauck, OH 43349

King of Kings Lutheran Church
Saturday, March 08, 2003
3621 Socialville Foster Rd.
Mason, OH 45040

Lebanon Presbyterian Church
Saturday, March 01, 2003
123 N. East Street
Lebanon, OH 45036

Messiah Lutheran Church
Saturday, March 15, 2003
1200 Waggoner Rd.
Reynoldsburg, OH 43068

New Albany First Church of Nazarene
Saturday, April 05, 2003
6000 Johnstown Rd.
New Albany, OH 43054

Northwest United Methodist Church
Saturday, March 01, 2003
5200 Riverside Dr.
Columbus, OH 43220

Olivet Lutheran Church
Saturday, March 08, 2003
5840 Monroe St.
Sylvania, OH 43560

Pleasant Hill Presbyterian Church
Saturday, March 08, 2003
3279 State Route 213
Steubenville, OH 43952

Salem Church of God
Saturday, March 01, 2003
6500 Southway Rd.
Clayton, OH 45315

Trinity Lutheran Church
Saturday, March 22, 2003
120 S. Henry
Malinta, OH 43535

Troy Abundant Life Assembly of God
Saturday, March 15, 2003
1586 McKaig Ave.
Troy, OH 45373

Upper Arlington Christian Church
Saturday, March 08, 2003
2211 Haviland Rd.
Columbus, OH 43220

OKLAHOMA

Church of the Nazarene
Saturday, March 01, 2003
414 Hill Dr.
Kingfisher, OK 73750

First Baptist Church
Saturday, March 29, 2003
212 North Main
Tonkawa, OK 74653

First Presbyterian Church
Saturday, April 05, 2003
1505 E. Grand
Ponca City, OK 74604

First United Methodist Church
Saturday, March 08, 2003
400 W. 7th Ave.
Stillwater, OK 74074

First United Methodist Church
Saturday, March 08, 2003
1001 Frisco Ave.
Clinton, OK 73601

Northside Christian Church
Saturday, March 01, 2003
1201 N. Elm Place
Broken Arrow, OK 74012

OREGON

Clackamas Park Evangelical Friends Church
Saturday, March 15, 2003
8120 SE Thiessen Road
Milwaukie, OR 97267

Community Presbyterian Church
Saturday, March 01, 2003
529 NW 19th St.
Redmond, OR 97756

Coquille Church of the Nazarene
Saturday, March 15, 2003
997 W. Central Blvd.
Coquille, OR 97423

Kingwood Bible Church
Saturday, March 01, 2003
1125 Elm St. NW
Salem, OR 97304

Mt. Scott Nazarene
Saturday, March 22, 2003
5535 SE Rhone
Portland, OR 97206

Mt. Tabor Presbyterian Church
Saturday, March 08, 2003
5441 SE Belmont
Portland, OR 97215

Southminster Presbyterian Church
Saturday, April 05, 2003
12250 SW Denney Road
Beaverton, OR 97008

PENNSYLVANIA

Calvary Full Gospel
Saturday, March 01, 2003
538 Hickory Grade Rd.
Bridgeville, PA 15017

Evangelical United Methodist Church
Saturday, March 15, 2003
305 South Centre St.
Pottsville, PA 17901

First United Methodist Church
Saturday, March 08, 2003
135 Decker Drive
New Castle, PA 16105

Kochenderfer United Methodist Church
Saturday, March 01, 2003
1105 Kochenderfer Rd.
Lebanon, PA 17046

St. John Evangelical Lutheran Church
Saturday, March 15, 2003
175 E. Main St.
New Freedom, PA 17349

St. Peter's United Methodist Church
Saturday, March 22, 2003
7860 Center St.
Emerald, PA 18080

St. Philip's Reformed Episcopal Church
Saturday, March 29, 2003
220 Norristown Rd.
Warminster, PA 18974

The Presbyterian Church
Saturday, March 22, 2003
414 Grant Street
Sewickley, PA 15143

The Salvation Army
Saturday, March 22, 2003
17 S. Pennsylvania Ave.
Wilkes-Barre, PA 18705

Trinity Evangelical Lutheran Church
Saturday, April 05, 2003
132 E. Main
Mechanicsburg, 17055

RHODE ISLAND

Evangelical Covenant Church
Saturday, March 15, 2003
165 Rounds Ave.
Riverside, RI 02915

SOUTH CAROLINA

Central First Wesleyan
Saturday, March 15, 2003
1020 SWU 453
Central, SC 29630

Clearview Baptist
Saturday, March 01, 2003
5611 State Park Rd.
Travelers Rest, SC 29690

Highland Park United Methodist Church
Saturday, March 08, 2003
1300 Second Loop Rd.
Florence, SC 29505

Pierpont Baptist Church
Saturday, March 15, 2003
2508 Ashley River Rd.
Charleston, SC 29414

St. David's Episcopal Church
Saturday, March 08, 2003
605 Polo Rd.
Columbia, SC

TENNESSEE

Bible Fellowship Church
Saturday, March 08, 2003
424 Maryville Hwy
Seymour, TN 37865

City Road Chapel United Methodist Church
Saturday, March 08, 2003
701 Gallatin Rd. S.
Madison, TN 37115

Cornerstone Baptist Church
Saturday, March 29, 2003
49 Golf Club Road
McMinnville, TN 37110

First Baptist Church of Chattanooga
Saturday, March 22, 2003
401 Gateway Ave.
Chattanooga, TN 37402

First Christian Church
Saturday, March 15, 2003
211 W. Fifth Ave.
Knoxville, TN 37917

Paris First United Methodist Church
Saturday, March 15, 2003
101 E. Blythe St.
Paris, TN 3824

Trinity Baptist Church
Saturday, March 29, 2003
260 Headtown Rd.
Jonesborough, TN 37659

heck www.groupvbs.com for additional locations!

- ✂

es, ReSeRVe a PLaCe FOR Me! PLEASE PRINT OR TYPE INFORMATION.

RTY I WILL ATTEND

URCH NAME | DATE

TY | STATE

UR NAME

UR CHURCH | CHURCH PHONE

NOMINATION

DRESS

☐ CHURCH ADDRESS ☐ HOME ADDRESS

TY | STATE | ZIP

YTIME PHONE

UR E-MAIL ADDRESS

ME AND ADDRESS OF ADDITIONAL ATTENDEE FROM YOUR CHURCH

ME

DRESS

TY | STATE | ZIP

MAIL ADDRESS

ase attach a separate page with additional names and addresses, if necessary.

3 WaYS TO ReGISTeR!

MAIL THIS FORM TO:
Group Publishing, C/O QMS
6840 Meadowridge Court
Alpharetta, GA 30005

ONLINE at www.groupvbs.com

CALL our toll-free registration hotline at
1-866-988-2883 (registration only please)

PaYMeNT INFORMaTION

REGISTRATION FEE: First person from each church, $20.00. Each additional attendee, $10.00.

Total attendees_____

Total amount due_____

☐ Check enclosed
(Make check payable to Group Publishing, Inc.)

Charge my: ☐ ☐ ☐ VISA ☐ MasterCard ☐ DISCOVER

Card Number

Expiration Date

Authorization Signature

Print name